ULTIMATE MUSIC THEORY
GLORY ST. GERMAIN ARCT RMT MYCC UMTC

Edited by Shelagh McKibbon-U'Ren RMT UMTC

INTERMEDIATE RUDIMENTS ANSWER BOOK

UltimateMusicTheory.com

Enriching Lives Through Music Education - *The Way To Score Success!*

ISBN: 978-0-9813101-6-9

Ultimate Music Theory Ltd. © COPYRIGHT 2021 Gloryland Publishing. All Rights Reserved.

ULTIMATE MUSIC THEORY: *The Way to Score Success!*

The Ultimate Music Theory workbooks are for all Musicians.

The more we understand the universal language of music, the more we are capable of communicating our ideas through performing and writing music, interpreting musical compositions of others, and developing a deeper appreciation of music. It is through music education that we progress from student to musician and are able to enjoy and understand music at a more comprehensive level.

Respect Copyright 2021 Glory St. Germain
All rights reserved. No part of this publication may be reproduced or transmitted in any form or by any means, electronic or mechanical, including photocopying, recording, or any information storage and retrieval system, without permission in writing from the author/publisher.

Published in 2021 by Gloryland Publishing

GlorylandPublishing.com

UltimateMusicTheory.com

Library and Archives Canada Cataloguing in Publication St. Germain, Glory 1953-
Ultimate Music Theory Series / Glory St. Germain

Gloryland Publishing - Ultimate Music Theory Series:

GP - UP1	ISBN: 978-0-9809556-6-8	Ultimate Prep 1 Rudiments
GP - UP1A	ISBN: 978-0-9809556-9-9	Ultimate Prep 1 Rudiments Answer Book
GP - UP2	ISBN: 978-0-9809556-7-5	Ultimate Prep 2 Rudiments
GP - UP2A	ISBN: 978-0-9813101-0-7	Ultimate Prep 2 Rudiments Answer Book
GP - UBR	ISBN: 978-0-9813101-3-8	Ultimate Basic Rudiments
GP - UBRA	ISBN: 978-0-9813101-4-5	Ultimate Basic Answer Book
GP - UIR	ISBN: 978-0-9813101-5-2	Ultimate Intermediate Rudiments
GP - UIRA	ISBN: 978-0-9813101-6-9	Ultimate Intermediate Answer Book
GP - UAR	ISBN: 978-0-9813101-7-6	Ultimate Advanced Rudiments
GP - UARA	ISBN: 978-0-9813101-8-3	Ultimate Advanced Answer Book
GP - UCR	ISBN: 978-0-9813101-1-4	Ultimate Complete Rudiments
GP - UCRA	ISBN: 978-0-9813101-2-1	Ultimate Complete Answer Book

♫ **Note:** The Ultimate Music Theory Program includes the UMT Workbook Series, Exam Series & Supplemental Series to help students successfully prepare for international theory exams.

Ultimate Music Theory Intermediate Rudiments
Table of Contents

Lesson 1	Basic Review	5
	Lesson 1 Review Test - Score: _____ / 100%	13
Lesson 2	Circle of Fifths, Major and Enharmonic Scales	17
	Lesson 2 Review Test - Score: _____ / 100%	27
Lesson 3	Double Sharps, Double Flats, Minor and Enharmonic Scales	31
	Lesson 3 Review Test - Score: _____ / 100%	42
Lesson 4	Technical Degree Names and Chromatic Scales	46
	Lesson 4 Review Test - Score: _____ / 100%	50
Lesson 5	Simple Time and Compound Time	54
	Lesson 5 Review Test - Score: _____ / 100%	69
Lesson 6	Intervals - Augmented, Diminished and Inversions	73
	Lesson 6 Review Test - Score: _____ / 100%	79
Lesson 7	Triads - Inversions, Close and Open Position	83
	Lesson 7 Review Test - Score: _____ / 100%	91
Lesson 8	Whole Tone, Pentatonic, Blues and Octatonic Scales	95
	Lesson 8 Review Test - Score: _____ / 100%	100
Lesson 9	Rewriting a Melody using a Key Signature	104
	Lesson 9 Review Test - Score: _____ / 100%	110
Lesson 10	Cadences - Perfect, Plagal and Imperfect	114
	Lesson 10 Review Test - Score: _____ / 100%	119
Lesson 11	Transposition - Major Key to Major Key	123
	Lesson 11 Review Test - Score: _____ / 100%	127
Lesson 12	Analysis, Italian Terms and Signs	132
	Lesson 12 Final Intermediate Exam - Score: _____ / 100% ...	140
Guide & Chart	UMT Guide & Chart - Intermediate Rudiments Flashcards	146

Score: 60 - 69 Pass; **70 - 79** Honors; **80 - 89** First Class Honors; **90 - 100** First Class Honors with Distinction

Ultimate Music Theory: *The Way to Score Success!*

ULTIMATE MUSIC THEORY: *The Way to Score Success!*

The focus of the **Ultimate Music Theory** Series is to simplify complex concepts and show the relativity of these concepts with practical application. These workbooks are designed to help teachers and students discover the excitement and benefits of a music theory education.

Ultimate Music Theory workbooks are based on a proven approach to the study of music theory that follows these **4 Ultimate Music Theory Learning Principles**:

♪ **Simplicity of Learning** - easy to understand instructions, examples and exercises.

♪ **Memory Joggers** - tips for all learning styles including visual, auditory, and kinaesthetic.

♪ **Tie it All Together** - helping musicians understand the universal language of music.

♪ **Make it Relevant** - applying theoretical concepts to pedagogical studies.

The **Ultimate Music Theory**™ Rudiments Workbooks, Supplemental Workbooks and Exams help students prepare for successful completion of internationally recognized theory examinations.

BONUS - Convenient and easy to use Ultimate Music Theory Answer Books - Identical to the student workbooks for quick, easy & accurate marking. UMT Answer Books available for all levels.

♫ **Note:** Each Ultimate Music Theory Rudiments Workbook has a corresponding Supplemental Workbook Level to enhance knowledge of analysis, develop a deeper understanding of music history, provide a proven step-by-step system in melody writing, and much more!

The Ultimate Music Theory Series includes these EXCLUSIVE BONUS features:

Ultimate Music Theory Guide & Chart - a convenient summarization to review concepts.

12 Comprehensive Review Tests & Final Exam - retention of concepts learned in previous lessons.

♫ **Notes:** point out important information and handy memory tips.

80 Music Theory Flashcards - Musical Terms & Signs, Rhythms, Key Signatures, Time Signatures, Note Naming, Dynamics, Tempos, Articulation, Triads, Chords, etc. (each workbook is different).

Ultimate Music Theory FREE Resources - Music History Videos, Worksheets, Music Theory Blogs, Free Ultimate Music Theory Teachers Guide & Free Teach Basic Rudiments Online Mini-Course.

Go To: **UltimateMusicTheory.com** Today!

Enriching Lives Through Music Education

Lesson 1 Basic Review

♭ B E A D
The order of flats

Circle of Fifths

♯ F C G D
The order of sharps

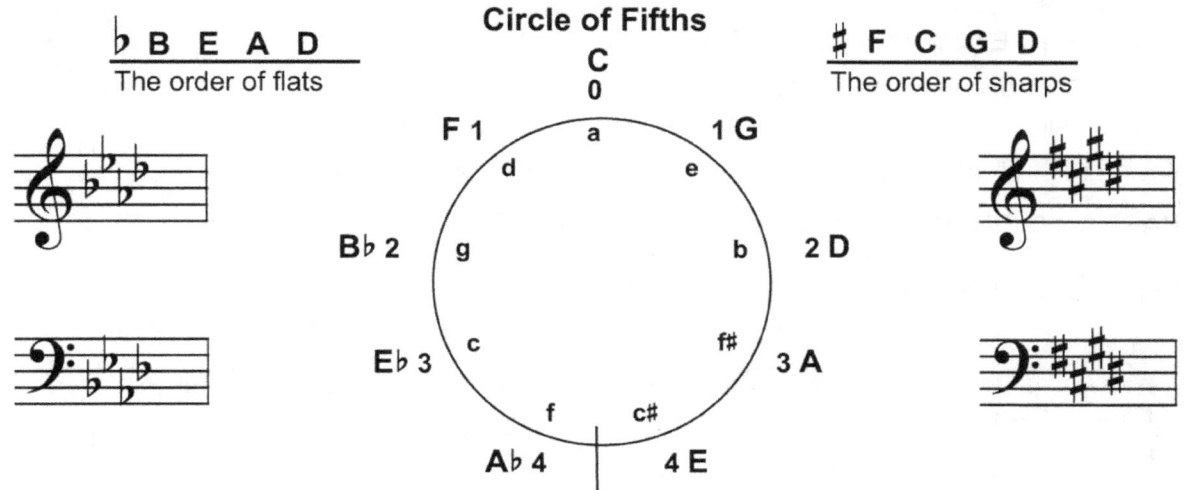

Circle of Fifths: OUTSIDE - Major keys, INSIDE - relative minor keys.
A Major key and its relative minor key have the SAME Key Signature.
A minor key is 3 semitones (and 3 letter names) BELOW its relative Major.

1. Name the Major key and its relative minor key for each of the following Key Signatures. Use UPPER case letters for Major keys and lower case letters for minor keys.

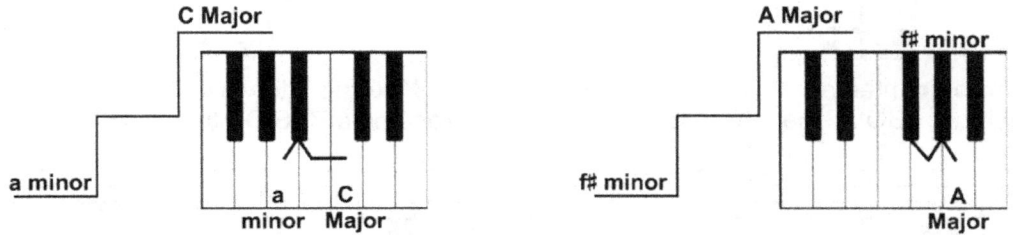

Maj key: G Maj, E♭Maj, E Maj, F Maj, D Maj, C Maj, B♭Maj, A Maj, A♭Maj

min key: e min, c min, c♯min, d min, b min, a min, g min, f♯min, f min

♪ **Note:** **Key Signatures** are placed after the clef, before the Time Signature. The Key Signature affects all the notes on the staff (and ledger lines) unless cancelled by an accidental.
Accidentals are placed in front of a note and apply only to the note on that specific line or space in the same measure. A **bar line** cancels the accidental but **NOT** the Key Signature.

2. Name the following notes.

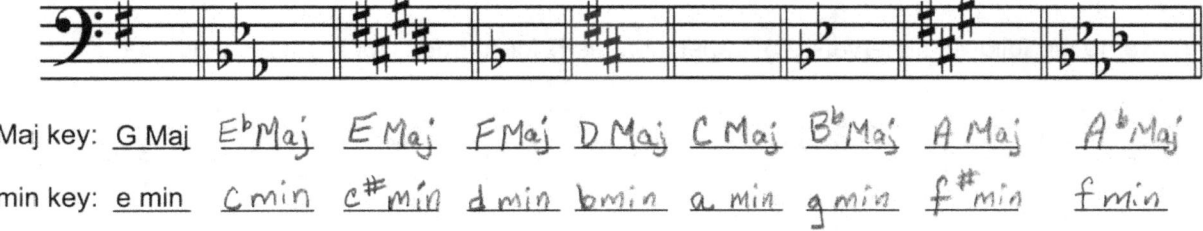

C♯, E♮, C♯, E♭, C, D♭, B♭, E♭, E♮

SEMITONE, WHOLE TONE, ENHARMONIC EQUIVALENT and INTERVALS

SEMITONE (Half Step): the shortest distance between two adjacent notes (black or white). Examples: C to C#, E to F, D♭ to D♮

Chromatic Semitone uses the SAME letter name. Example: C to C#
Diatonic Semitone uses a DIFFERENT letter name. Example: C to D♭
WHOLE TONE (Whole Step or Tone): equal to two semitones. Example: C to D

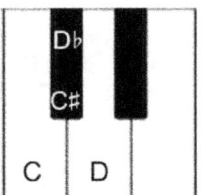

ENHARMONIC EQUIVALENT: SAME pitch with DIFFERENT letter names. Example: C# and D♭

1. Name each of the following as: **d.s.** (diatonic semitone), **c.s.** (chromatic semitone), **w.t.** (whole tone) or **e.e.** (enharmonic equivalent)

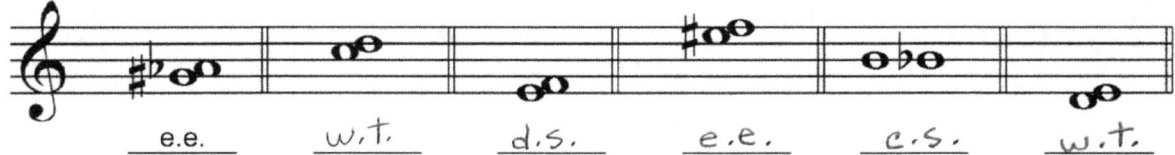

e.e.   w.t.   d.s.   e.e.   c.s.   w.t.

INTERVALS: the distance in pitch between two notes. The lowest note names the Major key. Intervals 1, 4, 5 and 8 are Perfect. Intervals 2, 3, 6 and 7 are Major or minor.

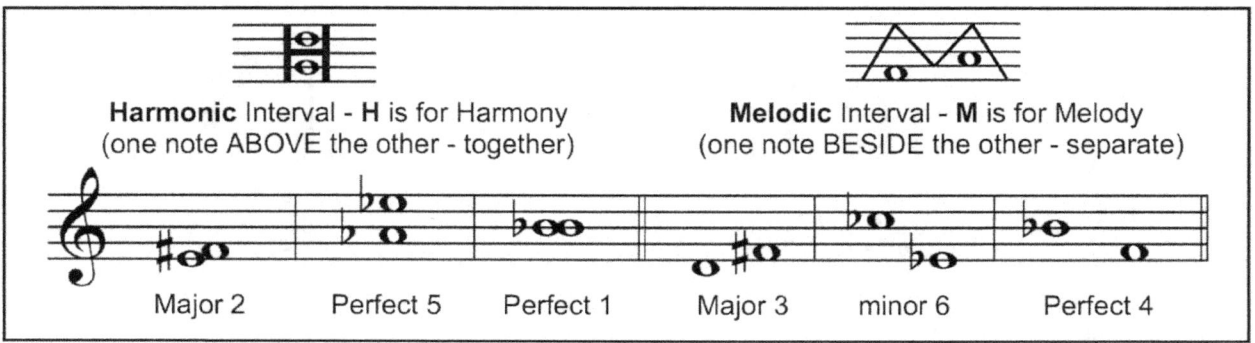

♪ **Note**: Abbreviations: Major = Maj; Perfect = Per; minor = min.

2. a) Name the following intervals. b) Label them as **H** for harmonic or **M** for melodic.

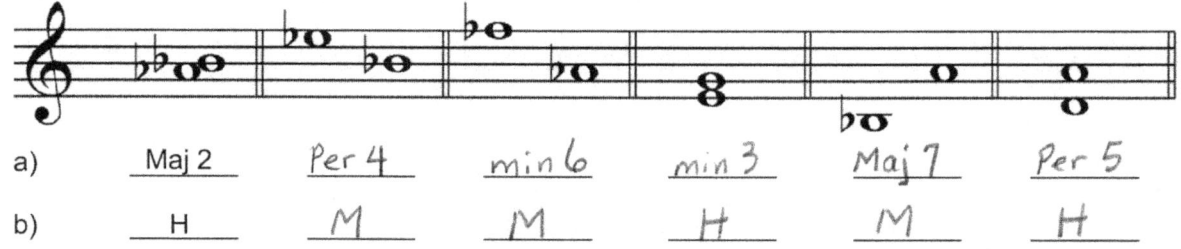

a) Maj 2   Per 4   min 6   min 3   Maj 7   Per 5
b)   H   M   M   H   M   H

♪ **Note**: A harmonic interval of a 1st or 2nd is written one note beside the other, touching.

3. Write the following harmonic intervals above the given notes.

Per 8   Maj 3   min 6   min 7   Maj 2   Per 1

SCALES, TECHNICAL DEGREE NAMES and ROMAN NUMERALS

SCALES - Major scales: eight notes based on a pattern of tones (whole steps) and semitones (half steps). A caret " ^ " sign (hat) above a number ($\hat{3}$) indicates the degree number of the scale.

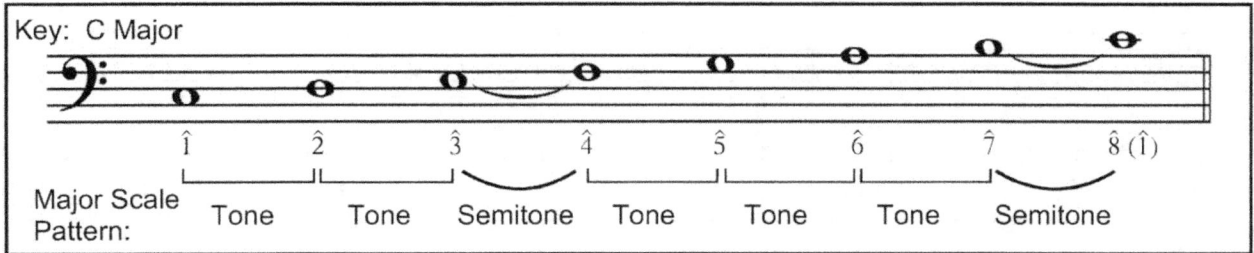

Natural minor scales have the SAME Key Signature as their relative Major. Nothing is added.

Harmonic minor scales have the SAME Key Signature as their relative Major. The 7th note is raised one chromatic semitone ascending and descending.

Melodic minor scales have the SAME Key Signature as their relative Major. The 6th and 7th notes are raised one chromatic semitone ascending and lowered one chromatic semitone descending.

TECHNICAL DEGREE NAMES: used to identify each degree of a scale.

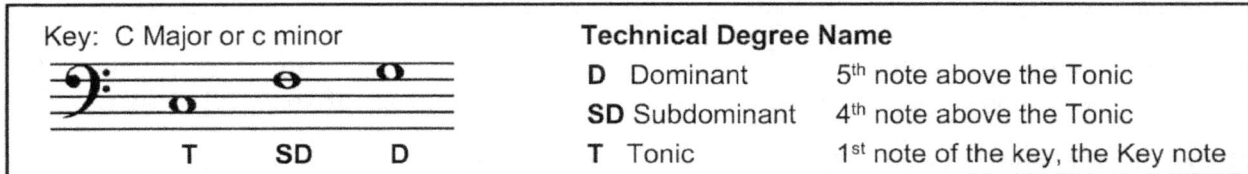

1. Name the (**T**) Tonic, (**SD**) Subdominant and (**D**) Dominant notes for the following keys.

   G Major: T - __G__ SD - __C__ D - __D__   g minor: T - __G__ SD - __C__ D - __D__

ROMAN NUMERALS (R.N.): identify the type/quality of a triad built on each degree of a scale. Type/quality - Major triads: UPPER case **I, IV, V**; minor triads: lower case **i, iv**. Solid triads (3 notes played together) or broken triads (one note played after the other) are built on any degree of a scale.

♪ **Note:** The Dominant triad of a harmonic minor key always contains the raised 7th note. The Dominant (V) triad is always Major.

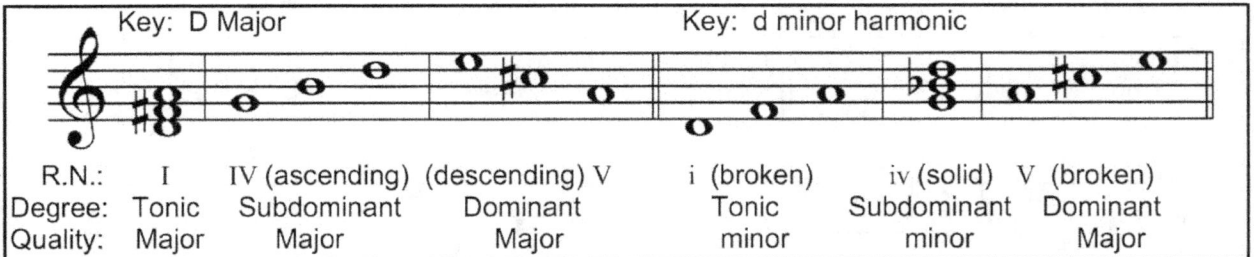

2. Write the g minor harmonic scale ascending only. Use a Key Signature and any necessary accidentals. Write the i, iv and V triads in solid root position. Use whole notes.

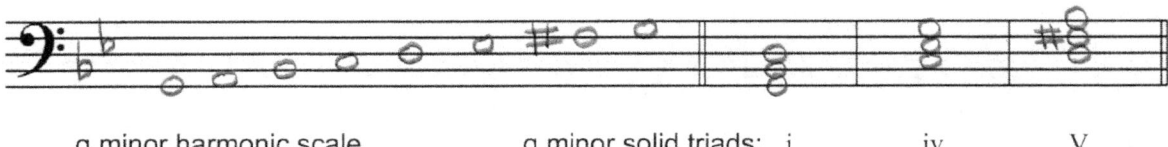

g minor harmonic scale   g minor solid triads: i   iv   V

NOTE and REST VALUES and TRANSPOSING

Each **NOTE** represents a specific time value of sound and each **REST** a specific time value of silence.

Note/Rest:	**Whole**	**Half**	**Quarter**	**Eighth**	**Sixteenth**	**Thirty-second**
Beats:	4 Beats	2 Beats	1 Beat	½ Beat	¼ Beat	⅛ Beat

Rests: ▬ hangs from line 4.   ▬ sits on line 3.   𝄽 and 𝄾 start in space 3.   𝄿 starts in space 4.

Flags: For an eighth, sixteenth and thirty-second note, the FLAG goes to the RIGHT.
When writing flags, the end of the flag does not touch the notehead.

1. Copy the notes and rests in the Bass Clef below. Write the number of beats for each note/rest.

Note/Rest:	**Whole**	**Half**	**Quarter**	**Eighth**	**Sixteenth**	**Thirty-second**
Beats:	4 Beats	2 Beats	1 Beat	½ Beat	¼ Beat	⅛ Beat

Stems: For beamed notes, the note farthest away from the third line (the middle line) determines the direction of all the stems. Notes above the middle line - the stems go down on the left; notes below the middle line - stems go up on the right; and notes on the middle line - stems go either way.

2. Copy the following beamed notes.

TRANSPOSING: A melody may be written one octave higher or lower in the same clef or in an alternate clef. A melody may also be rewritten at the same pitch in an alternate clef.

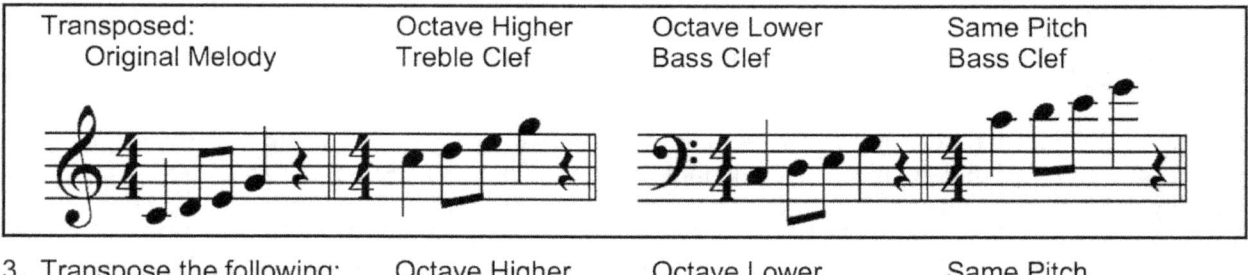

3. Transpose the following: Octave Higher   Octave Lower   Same Pitch
   Original Melody   Treble Clef   Bass Clef   Bass Clef

SIMPLE TIME

SIMPLE TIME SIGNATURE - Top Number

Top number is **2**, **3** or **4**.
The number of beats per measure.

Pulse is where the rhythmic emphasis falls.
S = Strong   **w** = weak   **M** = Medium

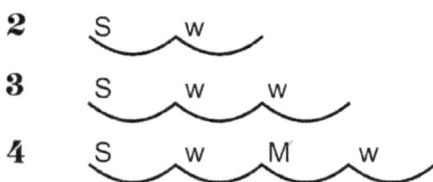

SIMPLE TIME SIGNATURE - Bottom Number

Bottom number is **2**, **4**, **8** or **16**.
The kind of note that equals ONE Basic Beat.

Basic Beat is a single note for each equal group.

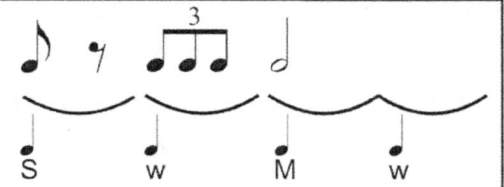

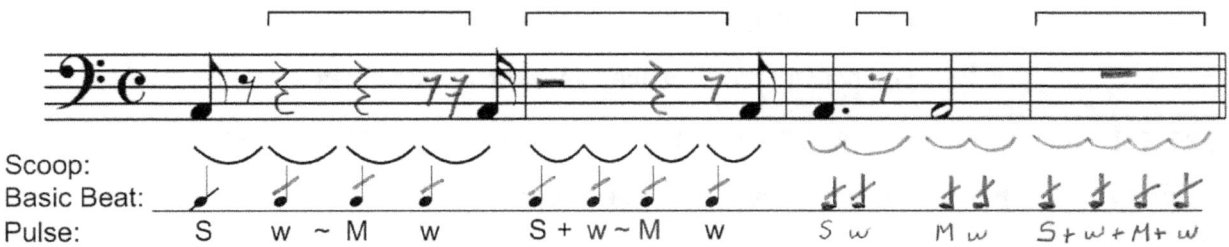

A **SCOOP** is a visual aid in grouping notes and/or rests into one beat.

Scoops are joined together when note or rest values equal more than one beat.

♪ **Note:** Plus (+) sign: **join** the **S + w** and the **M + w**.   Tilde (~) sign: do **NOT** join the **w ~ M** or **w ~ w**.

1. Scoop each beat. Write the Basic Beat and pulse below each scoop. Add rests below each bracket to complete the measure. Cross off the Basic Beat as each beat is completed.

Whole Rest Rules: A whole rest fills any measure with silence. There are 2 exceptions to the rule:

In **3/2** time: a **whole rest** receives 3 beats of silence and fills a whole measure (Strong+weak+weak).

        a **whole rest** receives 2 beats of silence for beats 1 and 2 (Strong+weak) when a half note value is on beat 3.

In **4/2** time: a **whole rest** receives 2 beats of silence for beats 1 and 2 (Strong+weak = 2 half notes) or 2 beats of silence for beats 3 and 4 (Medium+weak = 2 half notes).

        a **breve rest** (double whole rest ▬) receives 4 beats of silence and fills a whole measure.

        a **breve note** (double whole note ‖O‖) receives 4 beats of sound (4 half notes).

2. Add bar lines to complete the following measures.

MUSICAL TERMS and SIGNS

Articulation Terms	Definition	Sign
marcato, marc.	marked or stressed	♩ (marcato)
accent	a stressed note	♩ >
legato	smooth	
slur	play the notes *legato*	♩♩♩ (with slur)
staccato	detached	♩·
tenuto	held, sustained	♩—

Signs	Definition
D.C.	*da capo*, from the beginning
D.C. al Fine	repeat from the beginning and end at *Fine*
𝄋	*dal segno*, D.S., from the sign
M.D.	*mano destra*, right hand
M.S.	*mano sinistra*, left hand
8va- - - ⌐ *ottava, 8va*	play one octave above the written pitch
8va- - - ⌐ *ottava, 8va*	play one octave below the written pitch
Ped.	pedal marking
⌊_____⌋	pedal marking
♩‿♩	tie: hold for the combined value of the tied notes
𝄇 𝄆	repeat sign: repeat the music within the double bar lines
|	bar line: a vertical line separating measures
(measure)	measure/bar: a unit of musical time
‖	double bar line (2 thin lines): indicates the end of a section
𝄂	double bar line (final - 1 thin and 1 thick line): indicates the end of a piece

Terms	Definition	Sign
con pedale, con ped.	with pedal	⌊____⌋
pedale, ped.	pedal	Ped.
ottava, 8va	the interval of an octave	
tempo	speed at which music is performed	
fine	the end	

1. Articulation indicates the type of touch. Write the articulation term for each definition below.

   a) play the notes *legato*   b) held, sustained   c) detached   d) a stressed note

   _____slur_____   _____tenuto_____   _____staccato_____   _____accent_____

TEMPO, CHANGES in TEMPO and DYNAMICS

Tempo   **Definition** - arranged in order from slowest to fastest.
largo   very slow
larghetto   not as slow as *largo*
adagio   slow; slower than *andante*, but not as slow as *largo*
lento   slow

andante   moderately slow; at a walking pace
andantino   a little faster than *andante*
moderato   at a moderate tempo

allegretto   fairly fast; not as fast as *allegro*
allegro   fast
vivace   lively, brisk
presto   very fast
prestissimo   as fast as possible

1. Arrange the following tempos in order from slowest to fastest.

   andantino   adagio   presto   allegretto   largo

   <u>largo</u>   <u>adagio</u>   <u>andantino</u>   <u>allegretto</u>   <u>presto</u>

Changes in Tempo   **Definition**
accelerando, accel.   becoming quicker
a tempo   return to the original tempo
fermata, ⌒   pause; hold the note or rest longer than its written value
rallentando, rall.   slowing down
ritardando, rit.   slowing down gradually
Tempo primo, Tempo I   return to the original tempo

2. Write the abbreviation or sign for the following terms.

   <u>rall.</u>   <u>accel.</u>   <u>⌒</u>   <u>rit.</u>
   rallentando   accelerando   fermata   ritardando

Dynamics   **Definition**
crescendo, cresc.   becoming louder   <
decrescendo, decresc.   becoming softer
diminuendo, dim.   becoming softer   >
fortepiano, **fp**   loud, then suddenly soft

mezzo forte, **mf**   moderately loud   *mezzo piano,* **mp**   moderately soft
forte, **f**   loud   *piano,* **p**   soft
fortissimo, **ff**   very loud   *pianissimo,* **pp**   very soft

3. Write the opposite dynamic for each given dynamic sign.

   a) **f** - <u>**p**</u>   b) **pp** - <u>**ff**</u>   c) **mf** - <u>**mp**</u>   d) *dim.* - <u>*cresc.*</u>   e) < - <u>></u>

ANALYSIS REVIEW

ANALYSIS of a musical composition gives the performer a better understanding of the composers ideas in interpreting the piece. Musical terms and signs are used to convey the key, tempo, dynamics, articulation and other important elements of music.

1. Analyze the following piece of music by answering the questions below.

a) Add the correct Time Signature directly on the music.
b) Name the title of this piece. _Two Caterpillars_
c) Name the composers of this piece. _S. McKibbon and G. St. Germain_
d) Name the key of this piece. _e minor_
e) For the triad at the letter **A**, name: Root: _E_   Type/Quality: _minor_
f) Name the interval at the letter **B**. _Major 2_
g) Name the scale at the letter **C**. _e minor harmonic_
h) Name the scale at the letter **D**. _e minor melodic_
i) Name the scale at the letter **E**. _e minor natural (e minor melodic descending)_
j) Explain the sign at the letter **F**. _ritardando - slowing down gradually_

Lesson 1 Review Test

Total Score: ____ / 100

1. Complete the Circle of Fifths:
   a) Write the order of flats on the top left and the order of sharps on the top right.
   b) Write the Major keys on the OUTSIDE of the circle. (Use UPPER case for Major keys.)
   c) Write the relative minor keys on the INSIDE of the circle. (Use lower case for minor keys.)

____ / 10

♭ BEAD — The order of flats

♯ FCGD — The order of sharps

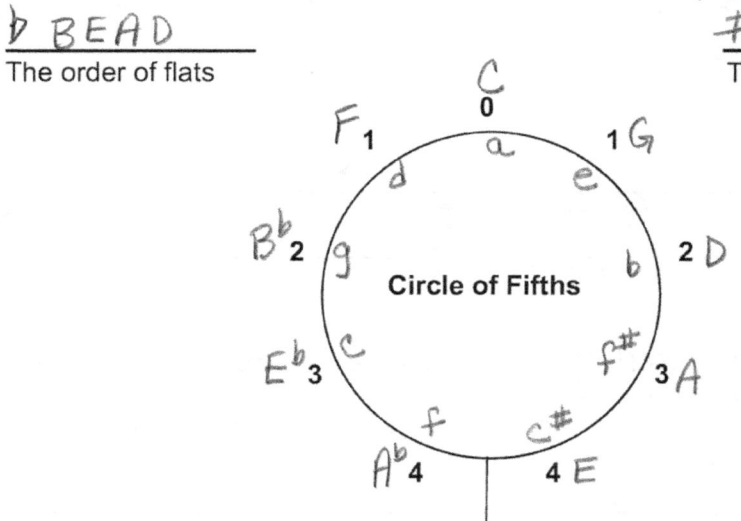

2. Write the Key Signature for each Major key and its relative minor key.

____ / 10

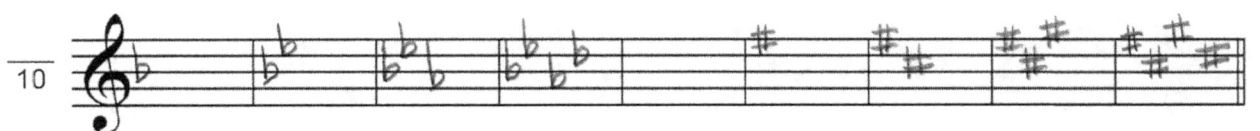

F Major   B♭ Major   E♭ Major   A♭ Major   C Major   G Major   D Major   A Major   E Major

d minor   g minor   c minor   f minor   a minor   e minor   b minor   f♯ minor   c♯ minor

3. Write the following **MELODIC** intervals **ABOVE** the given notes. Use whole notes.

____ / 10

minor 6   Perfect 4   minor 3   Major 7   minor 3

4. Name each of the following as: **d.s.** (diatonic semitone), **c.s.** (chromatic semitone), **w.t.** (whole tone) or **e.e.** (enharmonic equivalent)

____ / 10

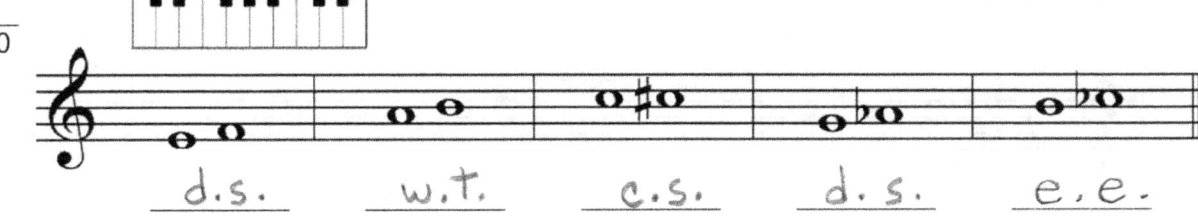

d.s.   w.t.   c.s.   d.s.   e.e.

5. Name the key of the following melody. Transpose it **DOWN** one octave into the Bass Clef using the correct Key Signature.

Key: D Major

6. Write a solid triad in **ROOT POSITION** above each of the given notes. Use whole notes.
   a) Name the **MAJOR** key for each of the following Key Signatures.
   b) Identify the technical degree name of the root as: **T** (Tonic), **SD** (Subdominant) or **D** (Dominant).

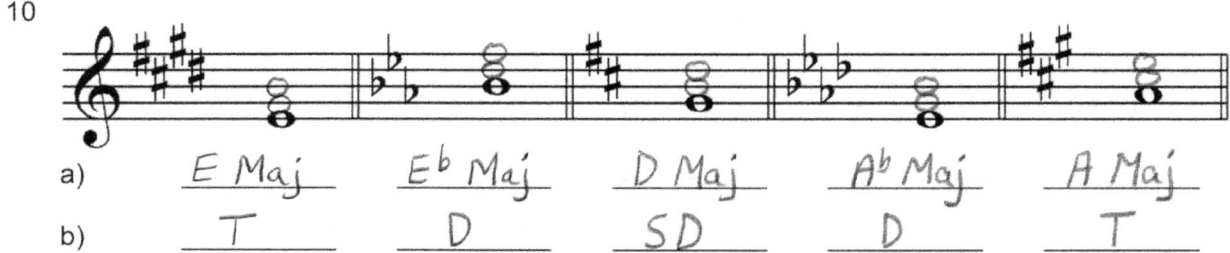

a) E Maj   Eb Maj   D Maj   Ab Maj   A Maj
b)   T   D   SD   D   T

7. Write the following scales, ascending and descending, using the correct **KEY SIGNATURE**. Use whole notes.

   a) B flat Major in the Treble Clef
   b) c minor melodic in the Bass Clef
   c) a minor harmonic in the Treble Clef

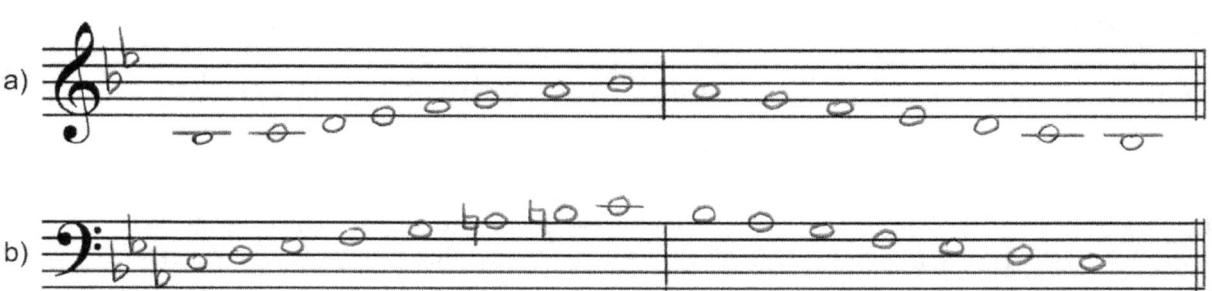

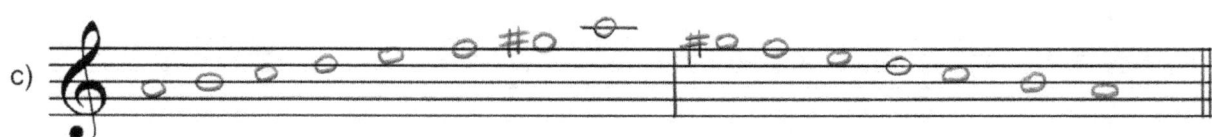

8. Write the **BASIC BEAT** and the **PULSE** below each measure. Add rests below each bracket to complete the measure. Cross off the Basic Beat as each beat is completed.

9. Match each musical term or sign with the English definition. (Not all definitions will be used.)

Term		Definition
andante	c	a) indicates the end of a piece
ritardando, rit.	e	b) the interval of an octave
tenuto, ♩	g	c) moderately slow; at a walking pace
legato	f	d) becoming quicker
fortepiano, *fp*	h	e) gradually getting slower
bar line	j	f) smooth
ottava, 8*va*	b	g) held, sustained
marcato, marc.	i	h) loud, then suddenly soft
double bar line	a	i) marked or stressed
accelerando	d	j) a vertical line separating measures
		k) playfully

15

10. Analyze the following piece of music by answering the questions below.

Minuet

Moderato

Leopold Mozart
(1719 - 1787)

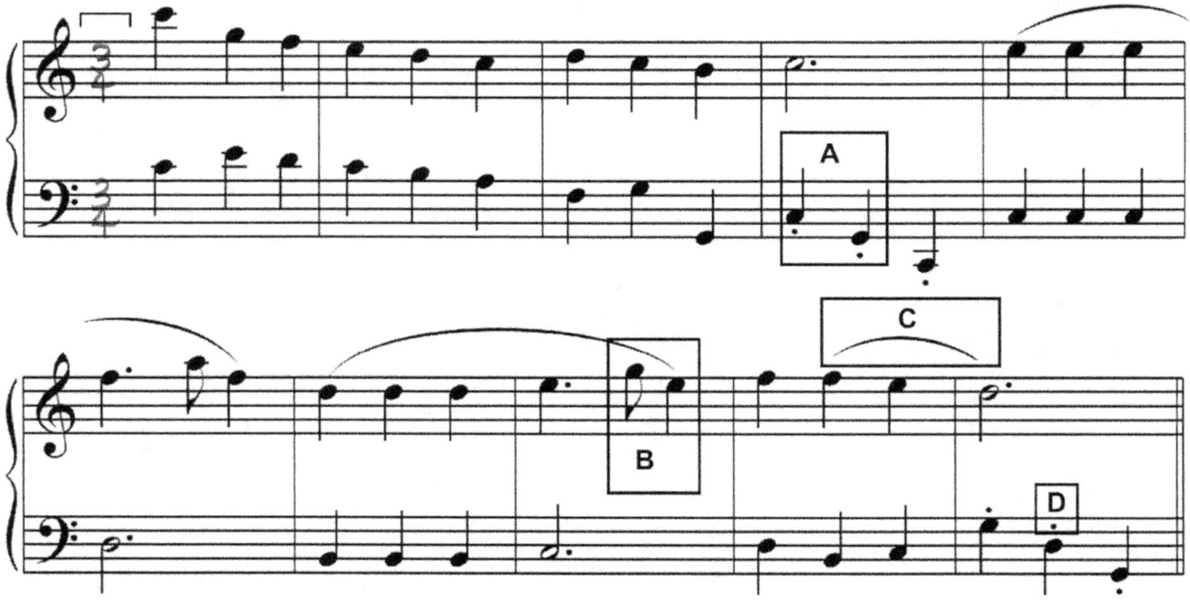

a) Add the correct Time Signature directly on the music.

b) Name the title of this piece. __Minuet__

c) Name the composer of this piece. __Leopold Mozart__

d) When did the composer live? __1719-1787__

e) Name the interval at the letter **A**. __Perfect 4__

f) Name the interval at the letter **B**. __minor 3__

g) How many measures are in this piece? __10__

h) Explain the meaning of **Moderato**. __at a moderate tempo__

i) Explain the sign at the letter **C**. __slur - play the notes legato__

j) Explain the sign at the letter **D**. __staccato - detached__

Lesson 2   Circle of Fifths, Major and Enharmonic Scales

The **CIRCLE of FIFTHS** is a map of the Major and minor Key Signatures. **MAJOR KEYS** are written around the outside of the circle using UPPER CASE letters. The numbers around the outside of the Circle of Fifths indicate how many flats or sharps are found in each key.

♪ **Note:** The distance from one key to the next key around the Circle of Fifths is a Perfect Fifth.

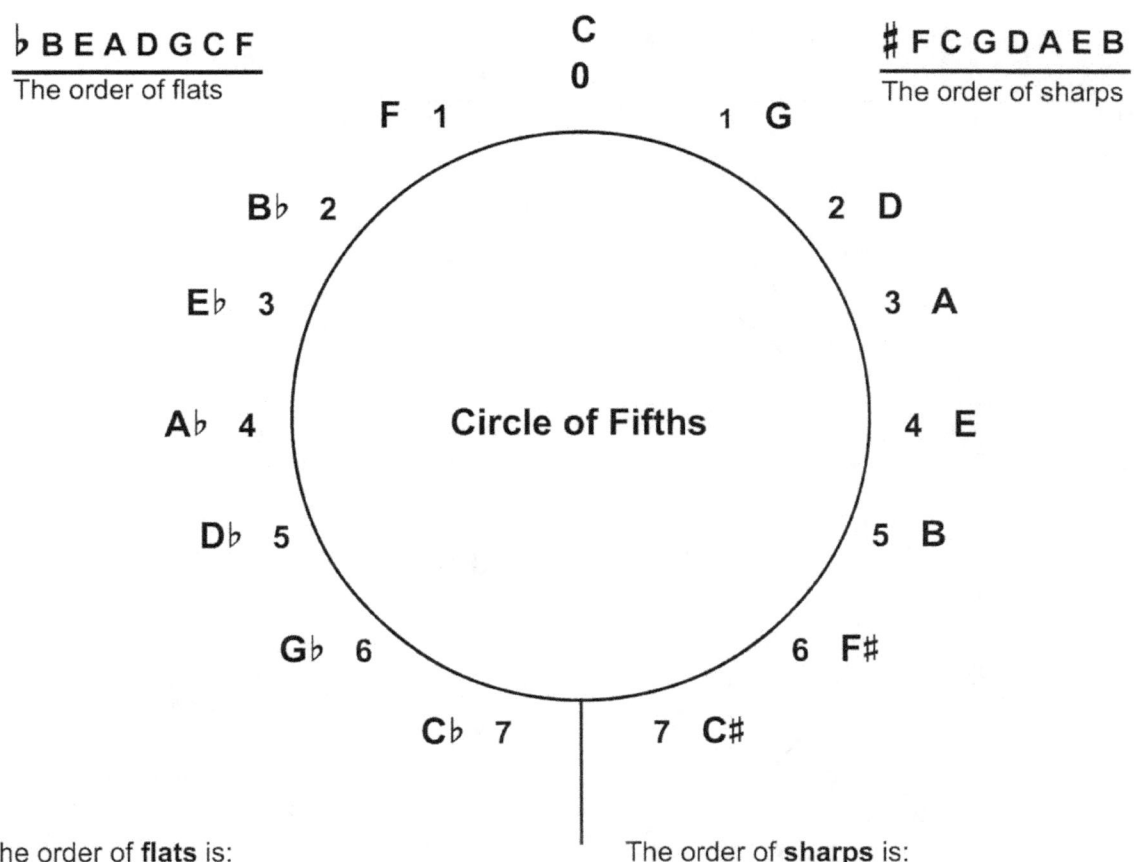

The order of **flats** is:

Battle Ends And Down Goes Charles Father

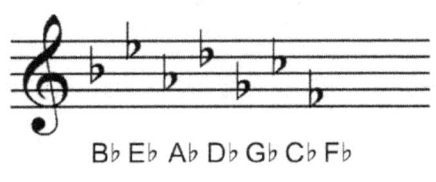

Bb Eb Ab Db Gb Cb Fb

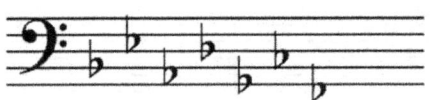

The order of **sharps** is:

Father Charles Goes Down And Ends Battle

F# C# G# D# A# E# B#

♪ **Note:** Always write the flats and sharps in the correct order.

1. Write the order of flats.

Bb Eb Ab Db Gb Cb Fb

2. Write the order of sharps.

F# C# G# D# A# E# B#

TRACE THE CIRCLE OF FIFTHS - MAJOR KEYS

Major keys are written on the OUTSIDE of the Circle of Fifths.

1. Complete the Circle of Fifths:
    a) Write the order of flats on the top left. Write the order of sharps on the top right.
    b) Start at the number "1" on the flat side with **F** (Father). Move clockwise (to the right) **UP** a **FIFTH** each time. Trace the given letters. Use this sentence to complete the Circle of Fifths:

Father Charles Goes Down And Ends Battle

♭ __BEADGCF__   # __FCGDAEB__
The order of flats   The order of sharps

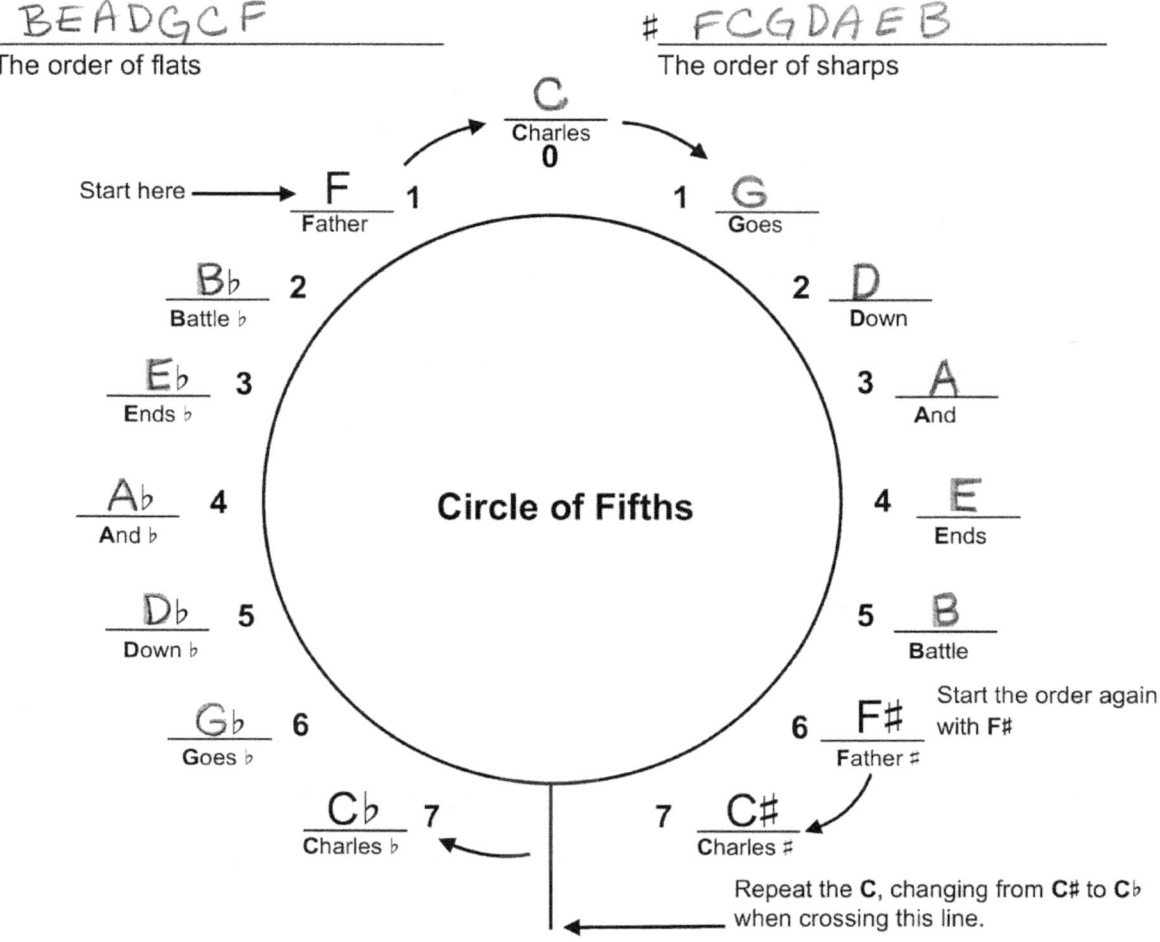

♫ **Note:** Always write the flats and sharps in the correct order.

2. a) Copy the order of flats in the Treble Clef.   b) Copy the order of sharps in the Treble Clef.

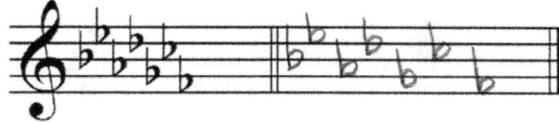 

♫ **Note:** This is called the **Circle of Fifths** as the distance between each key when moving clockwise around the circle is **five letter names** (a fifth).

F G A B **C** D E F **G** A B C D E F **G** A B C D **E** F G A **B** C D E **F**
1 2 3 4 5 2 3 4 5 2 3 4 5 2 3 4 5 2 3 4 5 2 3 4 5 2 3 4 5

18

WRITE THE CIRCLE OF FIFTHS - MAJOR KEYS

Major Keys are written on the OUTSIDE of the Circle of Fifths.

1. Complete the Circle of Fifths:
   a) Write the order of flats on the top left. Write the order of sharps on the top right.
   b) Start at the number "1" on the flat side with **F** (Father). Move clockwise (to the right) **UP** a **FIFTH** each time. Use upper case letters. Use this sentence to complete the Circle of Fifths:

Father Charles Goes Down And Ends Battle

♭ __BEADGCF__   ♯ __FCGDAEB__
The order of flats   The order of sharps

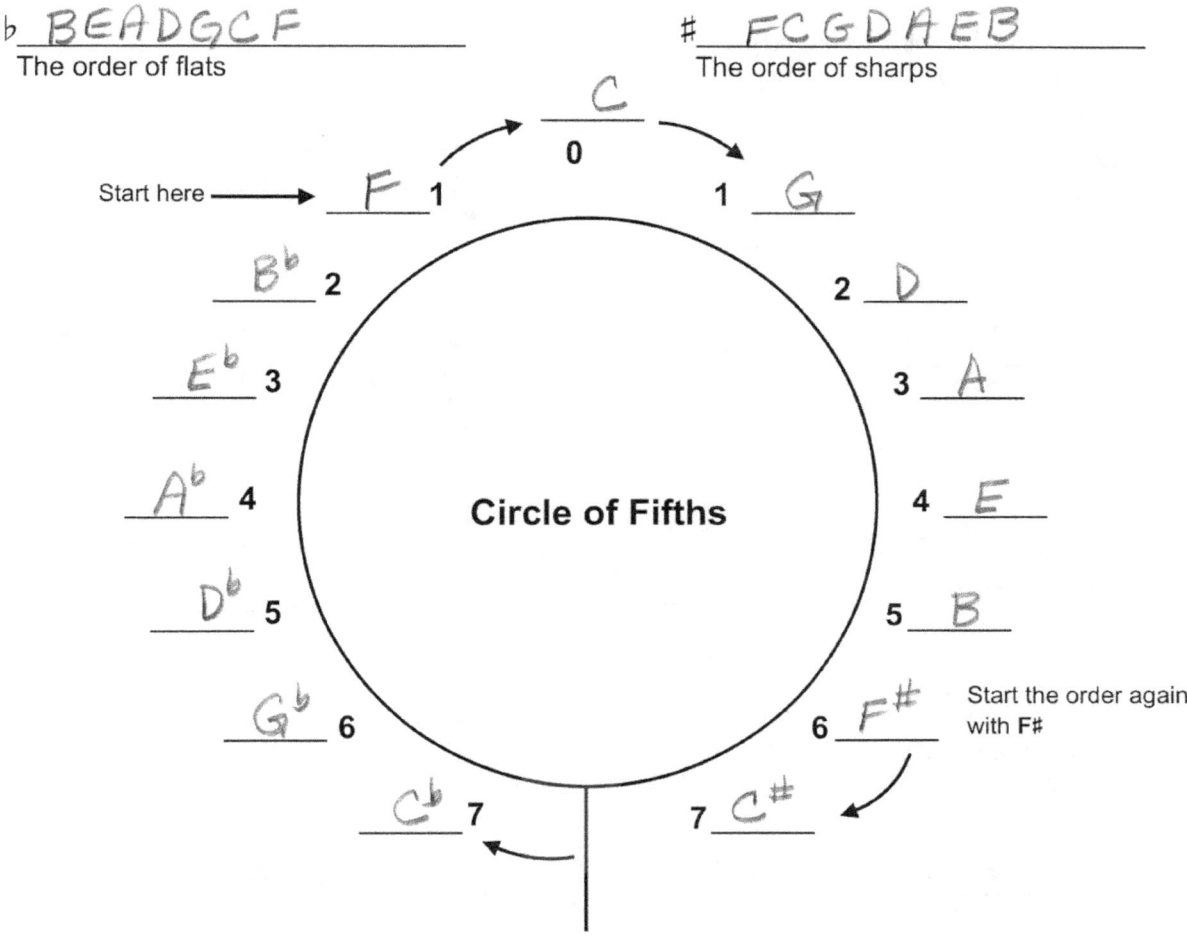

♪ **Note:** Always write the flats and sharps in the correct order.

2. a) Copy the order of flats in the Bass Clef.   b) Copy the order of sharps in the Bass Clef.

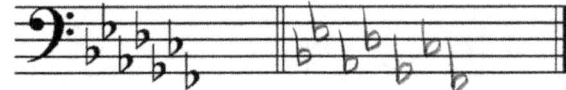   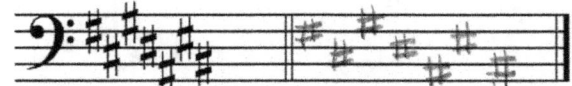

♪ **Note:** Always write **MAJOR** keys on the **OUTSIDE** of the circle **BESIDE** the numbers.
        Use UPPER CASE letters for Major key names.

The sentence for the order of flats is: The sentence for the order of sharps is:

Battle **E**nds **A**nd **D**own **G**oes **C**harles **F**ather   **F**ather **C**harles **G**oes **D**own **A**nd **E**nds **B**attle

MAJOR KEY SIGNATURES with FLATS

To name the **MAJOR KEY with FLATS**, go to the **SECOND LAST** flat of the Key Signature. That note is the name of the Major Key.

Example: Key Signature is B♭ E♭ A♭: the second last flat is E♭. That names the key as E♭ Major.
The exception to the rule is **F Major** which only has one flat, B♭.

♪ Note: The Key Signature is written at the beginning of the music after the clef.

1. a) Name the following Major keys.
   b) Copy the Treble Clef and Key Signature. Name the Major key again.

2. a) Name the following Major keys.
   b) Copy the Bass Clef and Key Signature. Name the Major key again.

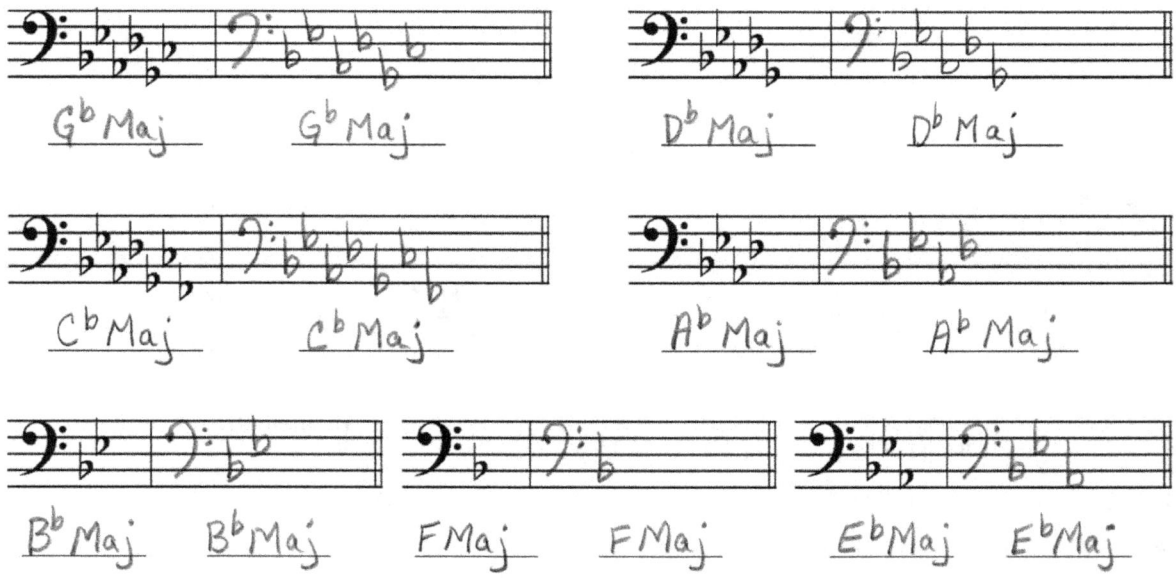

MAJOR KEY SIGNATURES with SHARPS

To name the **MAJOR KEY with SHARPS**, go to the LAST sharp of the Key Signature and go up one diatonic semitone (half step). That note is the name of the Major key.

Example: Key Signature is F# C#: last sharp is C#. From C#, go up one diatonic semitone to D. That names the key as D Major.

♪ **Note:** The Key Signature is written at the beginning of the music after the clef.

1. a) Name the following Major keys.
   b) Copy the Treble Clef and Key Signature. Name the Major key again.

2. a) Name the following Major keys.
   b) Copy the Bass Clef and Key Signature. Name the Major key again.

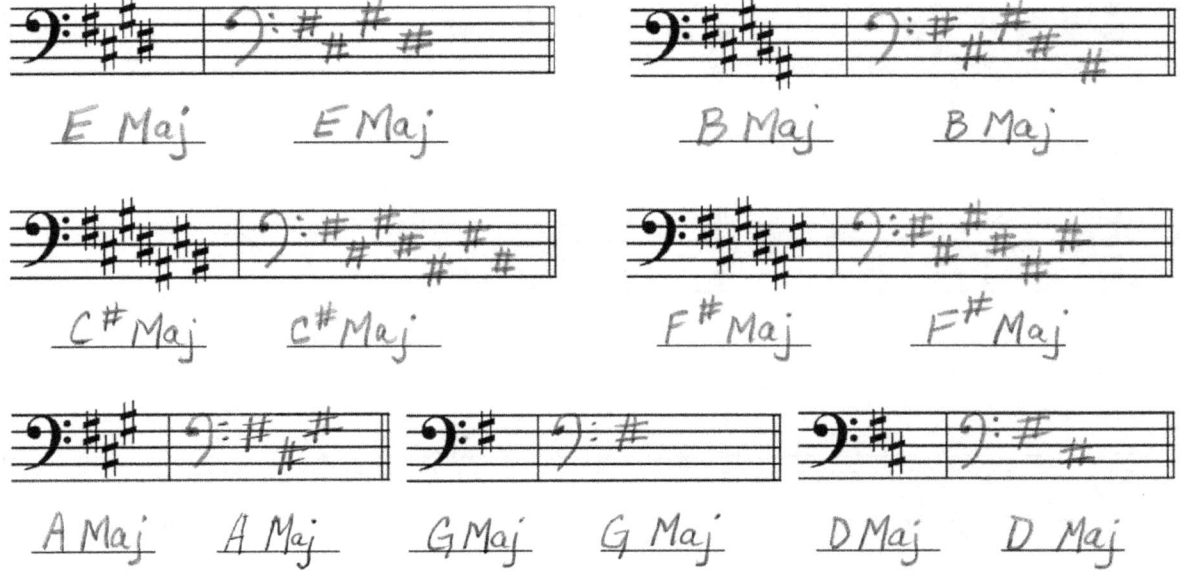

MAJOR SCALES using a KEY SIGNATURE with FLATS

MAJOR SCALES using a **KEY SIGNATURE** can be written with OR without a center bar line. When writing a scale WITH a center bar line, the bar line is written after the highest note.

♪ Note: Always write scales in the **SAME WAY**, either WITH or WITHOUT a center bar line.
Use a double bar line at the end of the staff.

1. Write the following Major scales with flats, ascending and descending, using the correct Key Signature. Use whole notes.

    a) D flat Major in the Treble Clef

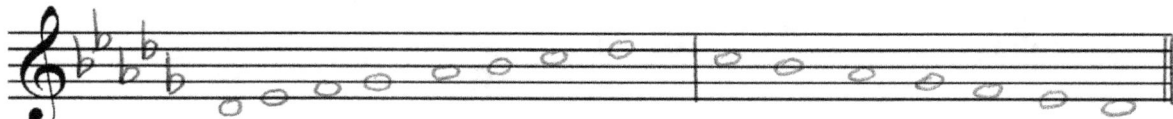

    b) G flat Major in the Treble Clef

    c) C flat Major in the Treble Clef

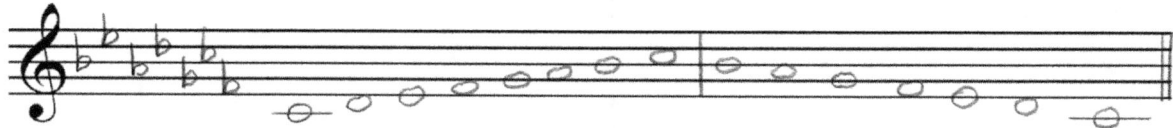

    d) D flat Major in the Bass Clef

    e) G flat Major in the Bass Clef

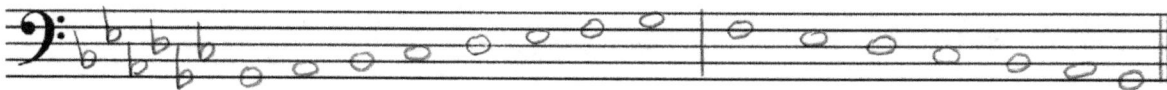

    f) C flat Major in the Bass Clef

MAJOR SCALES using a KEY SIGNATURE with SHARPS

When writing a **MAJOR SCALE** using a **KEY SIGNATURE**, with or without a center bar line, no accidentals are needed in the scale.

♪ **Note:** When writing a scale using a Key Signature, the notes begin **AFTER** the Key Signature.

1. Write the following Major scales with sharps, ascending and descending, using the correct Key Signature. Use whole notes.

    a) B Major in the Treble Clef

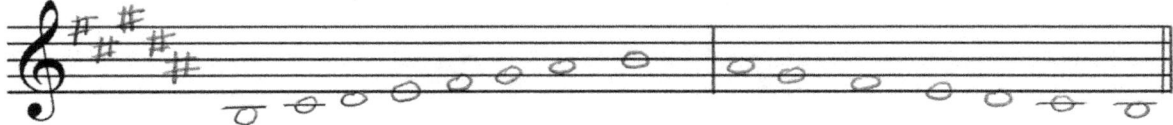

    b) F sharp Major in the Treble Clef

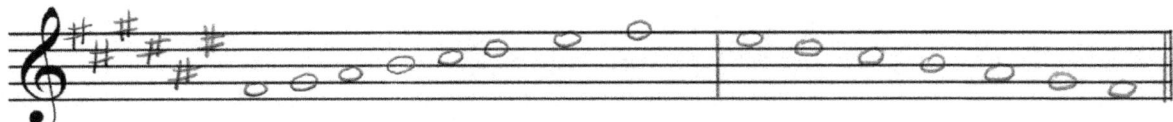

    c) C sharp Major in the Treble Clef

    d) B Major in the Bass Clef

    e) F sharp Major in the Bass Clef

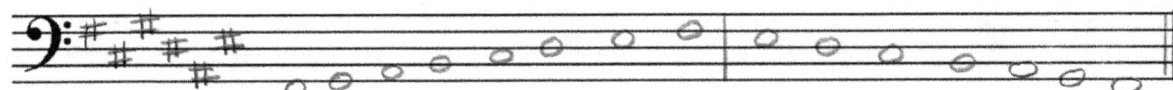

    f) C sharp Major in the Bass Clef

ENHARMONIC TONIC MAJOR SCALES

ENHARMONIC TONIC MAJOR SCALES are scales that use the SAME pitches but are written with notes using different letter names (enharmonic equivalents).
Example: D♭ Major scale and C♯ Major scale

♪ **Note:** The Circle of Fifths contains three enharmonic Major keys:
D♭ Major and C♯ Major; G♭ Major and F♯ Major; C♭ Major and B Major.

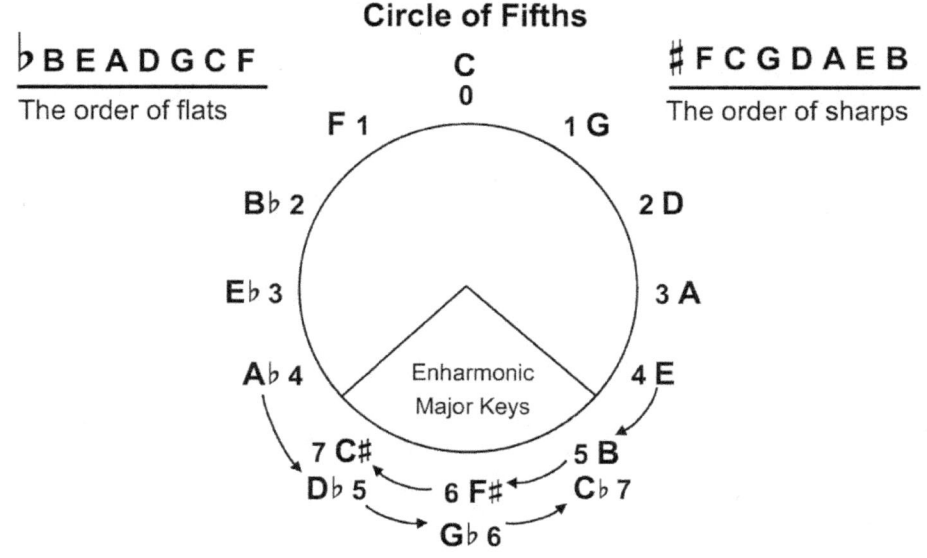

1. Name the enharmonic Tonic Major scale. Write the enharmonic Tonic Major scale, ascending and descending, using the correct Key Signature. Use whole notes.

a) the enharmonic Tonic Major scale of D flat Major is ___C♯ Major___

b) the enharmonic Tonic Major scale of F sharp Major is ___G♭ Major___

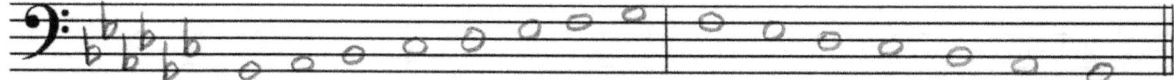

c) the enharmonic Tonic Major scale of C flat Major is ___B Major___

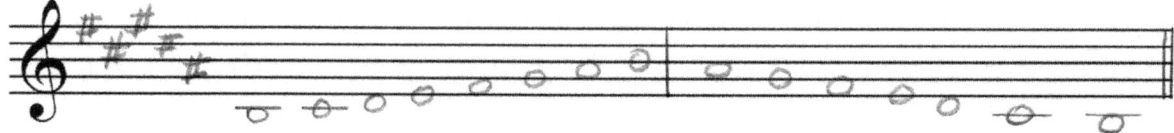

MAJOR SCALES using ACCIDENTALS

MAJOR SCALES may be written using **ACCIDENTALS** or a Key Signature. Scales may be written WITH or WITHOUT a center bar line. Scales always end with a double bar line.

WITH a center bar line: the center bar line **CANCELS** an accidental. Accidentals must be written in the ascending AND descending scale.

WITHOUT a center bar line: accidentals are written in the ascending scale only.

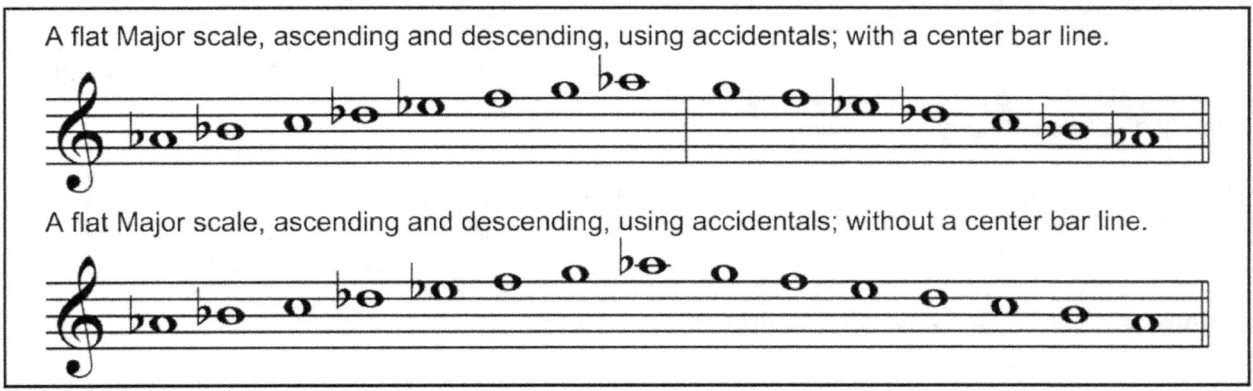

1. Write the following scales, ascending and descending, using accidentals. Use whole notes.

   a) E Major in the Treble Clef
   b) D flat Major in the Bass Clef
   c) enharmonic Tonic Major of B Major in the Treble Clef
   d) A Major in the Bass Clef
   e) enharmonic Tonic Major of G flat Major in the Bass Clef

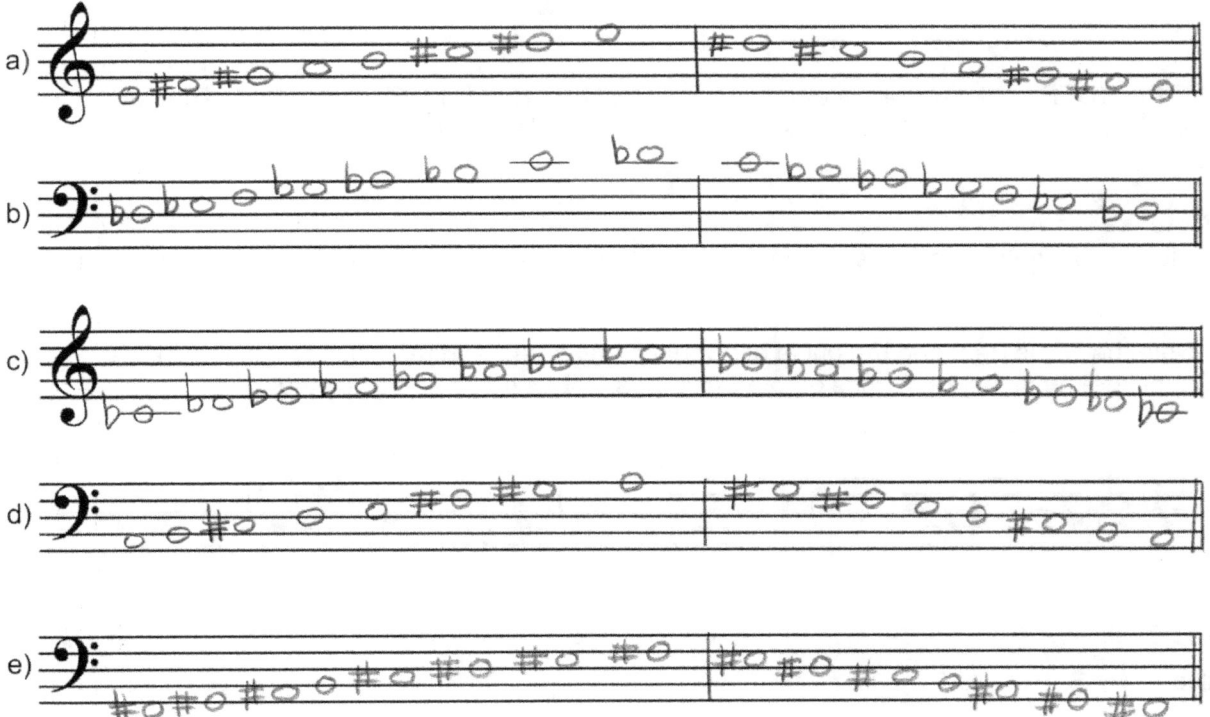

SLUR, TIE and DOTTED NOTE REVIEW

SLUR: a curved line connecting two or more notes of a **DIFFERENT PITCH**, played legato.

Only ONE slur is required, either above or below, for the notes of harmonic intervals or a chord that are to be played legato. Slurred repeated notes are indicated by a staccato and a slur. (A pedal may be used to connect the sound.)

TIE: a curved line connecting two or more notes of the **SAME PITCH**, held for the combined value of the tied notes.

A tie may be used to extend the note value over a bar line. Each tied note must have its own tie.

Ties and slurs may be used at the same time; the slur will connect notes of different pitches and the tie will connect notes of the same pitch.

♪ **Note:** A slur or a tie are written closest to the notehead.

1. Label the following as **S** (slur), **T** (tie) or **B** (both).

S   T   S   S   T   S   T   B

DOTTED NOTE: a dot placed after a note adds **"HALF THE VALUE"** of the note. The dot is written AFTER the note in the same space for a space note, and in the space above for a line note.

♪ **Note:**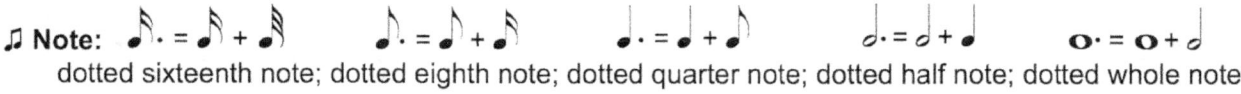

dotted sixteenth note; dotted eighth note; dotted quarter note; dotted half note; dotted whole note

2. Write the Basic Beat and the pulse below each measure. Add rests below each bracket to complete the measure. Cross off the Basic Beat as each beat is completed.

Basic Beat: ♩ ♩ ♩ ♩   ♩♩♩ ♩   ♩ ♩♩   ♩   ♩♩♩

Pulse: S w M w   S w M w S   w M w   S   w M w

Lesson 2 — Review Test

Total Score: ____ / 100

1. Complete the Circle of Fifths:
   a) Write the order of flats on the top left and the order of sharps on the top right.
   b) Write the numbers 1 - 7 around the sharp side and the flat side of the Circle of Fifths.
   c) Write the Major keys on the outside of the Circle of Fifths.

___ / 10

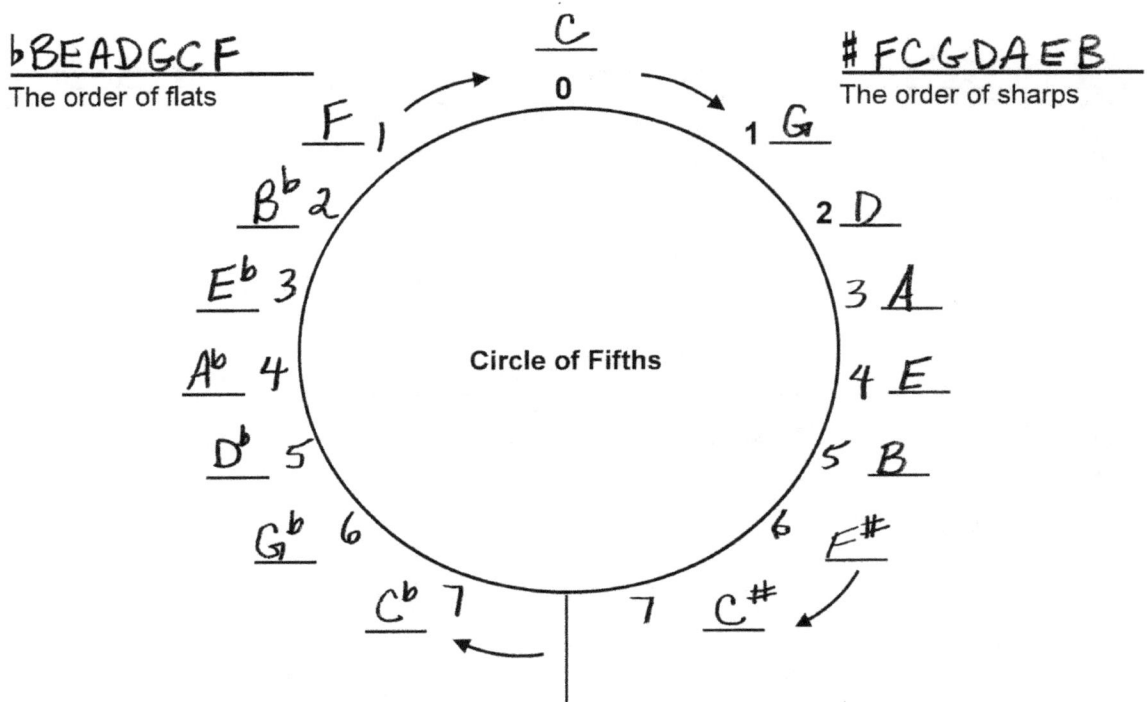

2. Write the **BASIC BEAT** and the **PULSE** below each measure. Add rests below each bracket to complete the measure. Cross off the Basic Beat as each beat is completed.

___ / 10

3. Write the following solid triads in **ROOT POSITION** in the Treble Clef, using the correct Key Signature. Use whole notes. Label the degree as: **I, IV** or **V** (Major triad); **i** or **iv** (minor triad).

10 a) the **TONIC** triad of c sharp minor harmonic
   b) the **DOMINANT** triad of e minor harmonic
   c) the **SUBDOMINANT** triad of b minor harmonic
   d) the **TONIC** triad of D flat Major
   e) the **DOMINANT** triad of C sharp Major

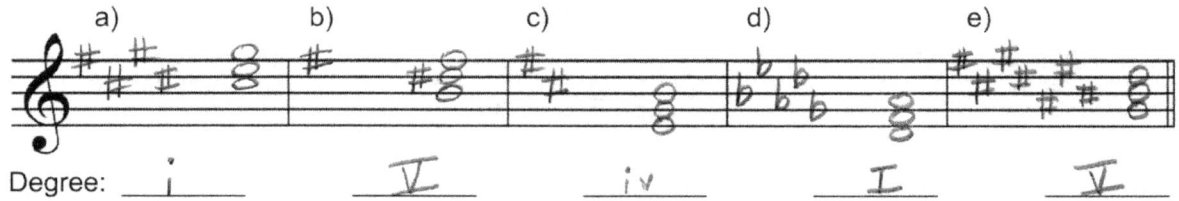

4. Name the key of the following melody. Transpose it **UP** one octave in the Treble Clef using the correct Key Signature.

10

5. Write the following **HARMONIC** intervals **ABOVE** the given notes. Use whole notes.

10

6. Write the following **MELODIC** intervals **ABOVE** the given notes. Use whole notes.

10

7. Write the following scales, ascending and descending, using **ACCIDENTALS**. Use whole notes.

   a) enharmonic Tonic Major of B Major in the Treble Clef
   b) D flat Major in the Treble Clef
   c) A Major in the Bass Clef
   d) C sharp Major in the Bass Clef
   e) enharmonic Tonic Major of G flat Major in the Bass Clef

8. Match each musical term or sign with the English definition. (Not all definitions will be used.)

Term		Definition
adagio	e	a) slur: play the notes *legato*
presto	j	b) left hand
♩ ♩	f	c) moderate tempo
mano sinistra, M.S.	b	d) slowing down
rallentando, rall.	d	e) slow; slower than *andante*, not as slow as *largo*
allegro	h	f) tie: hold for combined value of the tied notes
D.C. al Fine	i	g) loud
tempo	k	h) fast
forte, *f*	g	i) repeat from the beginning and end at *Fine*
♩♩♩	a	j) very fast
		k) speed at which music is performed

9. a) Write a whole tone (whole step) above each of the following notes. Use whole notes.

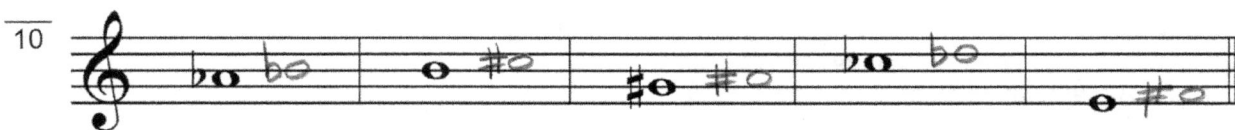

b) Name each of the following as: **d.s.** (diatonic semitone), **c.s.** (chromatic semitone),
   w.t. (whole tone)   or   **e.e.** (enharmonic equivalent)

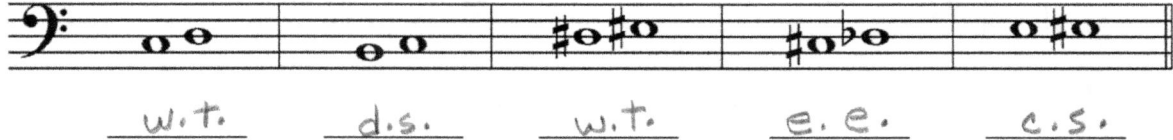

w.t.   d.s.   w.t.   e.e.   c.s.

10. Analyze the following piece by answering the questions below.

Andantino   Franz Joseph Haydn

a) Add the correct Time Signature directly on the music.
b) Name the key of this piece. __G Major__
c) Name the composer of this piece. __Franz Joseph Haydn__
d) Name the type of rest at the letter **A**. __quarter rest__
e) Name the interval at the letter **B**. __Perfect 4__
f) Give the technical degree name of the note at the letter **C**. __Tonic__
g) Name the highest note in this piece. __G__
h) Name the lowest note in this piece. __G__
i) Explain the meaning of **Andantino**. __a little faster than Andante__
j) How many measures are in this piece? __8__

Lesson 3 Double Sharps, Double Flats, Minor and Enharmonic Scales

ACCIDENTALS in front of a note raise or lower the PITCH of the note. An accidental applies only to notes on that specific line or in that specific space in a measure. A bar line CANCELS an accidental.

Double Sharp	𝄪	raises a sharp one chromatic semitone (half step) and raises a natural note one chromatic whole tone (whole step).
Sharp	♯	raises a natural note one chromatic semitone (half step).
Natural	♮	cancels an accidental and is always a white key.
Flat	♭	lowers a natural note one chromatic semitone (half step).
Double Flat	♭♭	lowers a flat one chromatic semitone (half step) and lowers a natural note one chromatic whole tone (whole step).

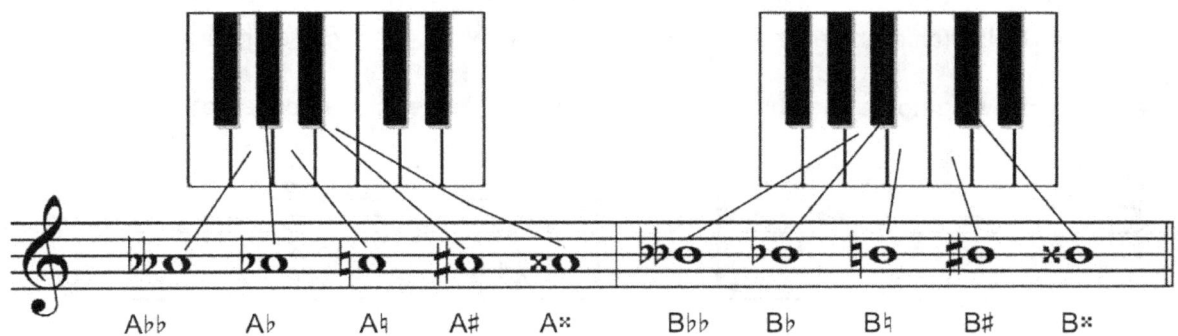

1. Write the following whole notes using accidentals. Draw corresponding lines to the keyboard.

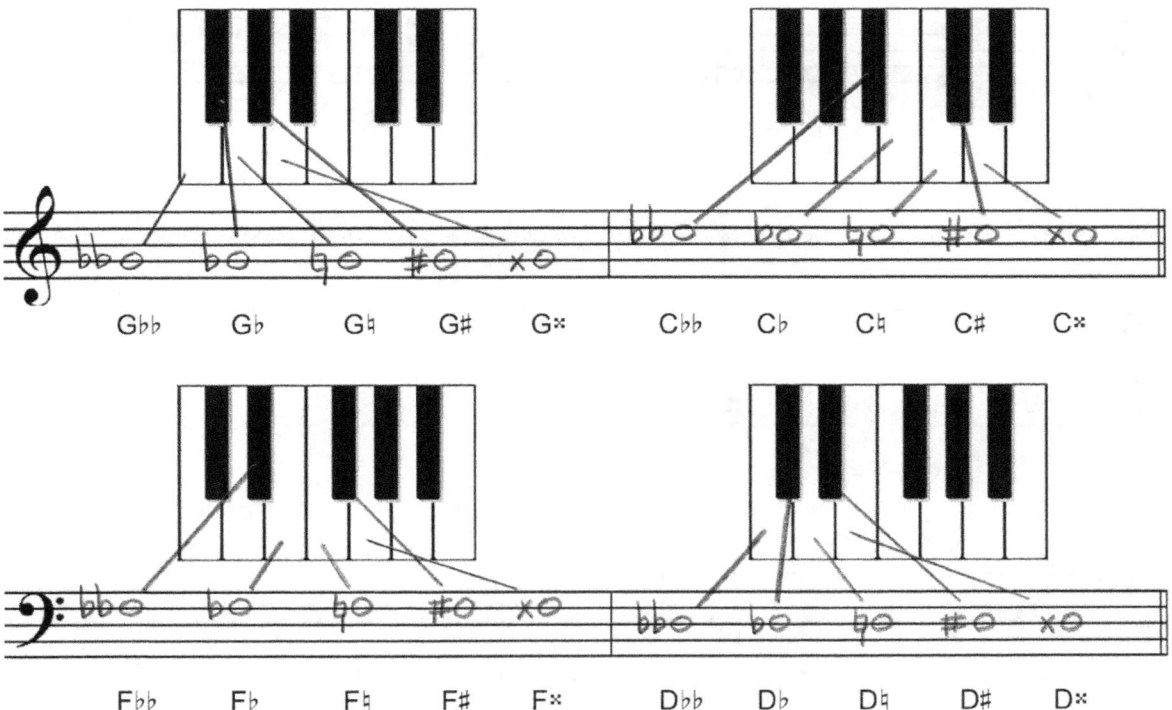

CHROMATIC and DIATONIC - WHOLE TONE (WHOLE STEP) and SEMITONE (HALF STEP)

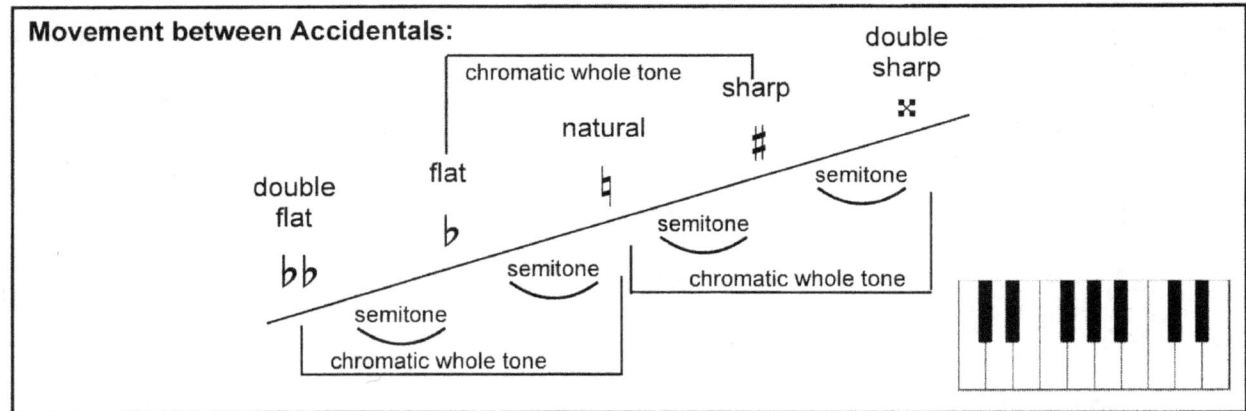

♪ **Note:** Two semitones (half steps) equal ONE whole tone (whole step), an interval of a 1st or a 2nd.
 CHROMATIC (same letter name) whole step - a 1st: C - C𝄪   half step - a 1st: C - C♯
 DIATONIC (different letter name) whole step - a 2nd: C - D   half step - a 2nd: C - D♭

1. Raise the following notes one chromatic whole tone (whole step). Name the notes.

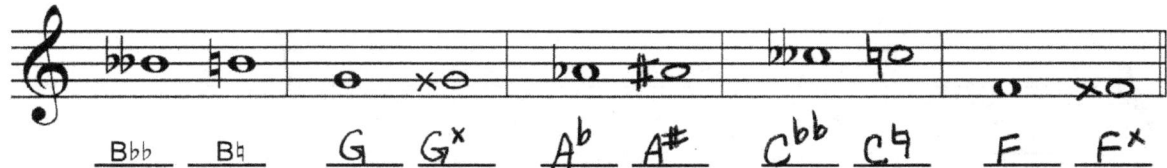

B♭♭, B♮, G, G𝄪, A♭, A♯, C♭♭, C♮, F, F𝄪

2. Lower the following notes one chromatic semitone (half step). Name the notes.

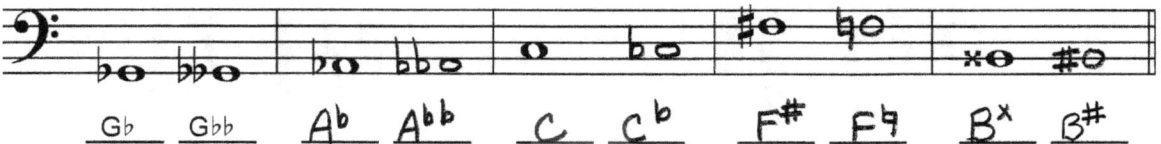

G♭, G♭♭, A♭, A♭♭, C, C♭, F♯, F♮, B𝄪, B♯

3. Raise the following notes one diatonic whole tone (whole step). Name the notes.

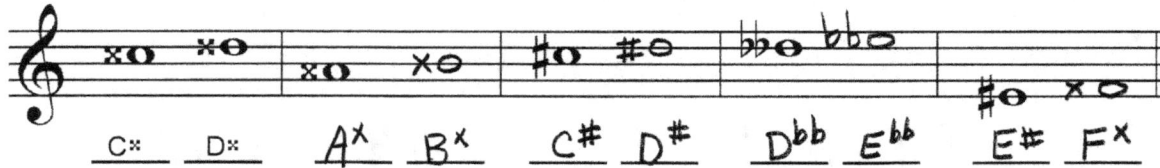

C𝄪, D𝄪, A𝄪, B𝄪, C♯, D♯, D♭♭, E♭♭, E♯, F𝄪

4. Lower the following notes one diatonic semitone (half step). Name the notes.

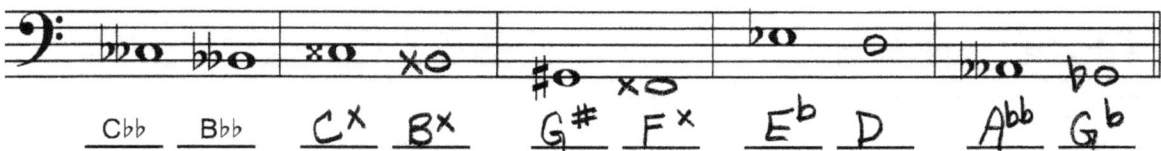

C♭♭, B♭♭, C𝄪, B𝄪, G♯, F𝄪, E♭, D, A♭♭, G♭

INTERVALS USING a DOUBLE FLAT

An **INTERVAL** uses a **DOUBLE FLAT** when a Major interval with the top note as a flat becomes a minor interval by lowering the top note one chromatic semitone. A flat is lowered to a double flat.

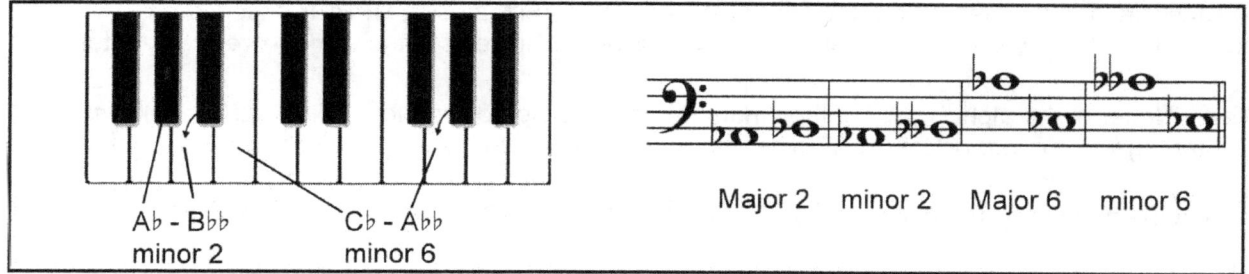

♪ **Note:** The bottom note of an interval names the Major key. Determine the Major interval first. Lower the top note one chromatic semitone (half step) to change a Major interval into a minor interval. If the top note is a flat, lower it to a double flat.

1. Name the following melodic intervals in the Treble Clef.

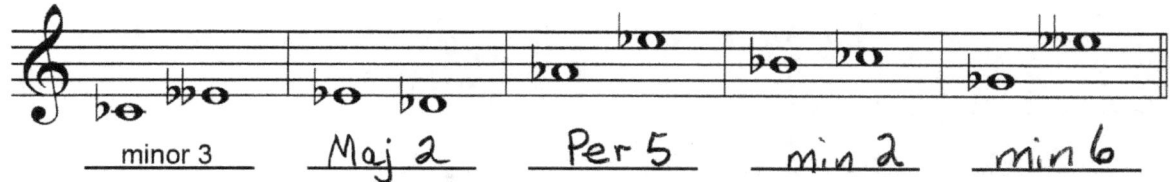

minor 3   Maj 2   Per 5   min 2   min 6

2. Write the following melodic intervals above the given notes. Use whole notes.

Major 3   minor 6   minor 2   Major 7   minor 3

For harmonic intervals of a 2, 3, 4, 5 and 6: when BOTH notes have accidentals, the accidental is written closest to the top note and further away from the bottom note.

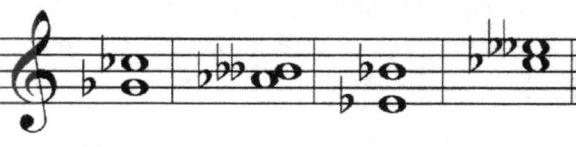

For harmonic intervals of a 7 and 8: when BOTH notes have accidentals, the accidentals are written lined up vertically (above each other).

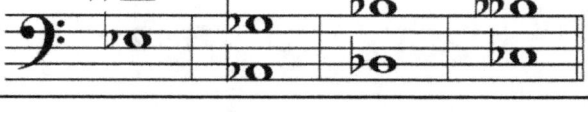

♪ **Note:** When writing a harmonic interval and there is **no room** for correct placement of accidentals, it is acceptable to place the accidental further away from the top note.

3. Write the following harmonic intervals above the given notes. Use whole notes.

minor 6   Perfect 1   Major 7   minor 6   minor 2

CIRCLE of FIFTHS with MINOR KEYS

A Major key and its relative minor key have the same Key Signature.

MAJOR keys are written on the **OUTSIDE** of the Circle of Fifths using **UPPER** case letters.
RELATIVE MINOR keys are written on the **INSIDE** of the Circle of Fifths using **lower** case letters.

The 1st letter of the alphabet "A" is the landmark and starting position for adding the minor keys.
Starting with f minor on the **FLAT** side, moving clockwise (to the right), minor keys are added.

Use the minor key sentence: **father charles goes down and ends battle**

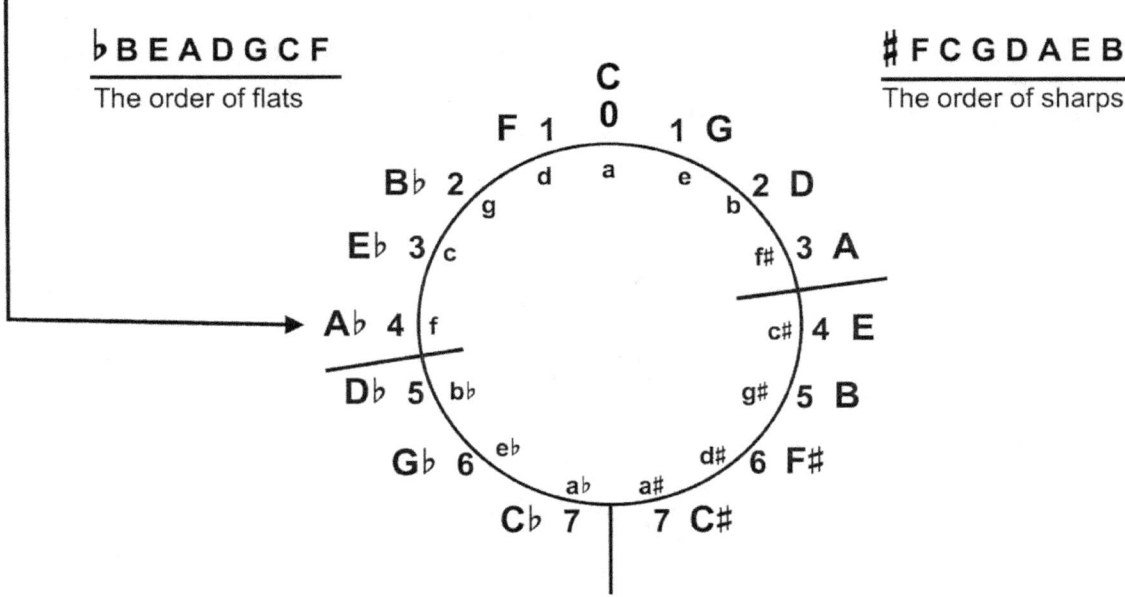

1. Complete the Circle of Fifths:
    a) Draw the landmark lines under the A flat Major and the A Major (A = 1st letter of the alphabet).
    b) Write the minor keys inside the circle, **f c g d a e b**; then start the sentence again adding the sharps, **f# c# g# d# a#** (change to flats) **a♭ e♭ b♭**.

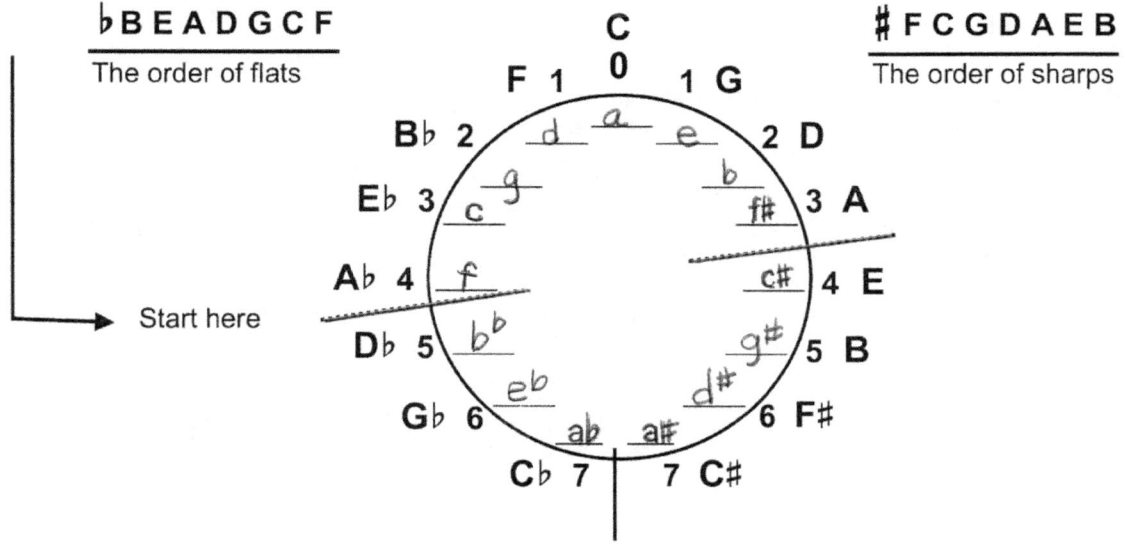

34

COMPLETING the CIRCLE of FIFTHS

The **Circle of Fifths** is a map of the **Major** keys and **minor** keys. A **Major** key and its **relative minor** key have the SAME Key Signature. Major key to relative minor key = 3 semitones (3 letter names).

1. Complete the Circle of Fifths:
   a) Write the order of flats on the top left and the order of sharps on the top right.
   b) Add the numbers on the outside of the circle. Start at the top with 0 and add the numbers 1 to 7 on the sharp side. Continue with 7 - 1 on the flat side.
   c) Write the Major Keys on the outside of the circle. Start with F Major and move clockwise: F, C, G, D, A, E, B. Then repeat the order again: F♯, C♯, C♭, G♭, D♭, A♭, E♭, B♭ (UPPER case).
   d) Draw the landmark line under the A♭ and under the A.
   e) Write the minor keys on the inside of the circle. Start with f minor (relative of A♭ Major) and move clockwise: f, c, g, d, a, e, b. Then repeat the order again: f♯, c♯, g♯, d♯, a♯, a♭, e♭, b♭ (lower case).

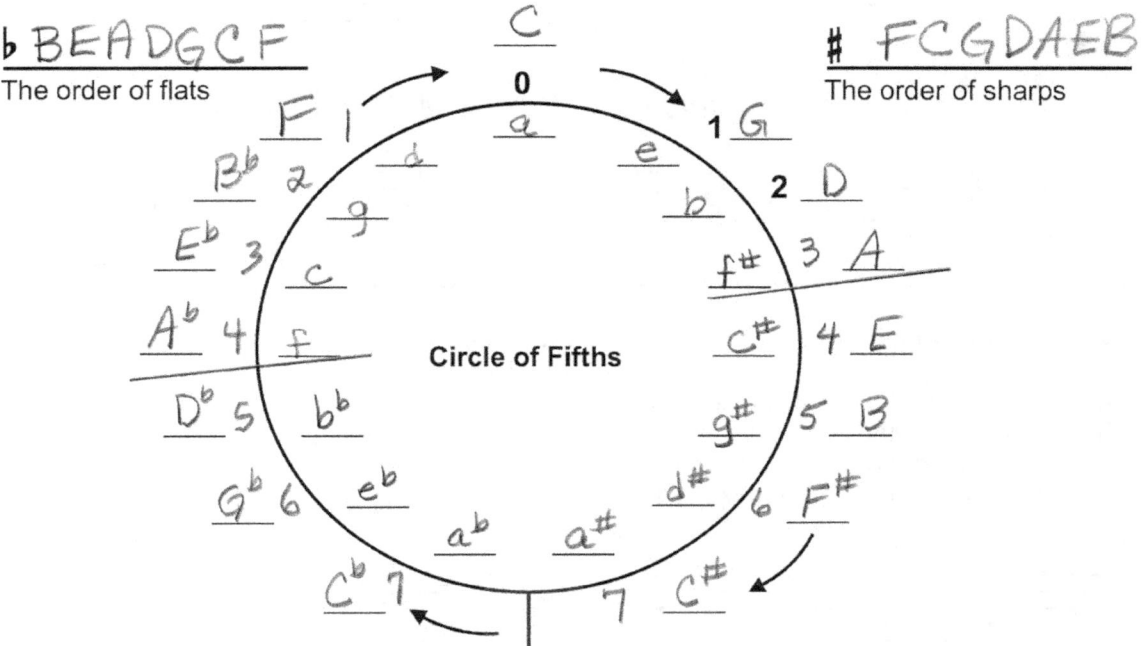

2. Use the Circle of Fifths to complete the following.

Seven sharps	Major Key: C♯	minor key: a♯
Six flats	Major Key: G♭	minor key: e♭
Five sharps	Major Key: B	minor key: g♯
Five flats	Major Key: D♭	minor key: b♭
Seven flats	Major Key: C♭	minor key: a♭
Six sharps	Major Key: F♯	minor key: d♯

   ♪ **Note:** Practice writing the **Circle of Fifths** on a blank piece of paper.
   Write it out many times until the order is memorized. Always write it in the same order.

MINOR SCALES with a DOUBLE SHARP

There are **SIX MINOR SCALES** that contain a **DOUBLE SHARP** (𝄪). They are the harmonic and melodic minor scales of g sharp minor, a sharp minor and d sharp minor.

Harmonic minor scale: the 7th note is raised one chromatic semitone ascending and descending.
Melodic minor scale: the 6th and 7th notes are raised one chromatic semitone ascending and are lowered one chromatic semitone descending.

♪ **Note:** When raising a sharp one chromatic semitone (half step), it becomes a double sharp (𝄪).

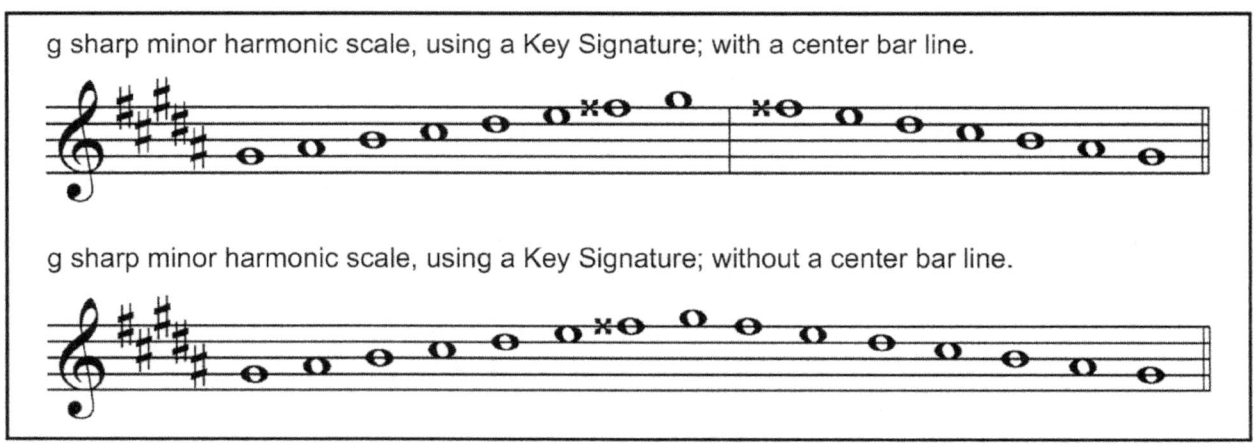

1. Write the following scales, ascending and descending, using a Key Signature. Use whole notes.

   a) d sharp minor harmonic in the Treble Clef
   b) a sharp minor melodic in the Bass Clef
   c) a sharp minor harmonic in the Treble Clef
   d) g sharp minor melodic in the Bass Clef

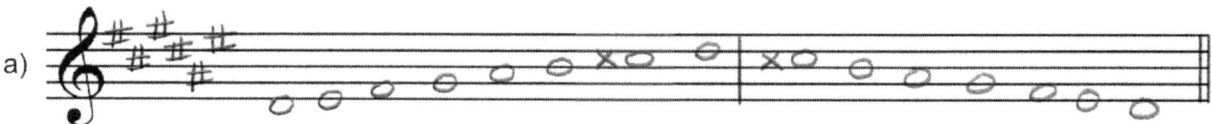

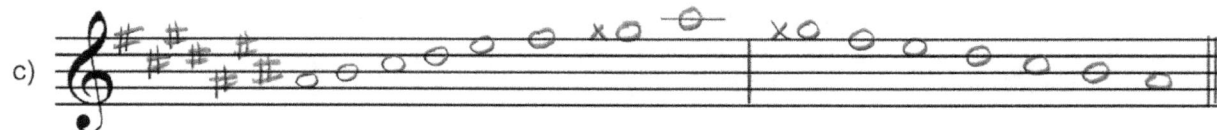

MINOR SCALES using ACCIDENTALS

MINOR SCALES may be written using **ACCIDENTALS** or a Key Signature.

WITH a center bar line: the center bar line **CANCELS** an accidental. Accidentals must be written in the ascending AND descending scale.

WITHOUT a center bar line: accidentals are written in the ascending scale; only accidentals for the lowered 6th and 7th are repeated in the descending scale.

♪ **Note:** When lowering a double sharp one chromatic semitone (half step), it becomes a sharp.

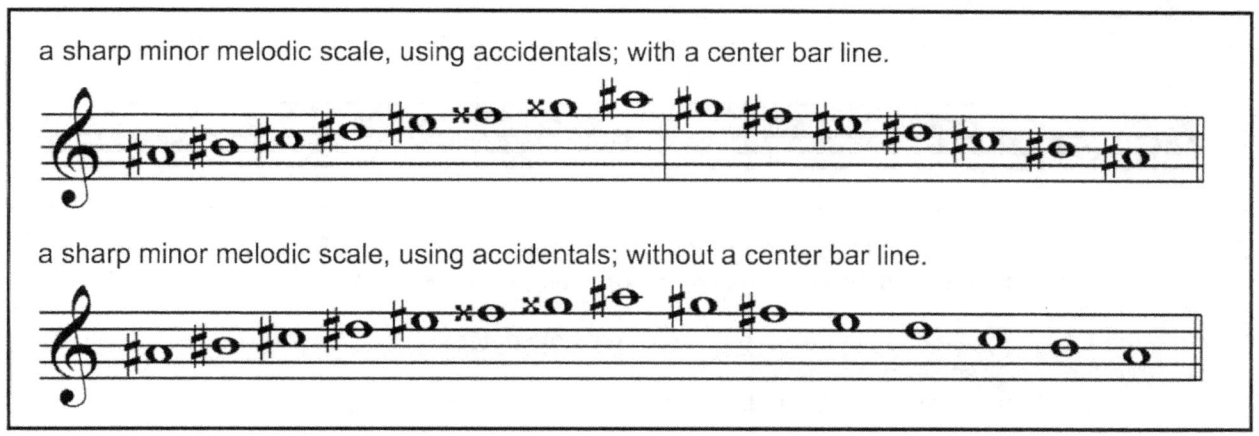

1. Write the following minor scales, ascending and descending, using accidentals. Use whole notes.

   a) a flat minor harmonic in the Treble Clef
   b) d sharp minor melodic in the Bass Clef
   c) g sharp minor melodic in the Treble Clef
   d) b flat minor harmonic in the Bass Clef

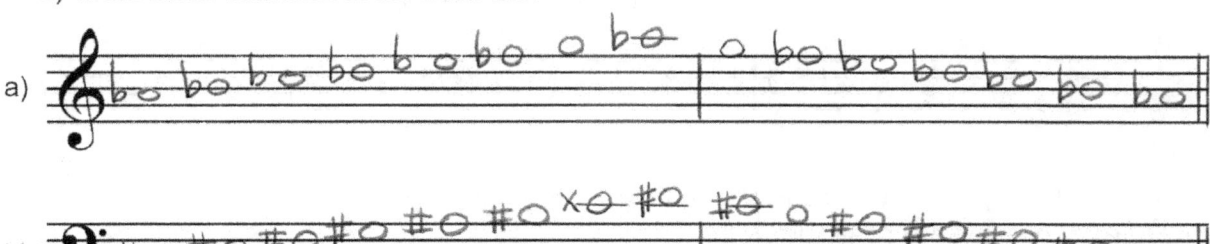

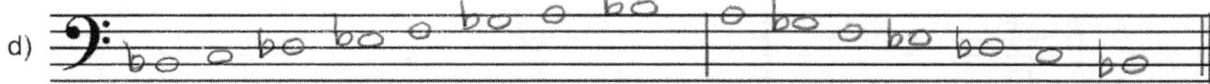

TONIC MAJOR and TONIC HARMONIC MINOR SCALES

TONIC MAJOR and **TONIC HARMONIC MINOR SCALES** have the **SAME** Tonic (first) note. They are **NOT** related keys. They do **NOT** use the same Key Signature. The Tonic minor key will have the same Key Signature as its relative Major key.

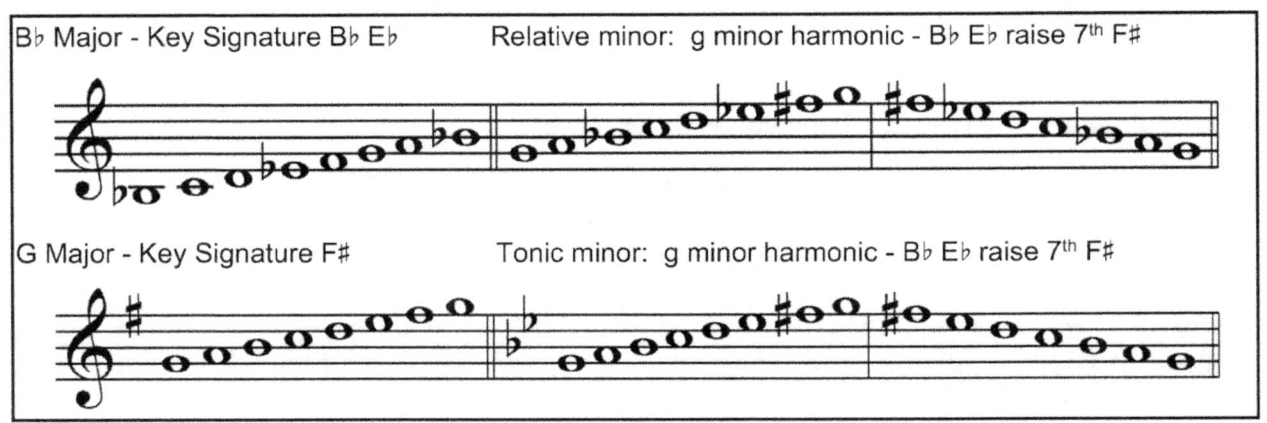

♪ **Note:** A Major scale and its relative harmonic minor scale have the SAME Key Signature.
   A Major scale and its Tonic harmonic minor scale have the SAME Tonic note.

1. Write the following scales using accidentals. Use whole notes.
   a) Write the Major scale, ascending only.
   b) Name the Tonic minor key. Write the Tonic harmonic minor scale, ascending and descending.

   a) F Major   b) Tonic minor key: __f__ harmonic minor

   a) D Major   b) Tonic minor key: __d__ harmonic minor

   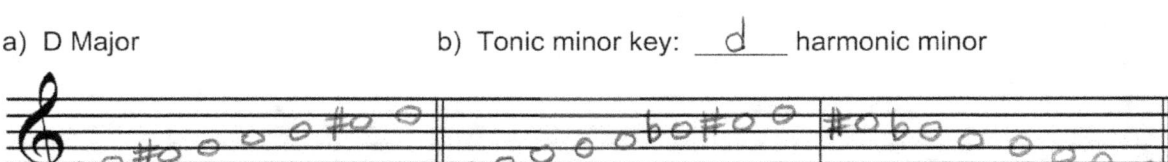

2. Write the following scales using a Key Signature. Use whole notes.
   a) Write the Major scale, ascending only.
   b) Name the Tonic minor key. Write the Tonic harmonic minor scale, ascending and descending.

   a) C# Major   b) Tonic minor key: __c#__ harmonic minor

   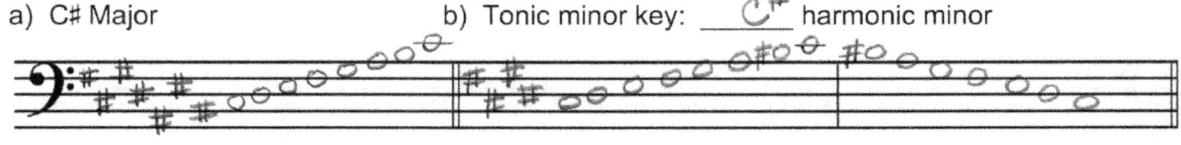

   a) A♭ Major   b) Tonic minor key: __a♭__ harmonic minor

   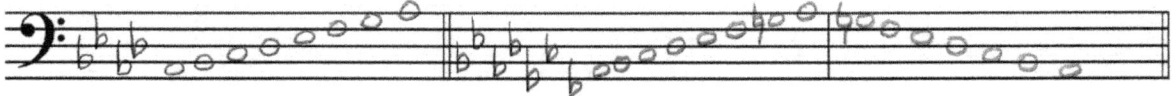

TONIC MAJOR and TONIC MELODIC MINOR SCALES

TONIC MAJOR and **TONIC MELODIC MINOR SCALES** have the **SAME** Tonic (first) note. They are **NOT** related keys. They do **NOT** use the same Key Signature. The Tonic minor key will have the same Key Signature as its relative Major key.

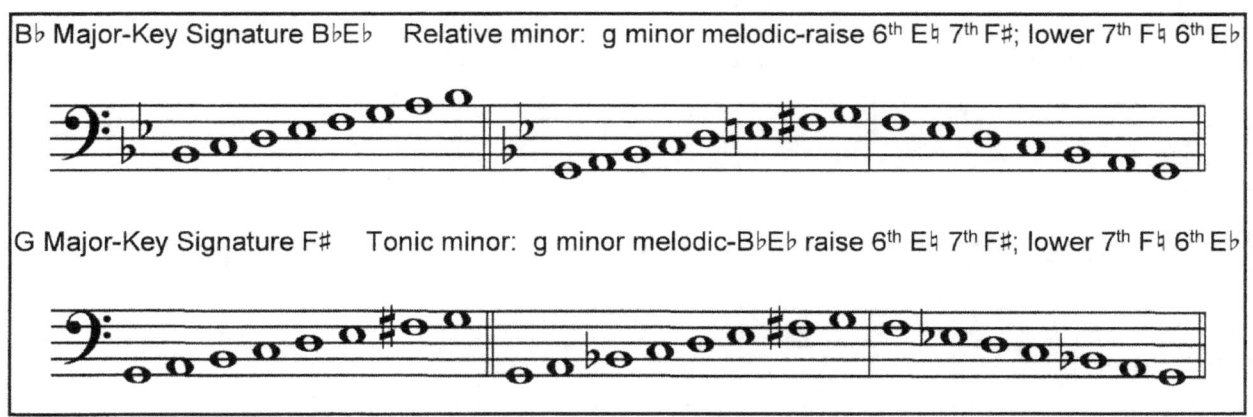

♪ **Note:** A Major scale and its relative melodic minor scale have the SAME Key Signature.
A Major scale and its Tonic melodic minor scale have the SAME Tonic note.

1. Write the following scales using a Key Signature. Use whole notes.
   a) Write the Major scale, ascending only.
   b) Name the Tonic minor key. Write the Tonic melodic minor scale, ascending and descending.

   a) E♭ Major   b) Tonic minor key: __e♭__ melodic minor

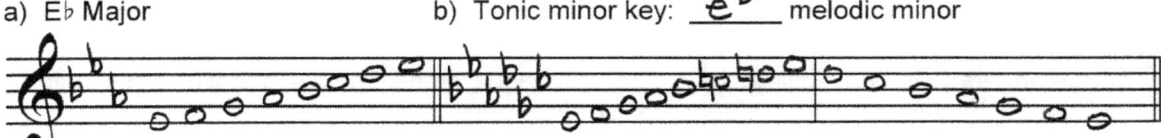

   a) F♯ Major   b) Tonic minor key: __f♯__ melodic minor

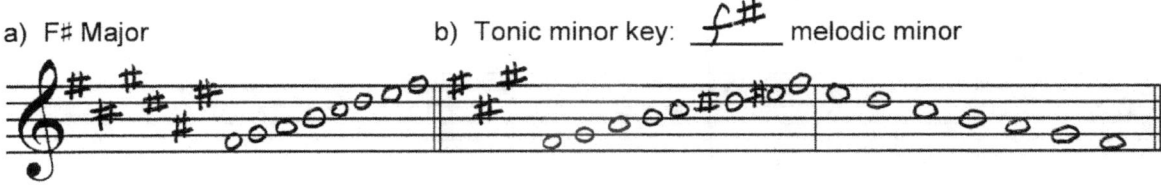

2. Write the following scales using accidentals. Use whole notes.
   a) Write the Major scale, ascending only.
   b) Name the Tonic minor key. Write the Tonic melodic minor scale, ascending and descending.

   a) G Major   b) Tonic minor key: __g__ melodic minor

   a) B Major   b) Tonic minor key: __b__ melodic minor

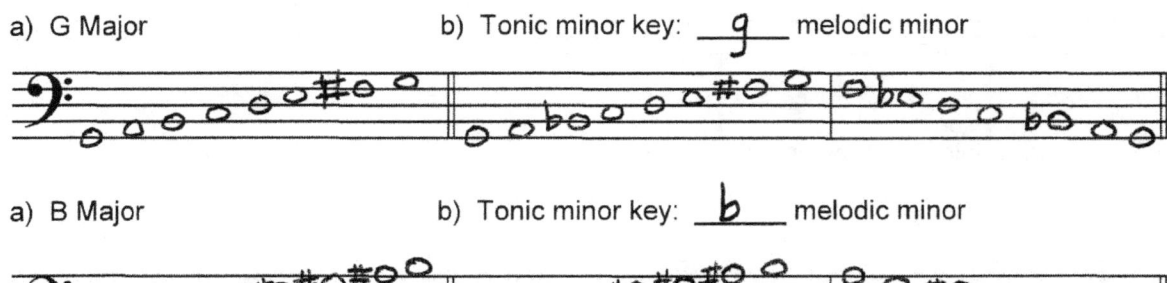

ENHARMONIC TONIC MINOR SCALES

ENHARMONIC TONIC MINOR SCALES are scales that use the SAME pitches but are written with notes using different letter names (enharmonic equivalents).
Example: b♭ minor scale and a♯ minor scale

♪ **Note:** The Circle of Fifths contains three enharmonic minor keys:
b♭ minor and a♯ minor; e♭ minor and d♯ minor; a♭ minor and g♯ minor

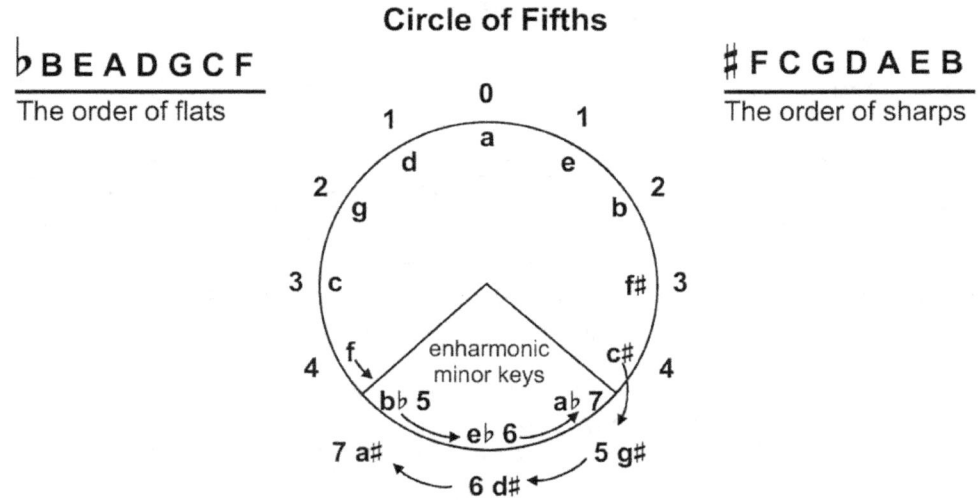

1. Name the enharmonic Tonic minor scale. Write the enharmonic Tonic minor scale, ascending and descending, using the correct Key Signature. Use whole notes.

   a) The enharmonic Tonic minor scale, melodic form, of a sharp minor is b♭ minor melodic

   b) The enharmonic Tonic minor scale, natural form, of e flat minor is d♯ minor natural

   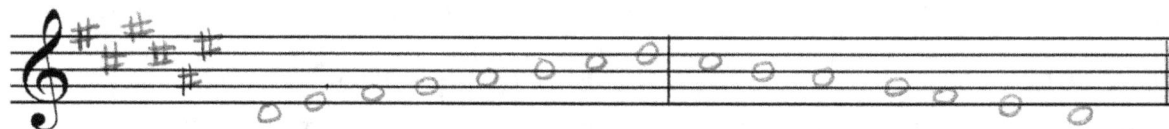

   c) The enharmonic Tonic minor scale, harmonic form, of g sharp minor is a♭ minor harmonic

   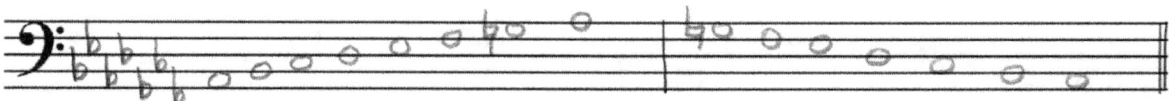

ENHARMONIC EQUIVALENTS - MAJOR or MINOR SCALES

ENHARMONIC EQUIVALENTS are the same pitch using different letter names.

1. Write the enharmonic equivalent names for each of the following keys directly on the keyboard.

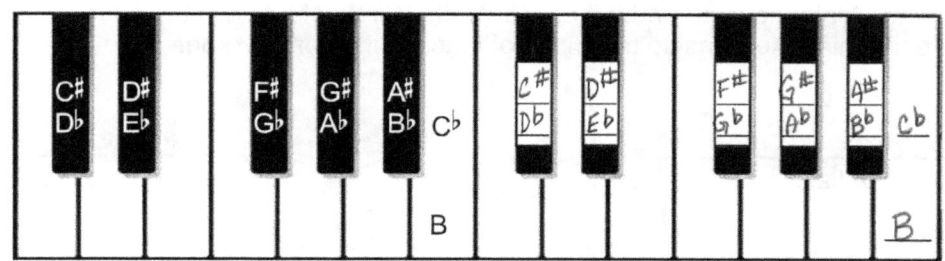

RELATIVE Major and minor scales have the SAME Key Signature. They are related.
 Example: Relative minor of C Major is a minor. Relative Major of c minor is E♭ Major.

TONIC Major and minor scales have the SAME Tonic note. They are NOT related. Tonic Major and minor scales are also called parallel Major and minor scales.
 Example: Tonic minor of C Major is c minor; Tonic Major of a minor is A Major.

ENHARMONIC TONIC Major and/or minor scales BEGIN on the SAME pitch as the given key but use different letter names. They are NOT related.
 Example: Enharmonic Major of D♭ Major is C♯ Major; Enharmonic minor of D♭ Major is c♯ minor.

ENHARMONIC RELATIVE Major and/or minor scales BEGIN on the SAME pitch as the relative Major or minor of the given key but use different letter names. They are NOT related.
 Example: Enharmonic relative minor of G♭ Major is d♯ minor.

---

2. For each of the following Major keys:
   a) Name the relative minor.
   b) Name the enharmonic relative minor.
   c) Name the enharmonic Tonic Major.

Major key:	B	G♭	C♯	D♭	F♯	C♭
a) Relative minor:	g♯	e♭	a♯	b♭	d♯	a♭
b) Enharmonic relative minor:	a♭	d♯	b♭	a♯	e♭	g♯
c) Enharmonic Tonic Major:	C♭	F♯	D♭	C♯	G♭	B

♪ **Note:** To determine the ENHARMONIC scale, first identify the name of the scale, and then change the name to its enharmonic equivalent.

3. Name each of the following keys. Name the Key Signature of the new key.
   a) The relative minor of B Major is __g♯ min__. Key Signature: F♯ C♯ G♯ D♯ A♯
   b) The enharmonic relative minor of C♯ Major is __b♭ min__. Key Signature: B♭ E♭ A♭ D♭ G♭
   c) The Tonic minor of G Major is __g min__. Key Signature: B♭ E♭
   d) The enharmonic Tonic Major of D♭ Major is __C♯ Maj__. Key Signature: F♯ C♯ G♯ D♯ A♯ E♯ B♯
   e) The enharmonic relative Major of d♯ minor is __G♭ Maj__. Key Signature: B♭ E♭ A♭ D♭ G♭ C♭

Lesson 3 — Review Test

Total Score: ____ / 100

1. Complete the Circle of Fifths with Major keys and minor keys:
    a) Write the order of flats on the top left and the order of sharps on the top right.
    b) Write the Major keys around the outside of the Circle of Fifths in the correct order.
    c) Write the minor keys inside the Circle of Fifths in the correct order.

___ / 10

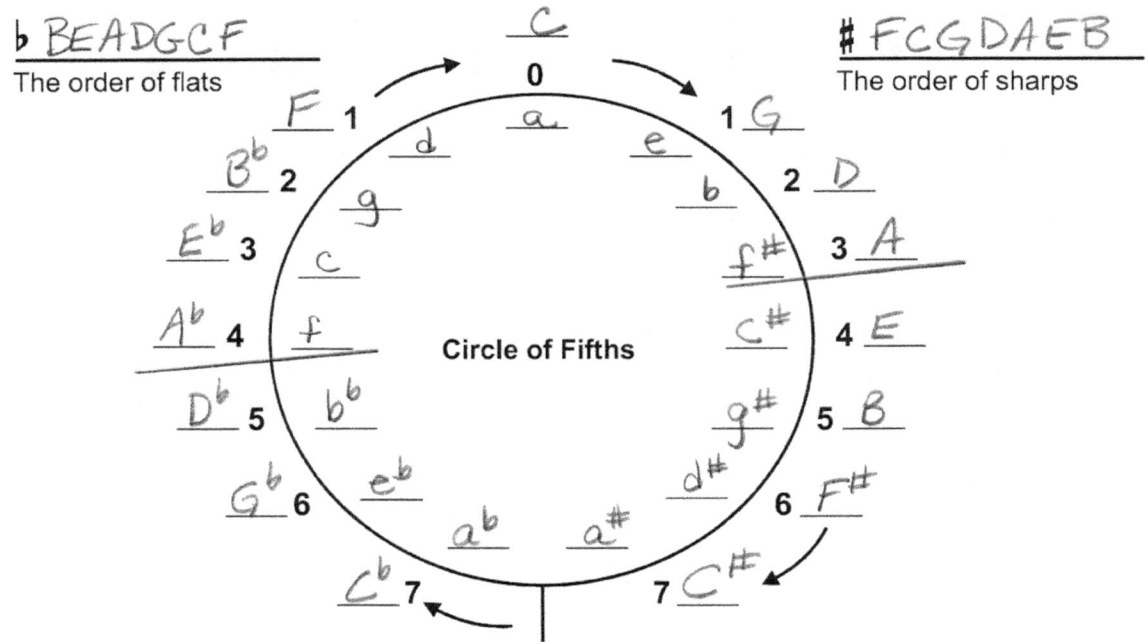

2. Write the following **HARMONIC** intervals **ABOVE** the given notes. Use whole notes.

___ / 10

Major 2   minor 6   Perfect 5   minor 7   minor 3

3. Raise the following notes a whole tone (whole step). **DO NOT** change the letter name.

___ / 10

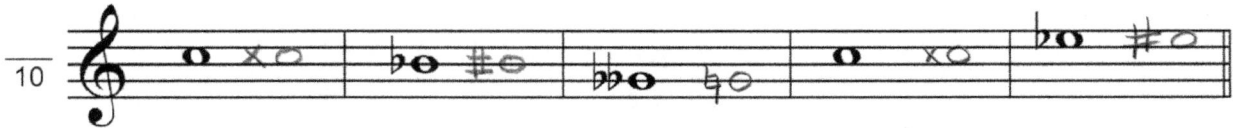

4. Write the following solid triads in **ROOT POSITION** in the Treble Clef using the correct Key Signature. Use whole notes.

___ / 10

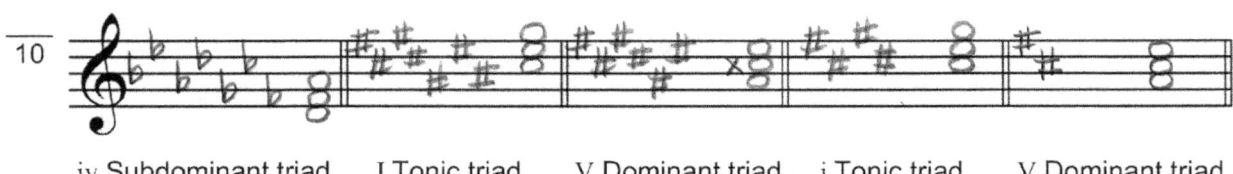

iv Subdominant triad   I Tonic triad   V Dominant triad   i Tonic triad   V Dominant triad
a flat minor   C sharp Major   d sharp minor   c sharp minor   D Major

5. Match each musical term or sign with the English definition. (Not all definitions will be used.)

   10

Term		Definition
andantino	e	a) very slow
con pedale, ped.	f	b) becoming softer
diminuendo	b	c) return to the original tempo
a tempo	c	d) moderately loud
mezzo forte, *mf*	d	e) a little faster than *andante*
largo	a	f) with pedal
staccato, ♪	h	g) right hand
mano destra, M.D.	g	h) detached
fine	j	i) without
pianissimo, **pp**	k	j) the end
		k) very soft

6. Write the following scales, ascending and descending, using the correct **KEY SIGNATURE**. Use whole notes.

   10
   a) Tonic minor, melodic form, of B flat Major in the Treble Clef
   b) relative minor, harmonic form, of C sharp Major in the Bass Clef
   c) enharmonic relative minor, natural form, of C flat Major in the Treble Clef
   d) enharmonic Tonic minor, melodic form, of e flat minor in the Treble Clef
   e) enharmonic Tonic Major of C sharp Major in the Bass Clef

a)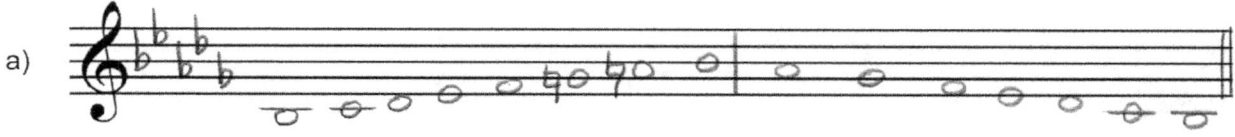

b)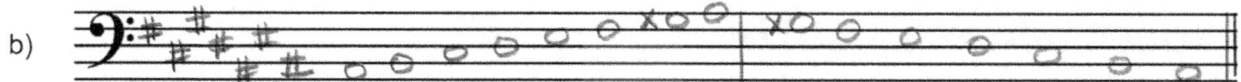

c)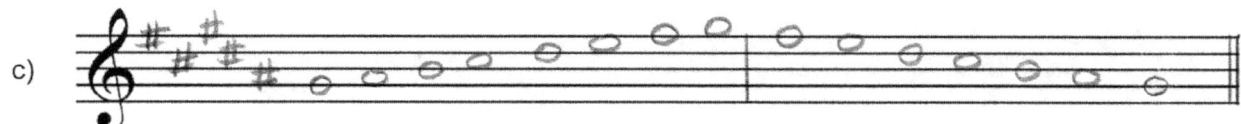

d)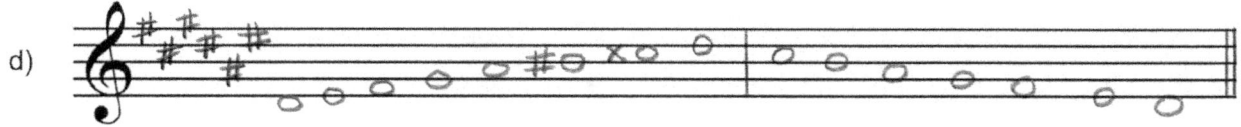

e)

7. Write the **BASIC BEAT** and the **PULSE** below each measure. Add rests below each bracket to complete the measure. Cross off the basic beat as each beat is completed.

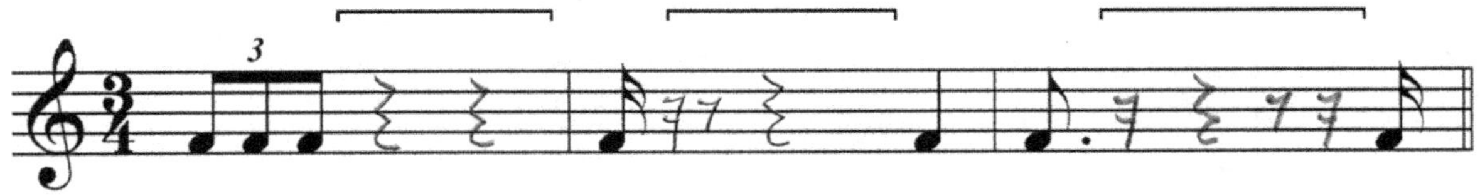

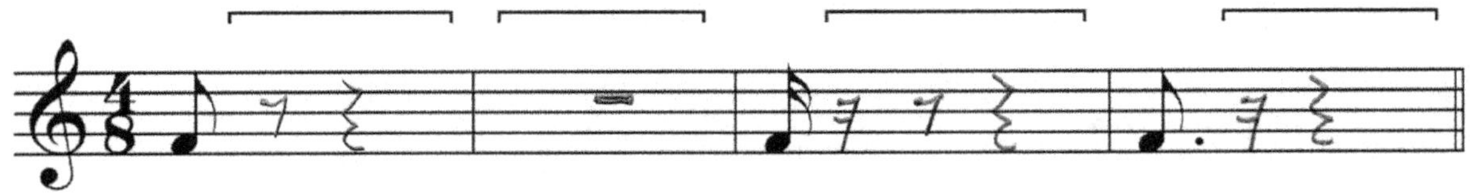

8. Name the key of the following melody. Transpose it **DOWN** one octave into the Bass Clef using the correct Key Signature.

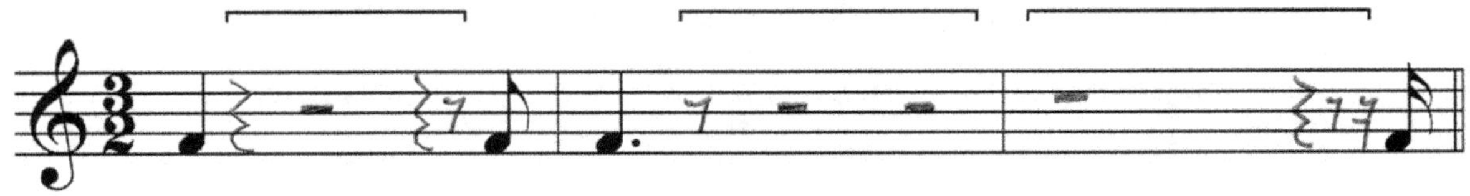

Key: g# min

9. a) Name the **MINOR KEY** for each of the following Key Signatures.
b) Identify the technical degree names as: **T** (Tonic), **SD** (Subdominant) or **D** (Dominant).

10

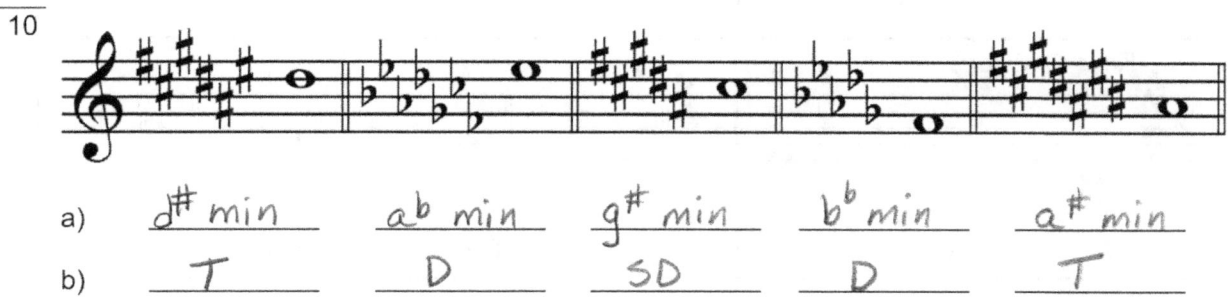

a)	d# min	ab min	g# min	bb min	a# min
b)	T	D	SD	D	T

10. Analyze the following piece by answering the questions below.

10

Lizzie the Lizard

Andante E. Sakowsky

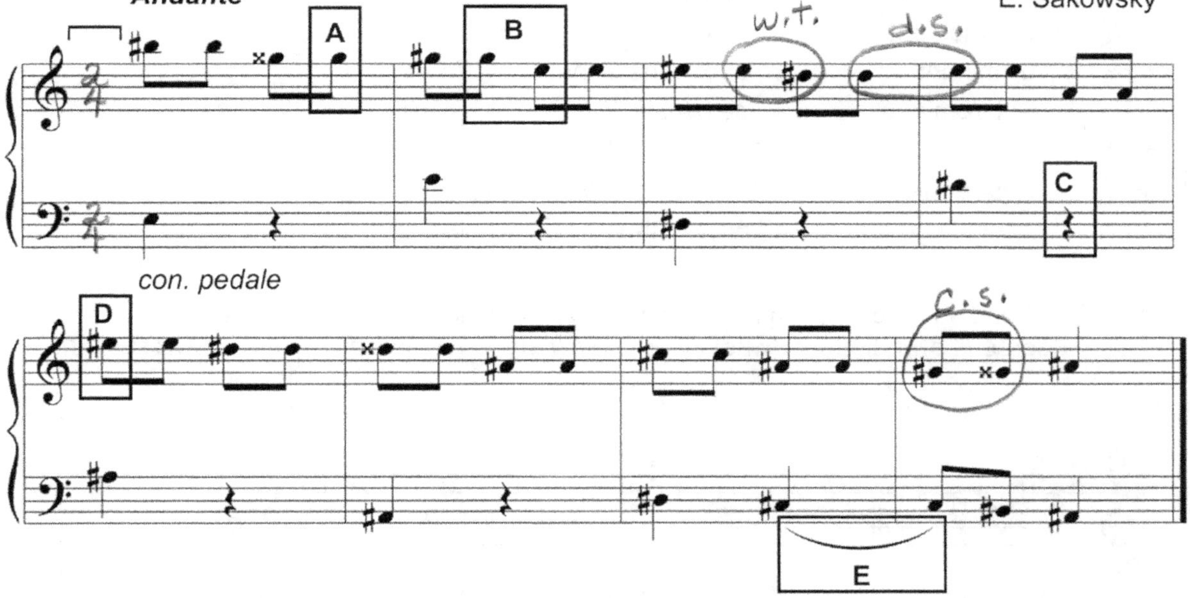

a) Add the correct Time Signature directly on the music.

b) Name the note at the letter **A**. G×

c) Name the interval at the letter **B**. Maj 3

d) Name the type of rest at the letter **C**. quarter rest

e) Name the enharmonic equivalent for the note at the letter **D**. F

f) Explain the sign at the letter **E**. tie - hold for the combined value of the tied notes

g) Locate and circle a whole tone in this piece. Label it as w.t.

h) Locate and circle a chromatic semitone in this piece. Label it as c.s.

i) Locate and circle a diatonic semitone in this piece. Label it as d.s.

j) How many measures are in this piece? 8

Lesson 4 Technical Degree Names and Chromatic Scales

TECHNICAL DEGREE NAMES are used to identify the degrees of a scale.

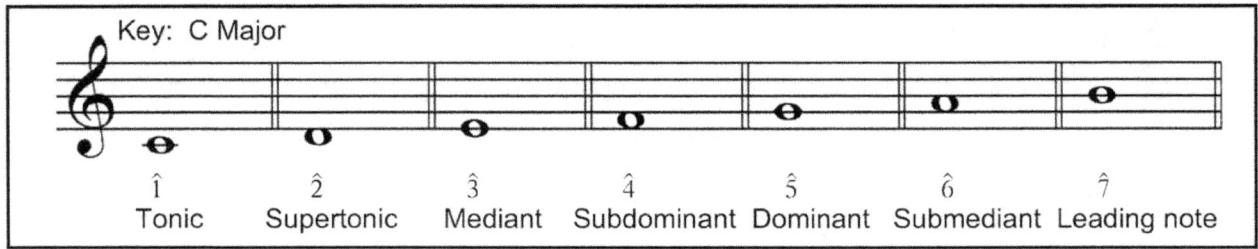

♫ **Note:** When identifying the technical degree name, start at the Tonic and count UP to determine the scale degree.

1. Write the technical degree name for each degree of the scale.

Scale Degree	Technical Degree Name		Scale Degree	Technical Degree Name
$\hat{8}$	Tonic	octave Tonic note	$\hat{8}$	Tonic
$\hat{7}$	Leading note	semitone below Tonic	$\hat{7}$	Leading note
$\hat{6}$	Submediant	3rd below the Tonic	$\hat{6}$	Submediant
$\hat{5}$	Dominant	5th above the Tonic	$\hat{5}$	Dominant
$\hat{4}$	Subdominant	5th below the Tonic	$\hat{4}$	Subdominant
$\hat{3}$	Mediant	3rd above the Tonic	$\hat{3}$	Mediant
$\hat{2}$	Supertonic	2nd above the Tonic	$\hat{2}$	Supertonic
$\hat{1}$	Tonic	1st note of the key (Key note)	$\hat{1}$	Tonic

♫ **Note:** The Leading note is a semitone (half step) below the Tonic. In the natural minor scale the $\hat{7}$ degree is a whole tone (whole step) below the Tonic and is called the **SUBTONIC**.

2. For each of the following, name the: a) Major key. b) technical degree name for each note.

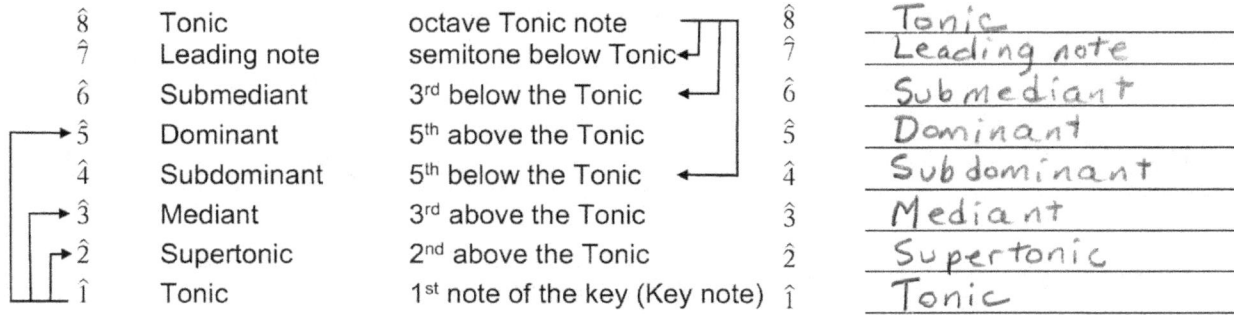

a) C# Major, Gb Maj, B Maj, Ab Maj, Db Maj, Eb Maj
b) Supertonic, Mediant, Submediant, Dominant, Subdominant, Leading note

3. For each of the following, name the: a) minor key. b) technical degree name for each note.

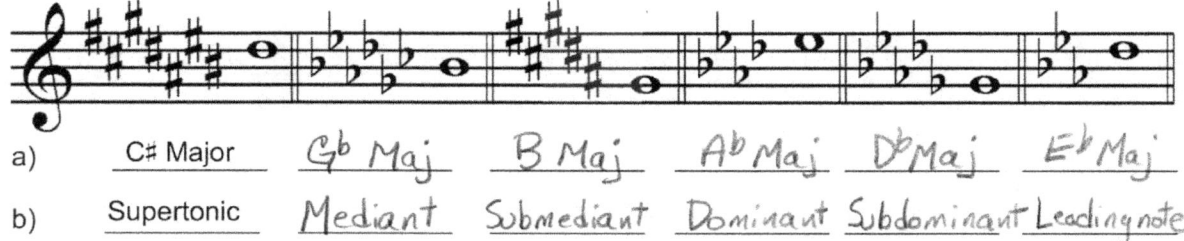

a) f minor, g# min, ab min, c# min, b min, d# min
b) Leading note, Supertonic, Leading note, Mediant, Submediant, Leading note

ROMAN NUMERALS, MAJOR and MINOR TRIADS

ROMAN NUMERALS are used to identify the type/quality of a triad built on each degree of a scale.
Type/Quality: Major triads - UPPER case (I, IV, V, VI); minor triads - lower case (i, ii, iii, iv, vi).

In the **MAJOR** scale, only triads built on the Tonic, Supertonic, Mediant, Subdominant, Dominant and Submediant are Major or minor triads. In the **HARMONIC MINOR** scale, only triads built on the Tonic, Subdominant, Dominant and Submediant are Major or minor triads.

♪ **Note:** The Dominant triad in the harmonic minor scale will contain the raised 7th (Leading note).

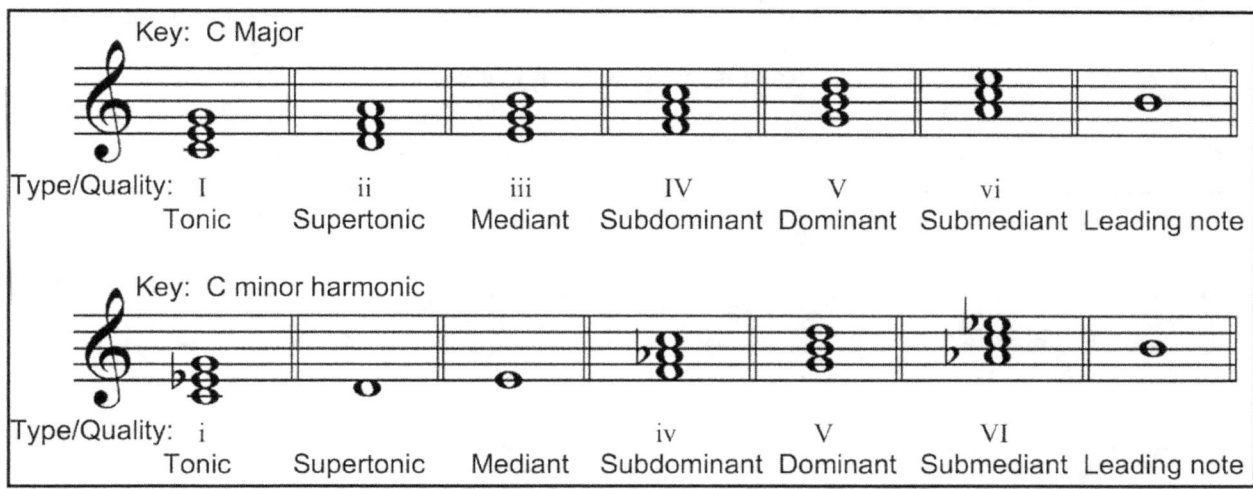

1. a) Write the following triads in E Major in root position. Use whole notes.
   b) Identify the type/quality of each triad using Roman Numerals.

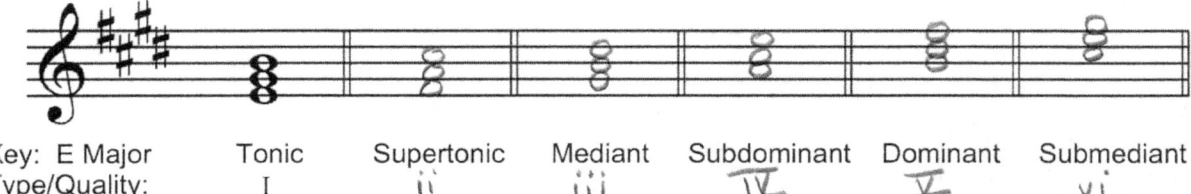

2. a) Name the minor key for each of the following Key Signatures.
   b) Identify the type/quality of each triad using Roman Numerals.

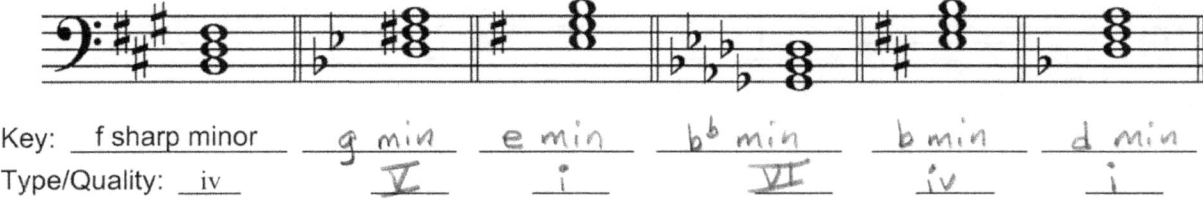

3. Write the Dominant triads in root position for each of the following harmonic minor keys. Use accidentals. Use whole notes.

g sharp minor   b flat minor   d sharp minor   a flat minor   f minor   f sharp minor

HARMONIC CHROMATIC SCALES

A **CHROMATIC** scale uses all 12 semitones in the octave, plus the upper Tonic for a total of 13 notes. A chromatic scale always begins and ends on the SAME Tonic note. Do not repeat a letter name more than twice. A chromatic scale may be written using accidentals or using the Major Key Signature of the Tonic note. A chromatic scale may be written with or without a center bar line.

There are two types of chromatic scales: **HARMONIC CHROMATIC** and **MELODIC CHROMATIC**.

A **HARMONIC CHROMATIC** scale has a set form. It uses a single Tonic, Dominant and upper Tonic note ascending, and a single Dominant and Tonic note descending. All other notes are used twice. Double sharps or double flats may be necessary to write a note twice.

♩ **Note:** A bar line CANCELS an accidental. Rewrite the accidentals in the descending scale.

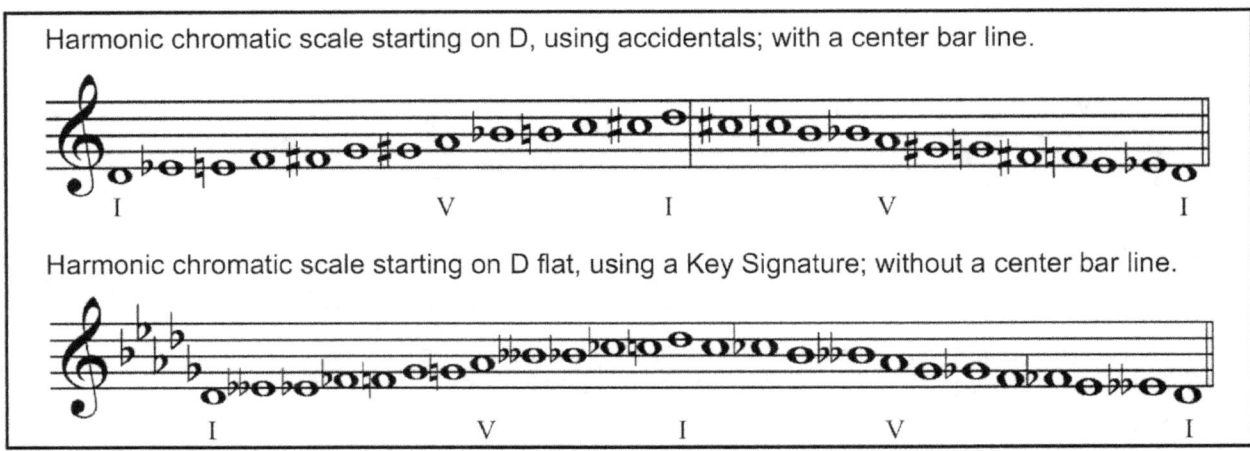

1. Write the following harmonic chromatic scales. Use whole notes.
   a) Write the notes first. Label the single Tonic (I) and Dominant (V) notes.
   b) Add accidentals to create the chromatic pattern.

harmonic chromatic scale starting on B flat, using a Key Signature

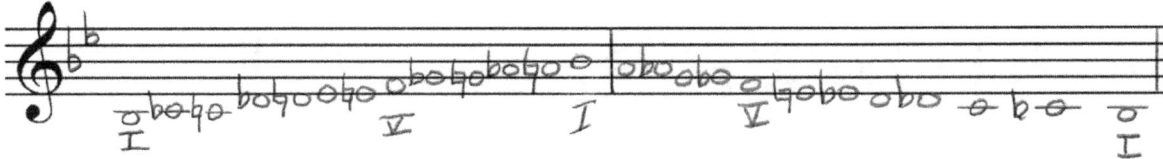

harmonic chromatic scale starting on G sharp, using accidentals

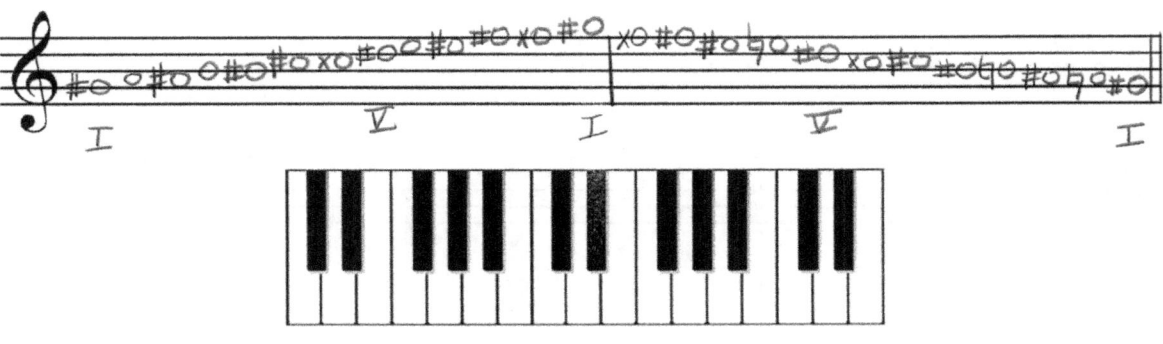

MELODIC CHROMATIC SCALES

A **MELODIC CHROMATIC** scale does not have a set form. One standard notation for writing a melodic chromatic scale is to raise the semitones on the way up (ascending) and lower them on the way down (descending). There will be 5 single notes and all other notes are used twice.

♪ **Note:** If a scale begins on a flat, switch to sharps as soon as possible in the ascending scale.

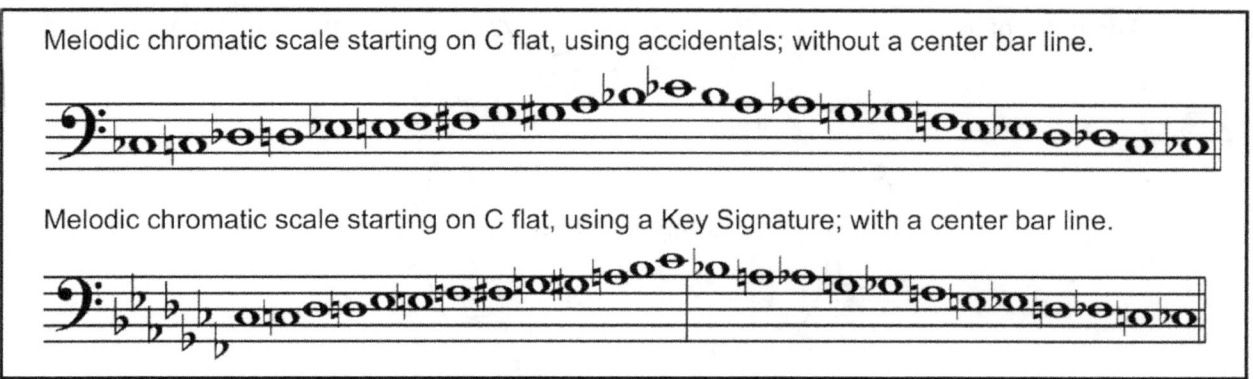

♪ **Note:** A melodic chromatic scale will not use the exact same notes ascending and descending.

A melodic chromatic scale may be written based on the Major scale using a single note for the Mediant (III), Leading Note (VII) and upper Tonic (VIII) ascending, and Subdominant (IV) and lower Tonic (I) descending. All other notes will be written twice.

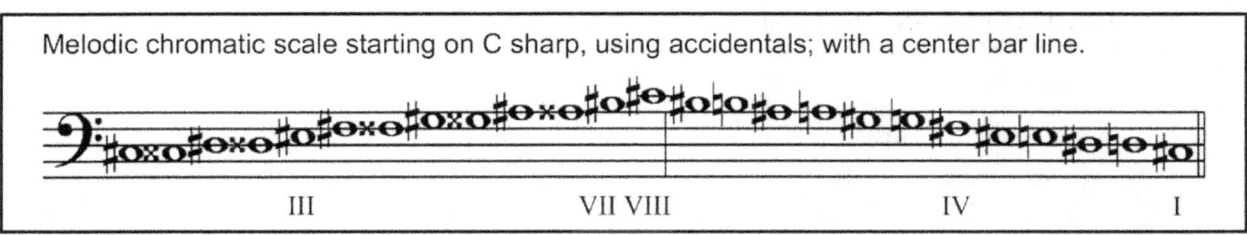

♪ **Note:** Any standard notation that starts and ends on the same Tonic note and does not use any letter (degree) name more than twice is considered correct.

1. Write the following melodic chromatic scales. Use any standard notation. Use whole notes.

   a) melodic chromatic scale starting on F sharp, using accidentals

   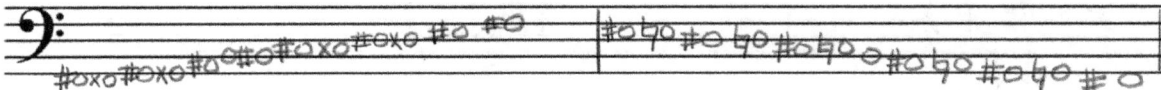

   b) melodic chromatic scale starting on E flat, using a Key Signature

   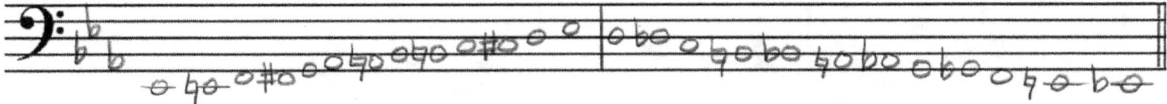

Lesson 4 — Review Test

Total Score: ____ / 100

1. Complete the Circle of Fifths with Major keys and minor keys:
   a) Write the order of flats on the top left and the order of sharps on the top right.
   b) Write the numbers 1 - 7 around the outside of the Circle of Fifths (both sides).
   c) Write the Major and minor keys around the Circle of Fifths in the correct order.

___/10

♭ B E A D G C F
The order of flats

♯ F C G D A E B
The order of sharps

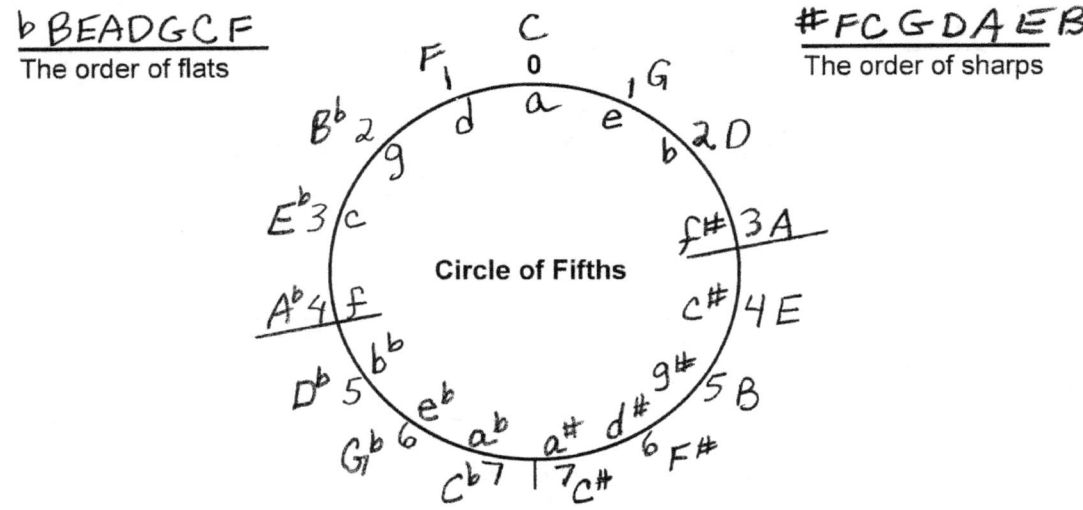

2. Write the following solid triads in **ROOT POSITION** in the Treble Clef, using the correct Key Signature. Use whole notes.

   a) the **SUBMEDIANT** triad of E Major
   b) the **SUBDOMINANT** triad of g sharp minor harmonic
   c) the **SUBDOMINANT** triad of g minor harmonic
   d) the **DOMINANT** triad of f sharp minor harmonic
   e) the **MEDIANT** triad of A Major

___/10

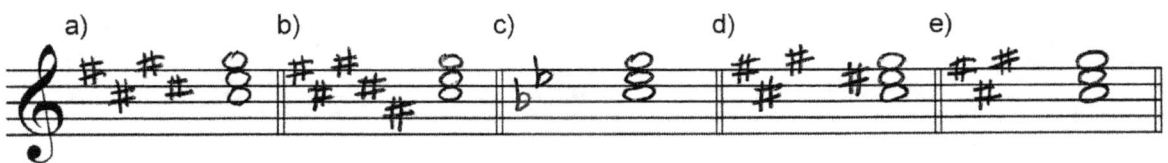

3. Name the key of the following melody. Rewrite it at the **SAME PITCH** in the Treble Clef using the correct Key Signature.

___/10

Key: F♯ Major

4. Write the following scales, ascending and descending. Use whole notes.

   a) Tonic Major of e minor in the Treble Clef, using the correct Key Signature
   b) f sharp minor melodic in the Bass Clef, using accidentals
   c) d minor harmonic in the Treble Clef, using the correct Key Signature
   d) harmonic chromatic scale beginning on C sharp, using the correct Key Signature
   e) melodic chromatic scale (any standard version) beginning on A flat, using accidentals

10

a)

b)

c)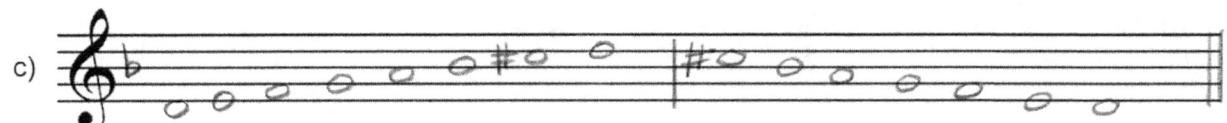

d)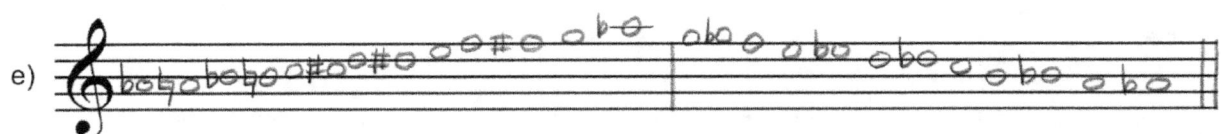

e)

5. Match each musical term or sign with the English definition. (Not all definitions will be used.)

10

Term		Definition
allegretto	h	a) very loud
prestissimo	e	b) becoming louder
pedale, ped.	k	c) slow
decrescendo, decresc.	g	d) moderately soft
fortissimo, *ff*	a	e) as fast as possible
crescendo, cresc.	b	f) in a singing style
da capo, D.C.	j	g) becoming softer
mezzo piano, *mp*	d	h) fairly fast; not as fast as *allegro*
lento	c	i) a stressed note
accent	i	j) from the beginning
		k) pedal

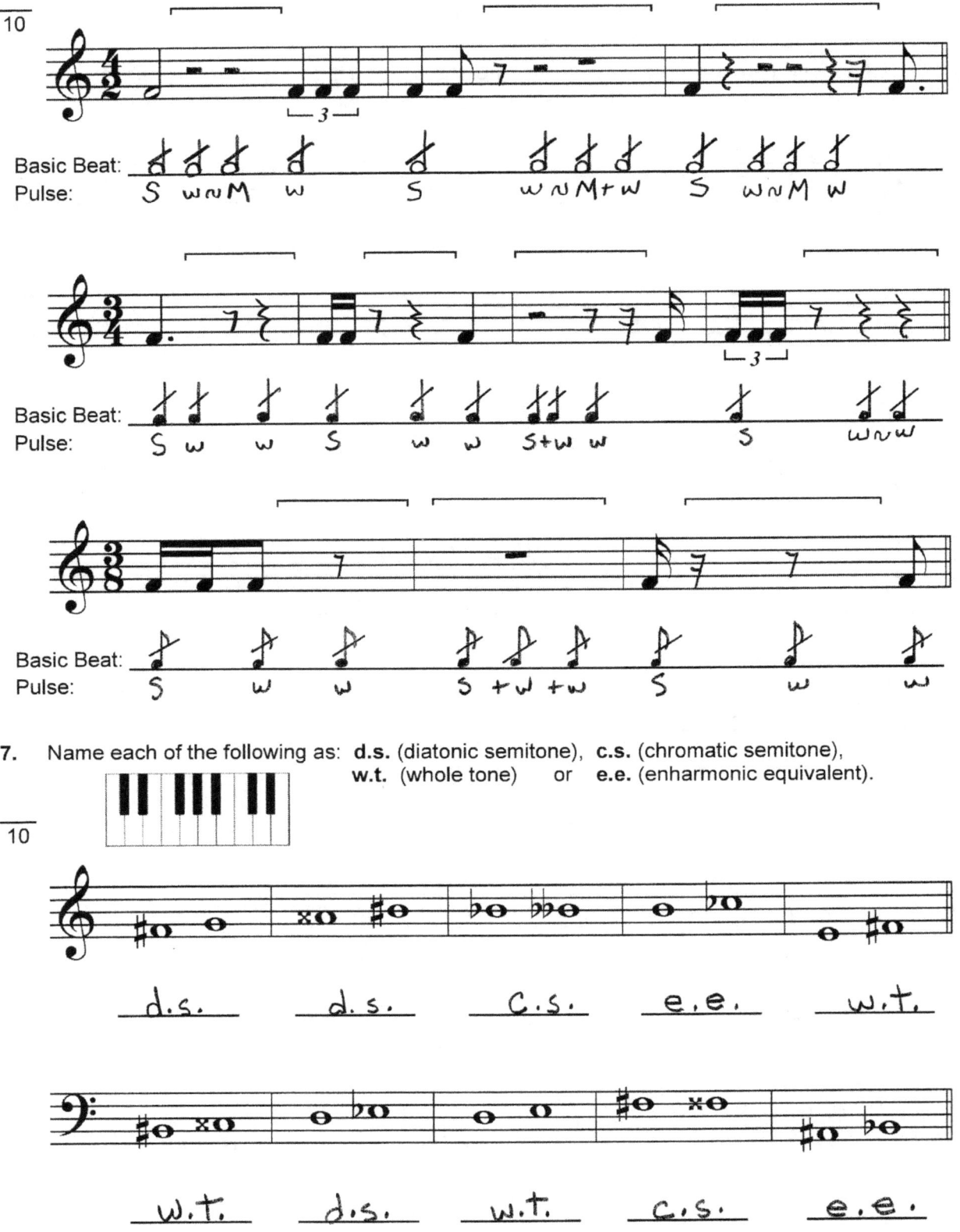

8. Give the **TECHNICAL DEGREE NAME** for each note. (Tonic, Supertonic, etc.)

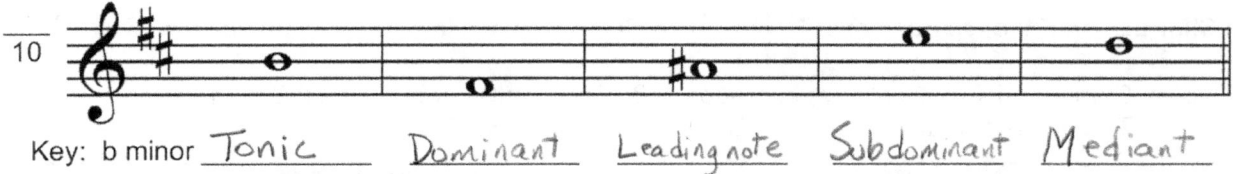

Key: b minor Tonic   Dominant   Leading note   Subdominant   Mediant

9. Write the following **HARMONIC** intervals **ABOVE** the given notes. Use whole notes.

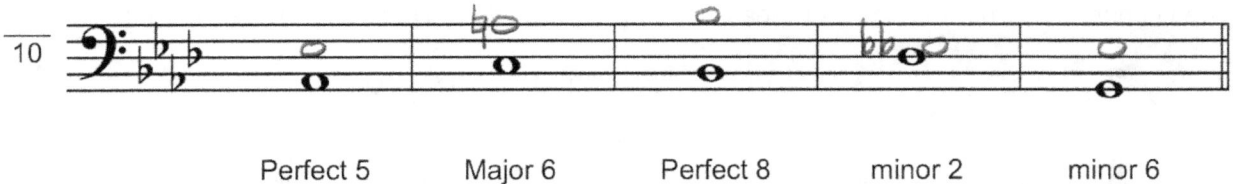

   Perfect 5   Major 6   Perfect 8   minor 2   minor 6

10. Analyze the following piece of music by answering the questions below.

Andante   Domenico Scarlatti

a) Add the correct Time Signature directly on the music.
b) Name the key of this piece.   d minor
c) Name the composer of this piece.   Domenico Scarlatti
d) Explain the meaning of **Andante**.   at a walking pace (moderately slow)
e) What is the shortest note value in this piece?   32nd note
f) What is the longest note value in this piece?   dotted quarter note
g) Explain the dynamic marking *mp*.   mezzo piano - moderately soft
h) Explain the dynamic marking *mf*.   mezzo forte - moderately loud
i) For the triad at **A**, name: Root: G   Type/Quality: minor
j) Name the interval at the letter **B**.   minor 2

Lesson 5 Simple Time and Compound Time

In **SIMPLE TIME** the top number is **2, 3** or **4**. In **COMPOUND TIME** the top number is **6, 9** or **12**.

♪ **Note:** Compound Time is always in groups of 3. Three pulses equal one DOTTED pulse.
Three Basic Beats equal one DOTTED Compound Basic Beat.

SIMPLE TIME	COMPOUND TIME (groups of 3)
Pulse: S = Strong w = weak M = Medium	Compound Dotted Pulse: S• = Sww w• = Mww M• = Mww
Top Number: Number of beats per measure	Top Number: Number of beats per measure
2 S w	**6** Sww Mww S• w•
3 S w w	**9** Sww Mww Mww S• w• w•
4 S w M w	**12** Sww Mww Mww Mww S• w• M• w•
Bottom Number: Basic Beat = 1 count	Bottom Number: Basic Beat = 1 count
Bottom Number Basic Beat	Bottom Number Basic Beat (group of 3) = Compound Basic Beat
2 𝅗𝅥	**4** ♩ (♩♩♩) = 𝅗𝅥.
4 ♩	**8** ♪ (♪♪♪) = ♩.
8 ♪	**16** ♬ (♬♬♬) = ♪.
16 ♬	
Simple Time: Basic Beat = one note (**NO DOT**)	Compound Time: (group of 3) Compound B.B. (Basic Beat) = one **DOTTED** note

1. Write one DOTTED pulse equal to each group of three pulses in $\frac{12}{8}$ time. (S• w• or M•)

   $\frac{12}{8}$ Pulse: Sww   Mww   Mww   Mww

   Compound Pulse: __S•__   __w•__   __M•__   __w•__

2. Write one DOTTED note (Compound B.B.) equal to each group of 3 Basic Beats.

   Basic Beat: ♩♩♩   Basic Beat: ♪♪♪   Basic Beat: ♬♬♬

   Compound B. B.: __𝅗𝅥.__   Compound B. B.: __♩.__   Compound B. B.: __♪.__

COMPOUND TIME: DOTTED REST

A **DOTTED REST** is ONLY used in **COMPOUND TIME** and is used for complete GROUPS of three beats or pulses. S+w+w or M+w+w. A dot after a rest ALWAYS goes in space three.

1. Write one dotted rest below the bracket that has the same value as the dotted note in the measure.

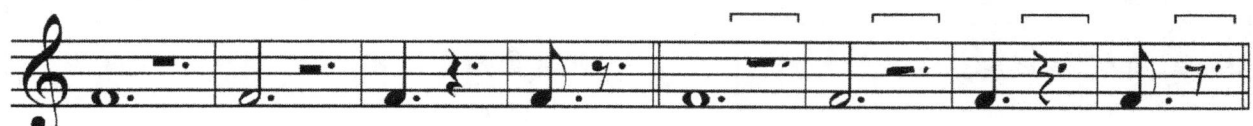

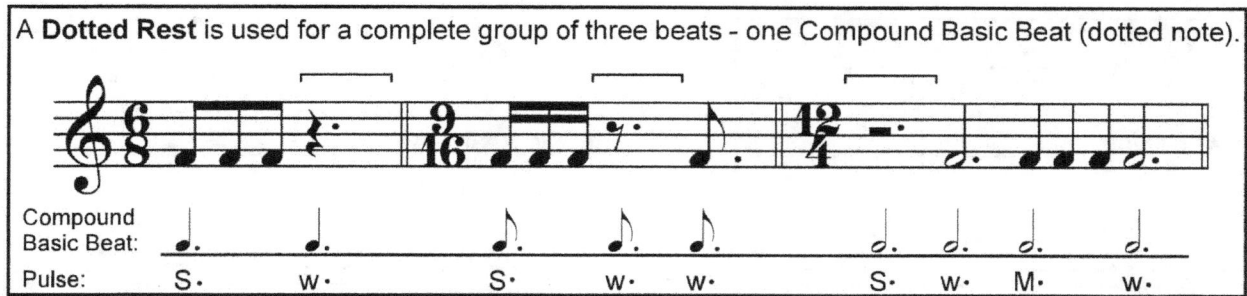

2. Add one dotted rest below each bracket to complete the measure. Cross off the Compound Basic Beat (Compound B.B.) as each beat is completed.

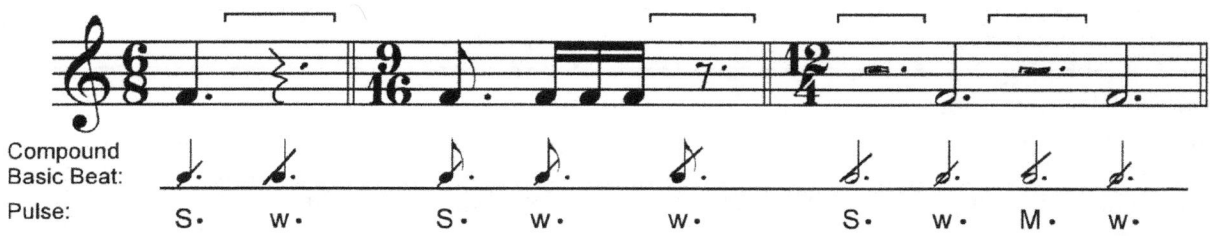

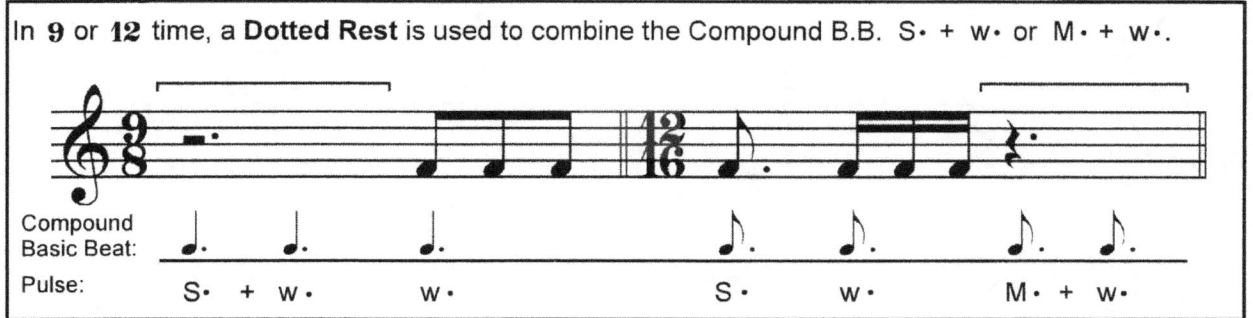

3. Add one dotted rest below each bracket to complete the measure. Cross off the Compound Basic Beat (Compound B.B.) as each beat is completed.

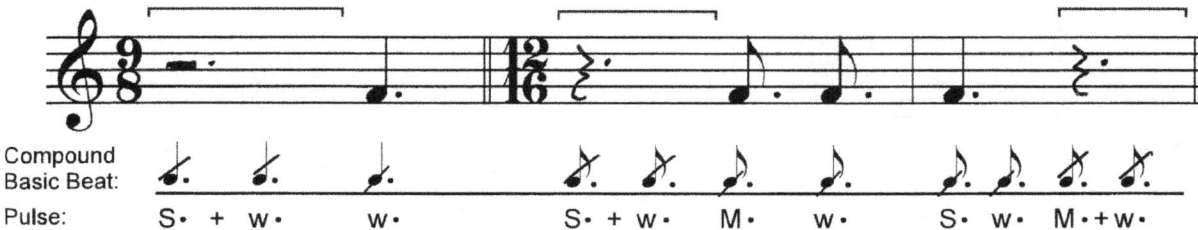

55

SIMPLE "DUPLE" TIME and COMPOUND "DUPLE" TIME (TWO EQUAL GROUPS)

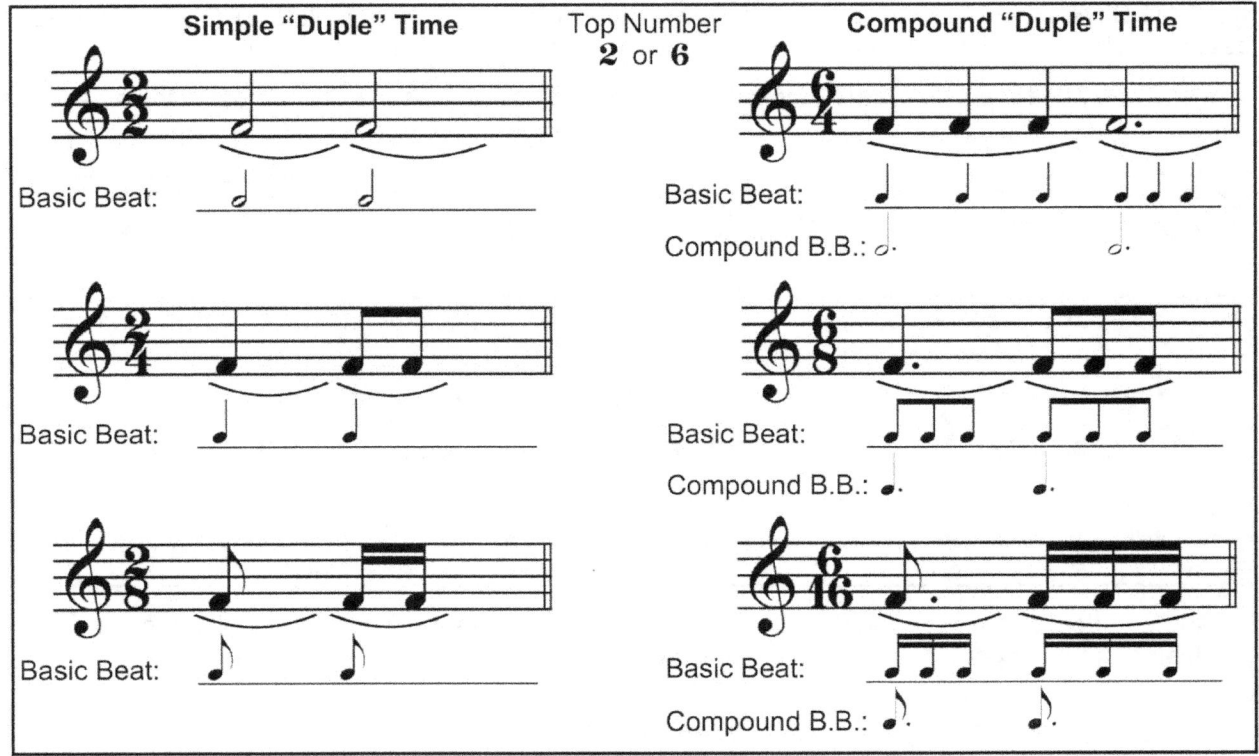

In Simple Time each group will equal one Basic Beat. (one note - no dot)
In Compound Time each group will equal one Compound Basic Beat. (one DOTTED note)

1. Scoop the equal groups. Write the Basic Beat and (when necessary) write the Compound B.B. (Basic Beat) below each measure. Add the correct Time Signature below each bracket.

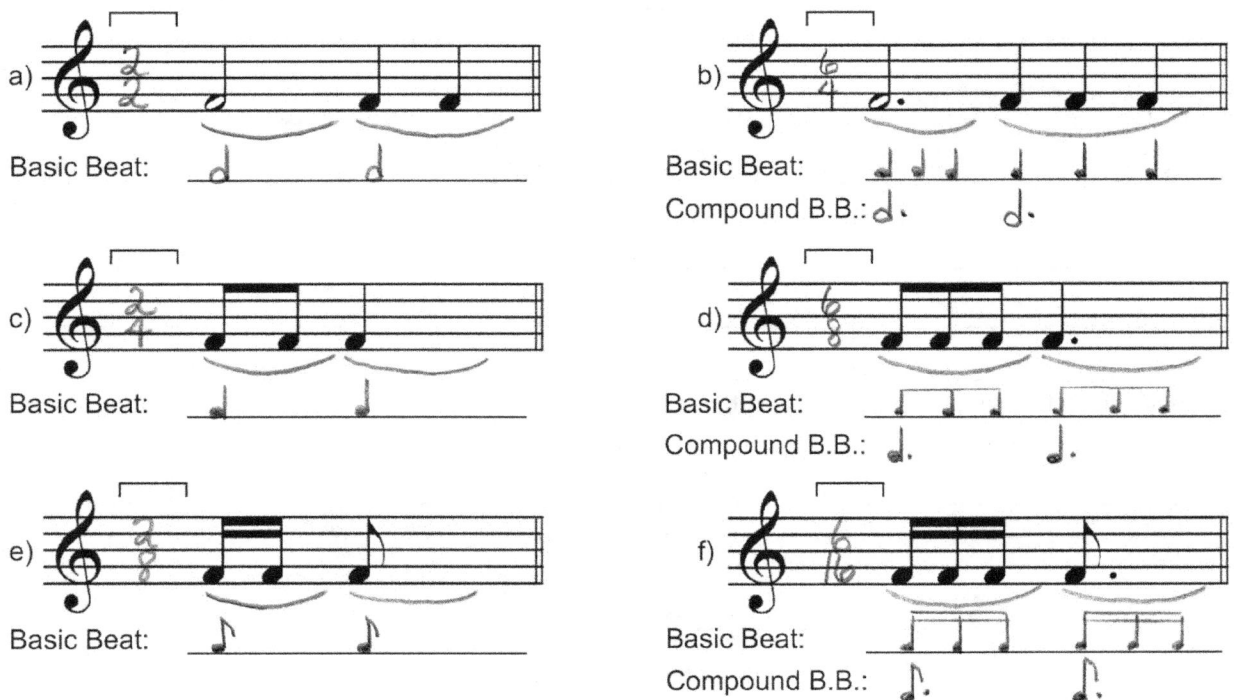

56

COMPOUND "DUPLE" TIME (TWO GROUPS of THREE)

In $\frac{6}{4}$ time, there are 6 ♩ notes in each measure. This is the Basic Beat. These 6 ♩ notes are divided into 2 groups of 3 ♩♩♩ notes, and equal 2 ♩. notes. This is the Compound Basic Beat. 2 x 3 = 6.

$\frac{6}{8}$ = 6 ♪ notes (Basic Beat); 2 groups of 3 ♪♪♪ notes = 2 ♩. notes (Compound B.B.)

$\frac{6}{16}$ = 6 ♬ notes (Basic Beat); 2 groups of 3 ♬♬♬ notes = 2 ♪. notes (Compound B.B.)

1. Scoop the equal groups. Write the Basic Beat and Compound Basic Beat below each measure. Add the correct Time Signature below each bracket.

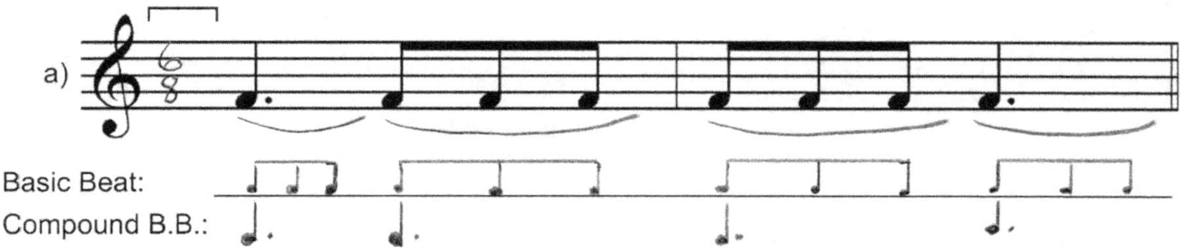

57

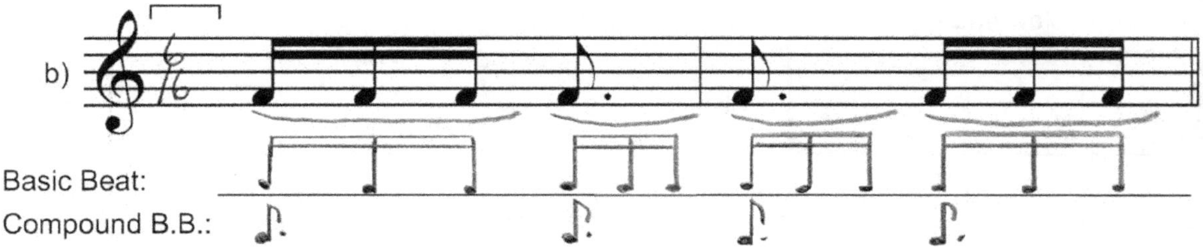

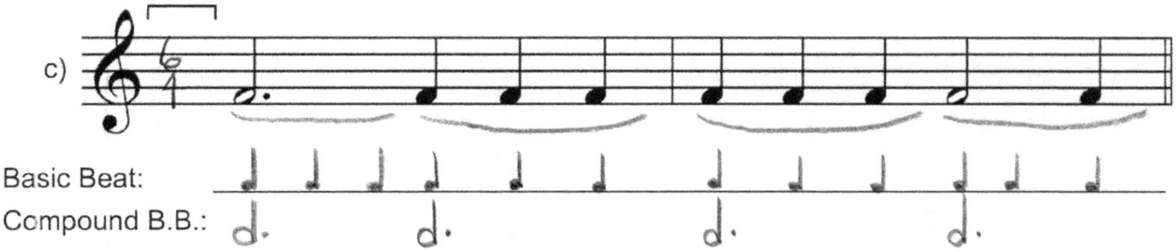

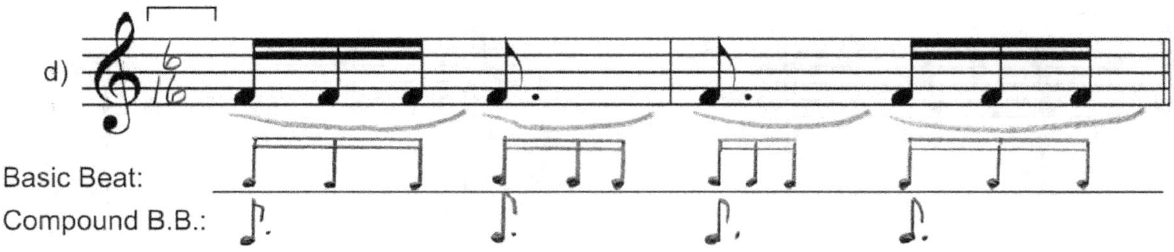

SIMPLE "TRIPLE" TIME and COMPOUND "TRIPLE" TIME (THREE EQUAL GROUPS)

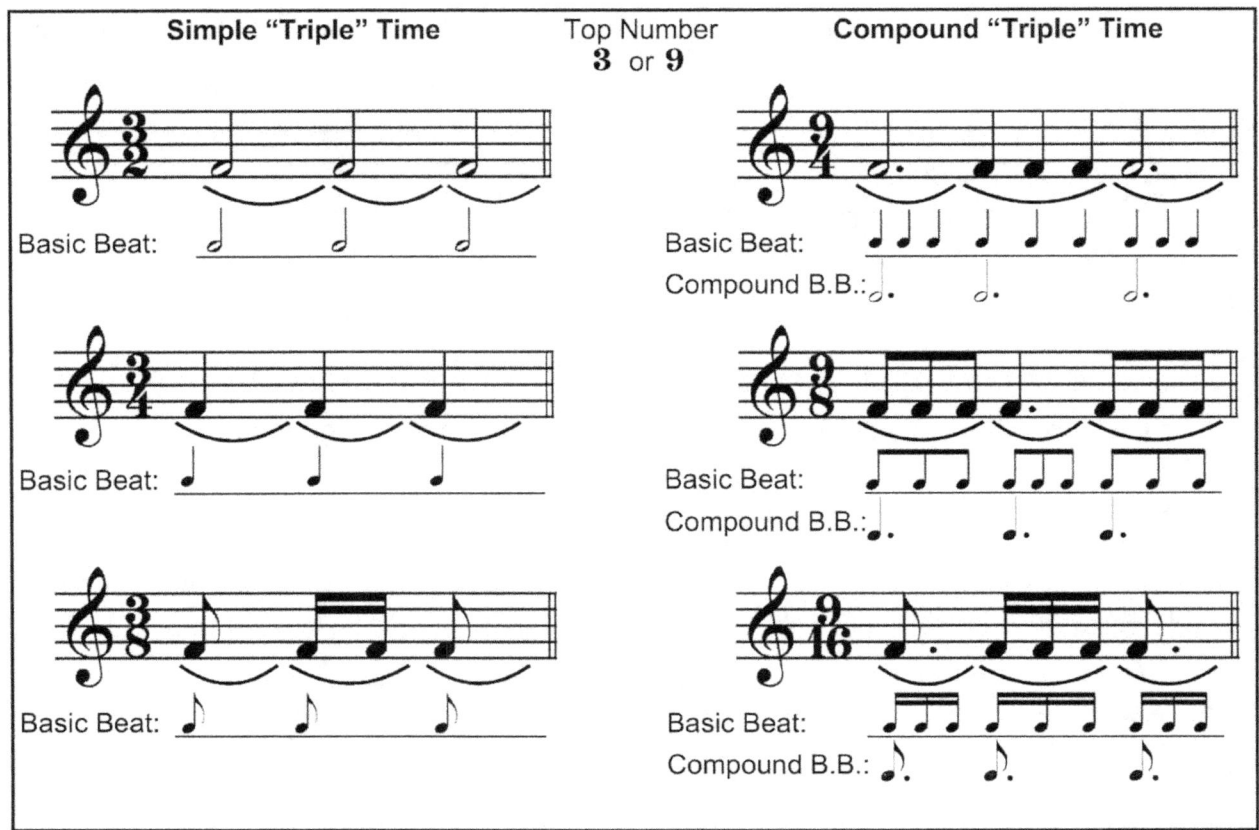

1. Scoop the equal groups. Write the Basic Beat and (when necessary) write the Compound B.B. (Basic Beat) below each measure. Add the correct Time Signature below each bracket.

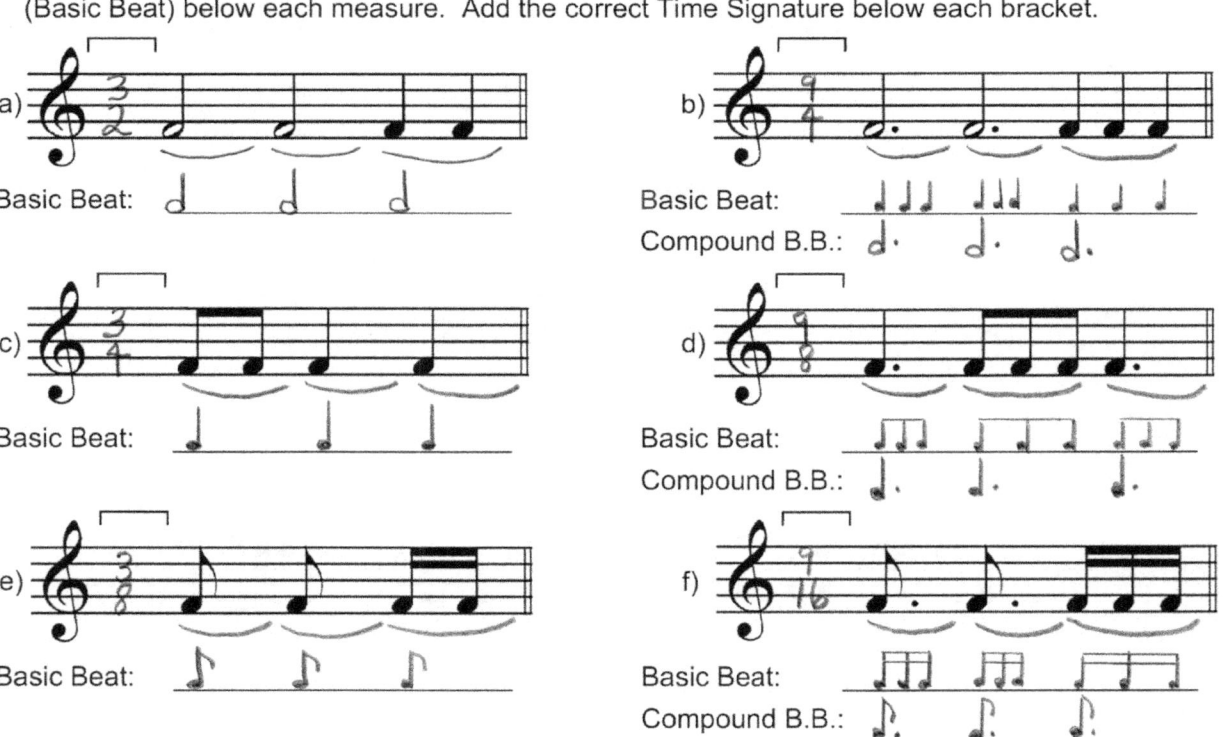

COMPOUND "TRIPLE" TIME (THREE GROUPS of THREE)

In $\frac{9}{4}$ time, there are 9 ♩ notes in each measure. This is the Basic Beat. These 9 ♩ notes are divided into 3 groups of 3 ♩♩♩ notes, and equal 3 ♩. notes. This is the Compound Basic Beat. 3 x 3 = 9.

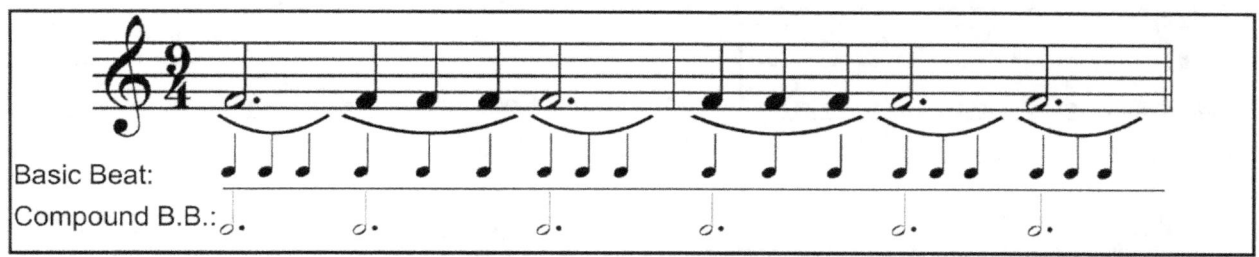

$\frac{9}{8}$ = 9 ♪ notes (Basic Beat); 3 groups of 3 ♪♪♪ notes = 3 ♩. notes (Compound B.B.)

$\frac{9}{16}$ = 9 ♬ notes (Basic Beat); 3 groups of 3 ♬♬♬ notes = 3 ♪. notes (Compound B.B.)

1. Scoop the equal groups. Write the Basic Beat and Compound Basic Beat below each measure. Add the correct Time Signature below each bracket.

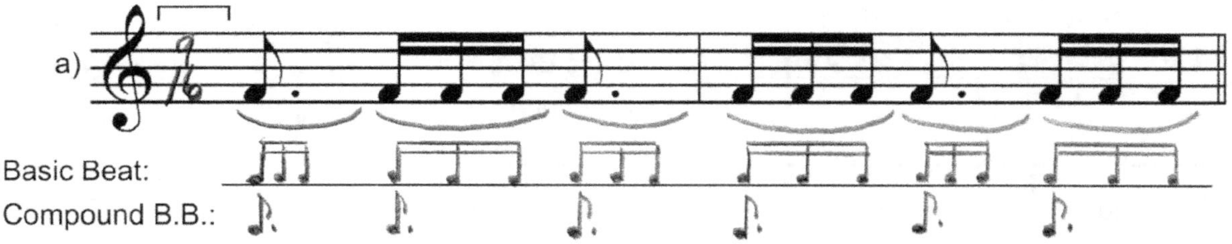

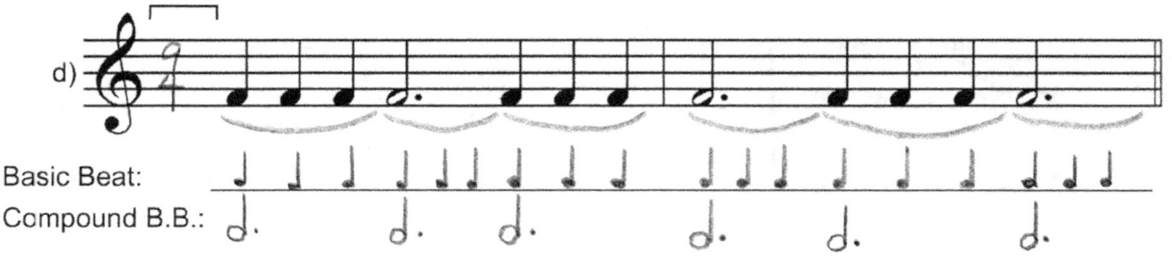

SIMPLE "QUADRUPLE" TIME and COMPOUND "QUADRUPLE" TIME (FOUR EQUAL GROUPS)

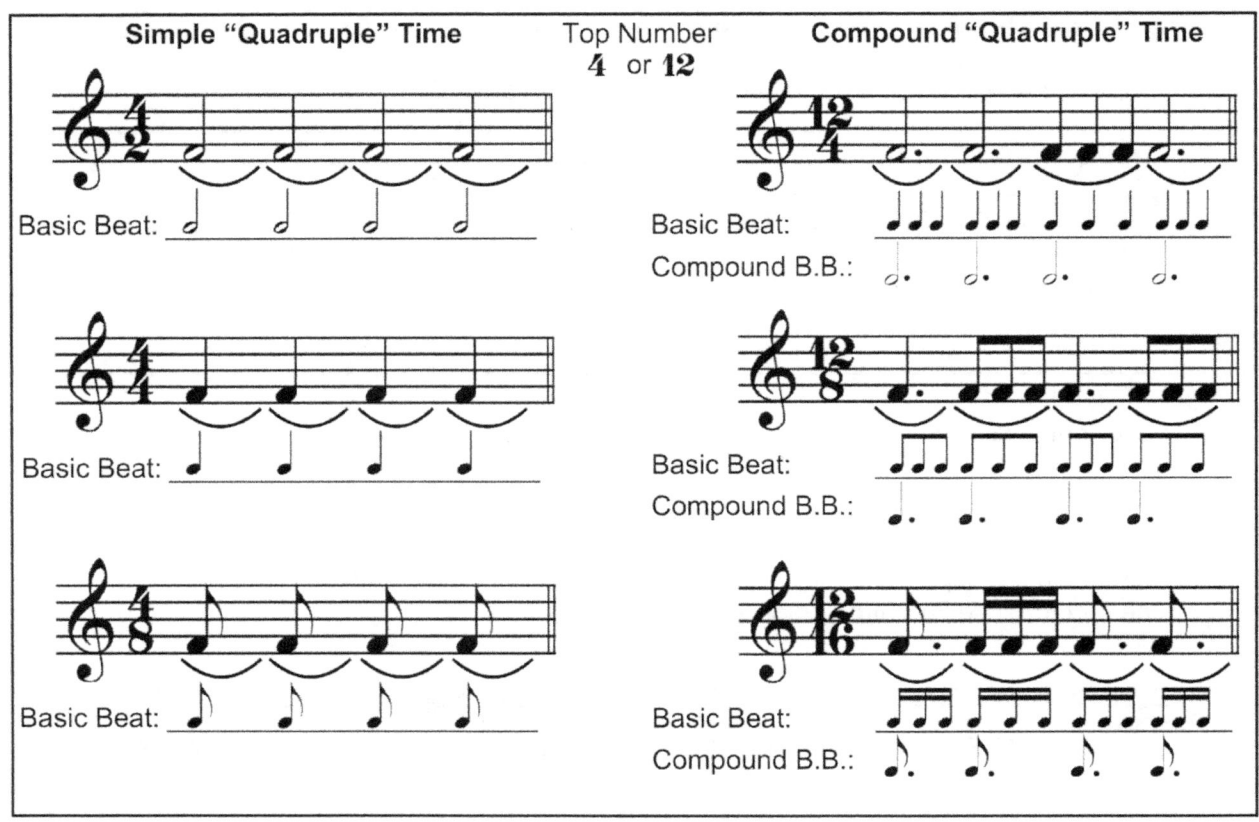

1. Scoop the equal groups. Write the Basic Beat and (when necessary) write the Compound B.B. (Basic Beat) below each measure. Add the correct Time Signature below each bracket.

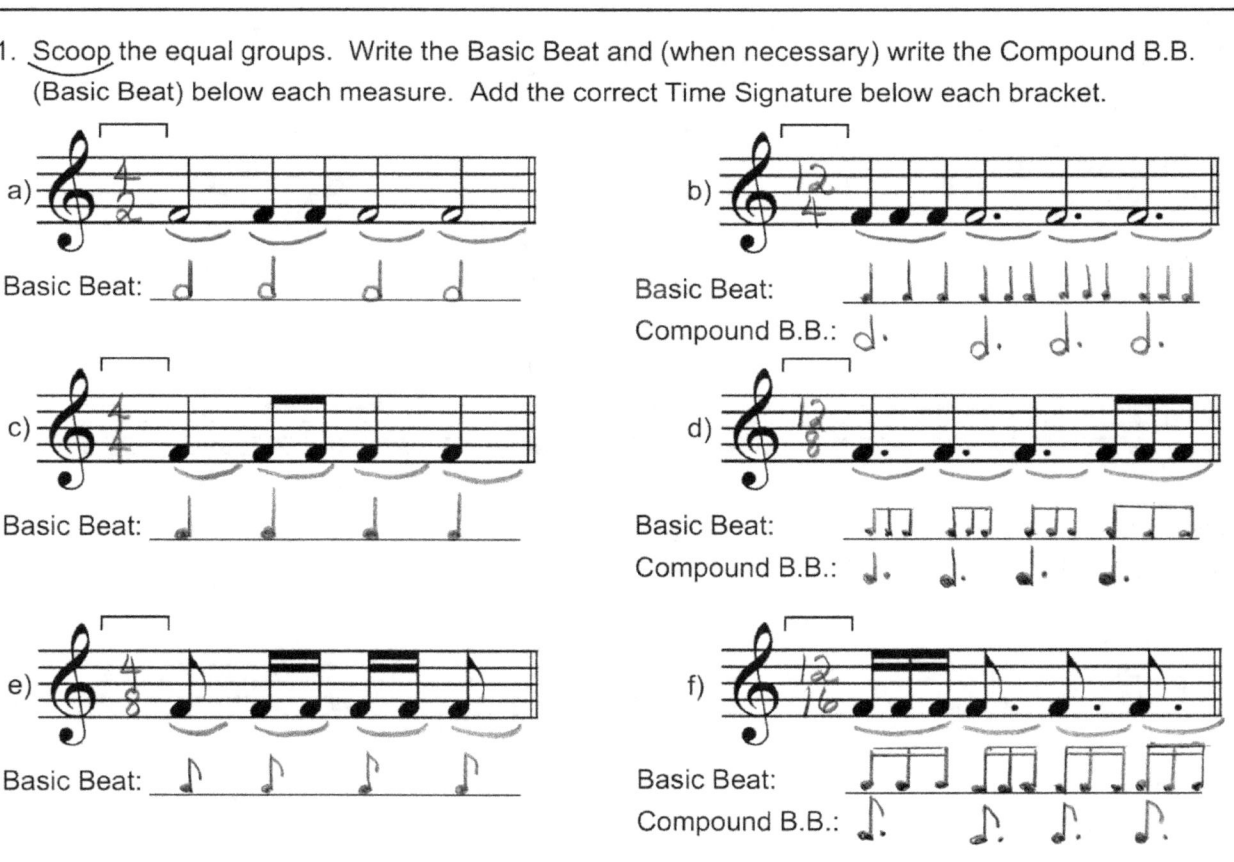

COMPOUND "QUADRUPLE" TIME (FOUR GROUPS of THREE)

In $\frac{12}{4}$ time, there are 12 ♩ notes in each measure. This is the Basic Beat. These 12 ♩ notes are divided into 4 groups of 3 ♩♩♩ notes, and equal 4 ♩. notes. This is the Compound B.B. 4 x 3 = 12.

$\frac{12}{8}$ = 12 ♪ notes (Basic Beat); 4 groups of 3 ♪♪♪ notes = 4 ♩. notes (Compound B.B.)

$\frac{12}{16}$ = 12 ♬ notes (Basic Beat); 4 groups of 3 ♬♬♬ notes = 4 ♪. notes (Compound B.B.)

1. Scoop the equal groups. Write the Basic Beat and Compound Basic Beat below each measure. Add the correct Time Signature below each bracket.

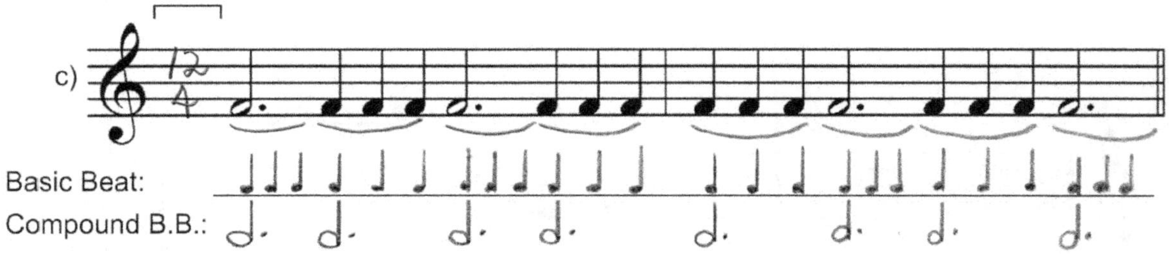

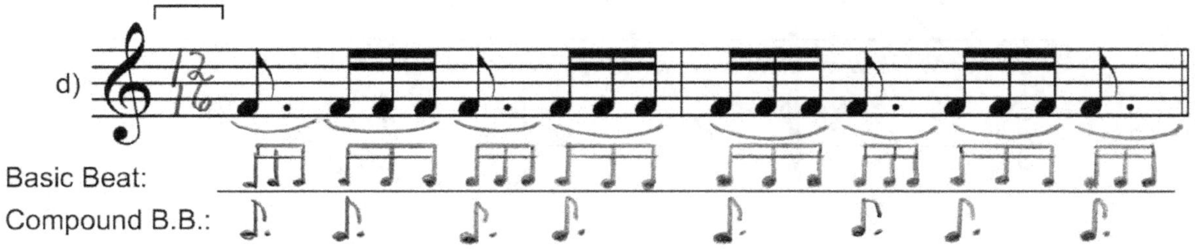

61

COMBINING BASIC BEATS and COMPOUND BASIC BEATS USING RESTS

> When **COMBINING BASIC BEATS** using **RESTS**:
> A Strong pulse joins a weak pulse or two weak pulses into one rest.   S + w or S + w + w
> A Medium pulse joins a weak pulse or two weak pulses into one rest.   M + w or M + w + w
> A weak pulse can NOT be joined to a Medium or a weak pulse.   w ~ M or w ~ w

♪ Note: Plus (+) sign: **join** the S + w (+ w) and M + w (+ w)
   Tilde (~) sign: do **NOT** join the w ~ M or w ~ w

1. a) Write the Basic Beat and pulse AND the Compound Basic Beat and pulse below each measure.
   b) Add rests below each bracket to complete the measure.
   c) Cross off the Basic Beat and the Compound B.B. as each beat is completed.

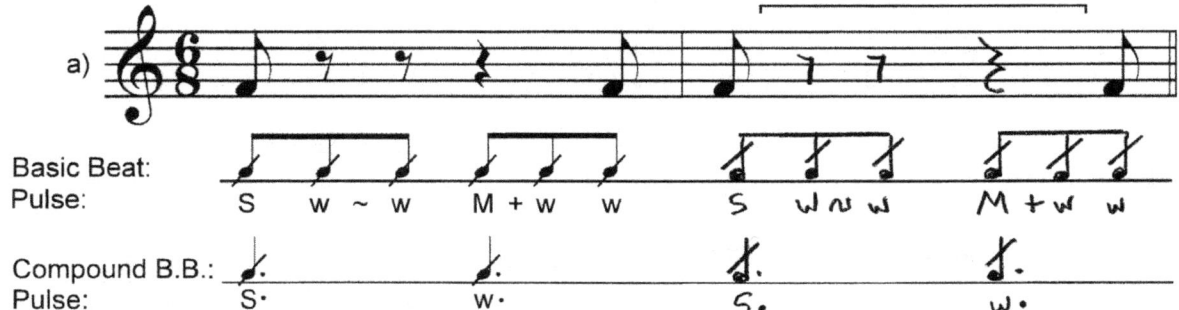

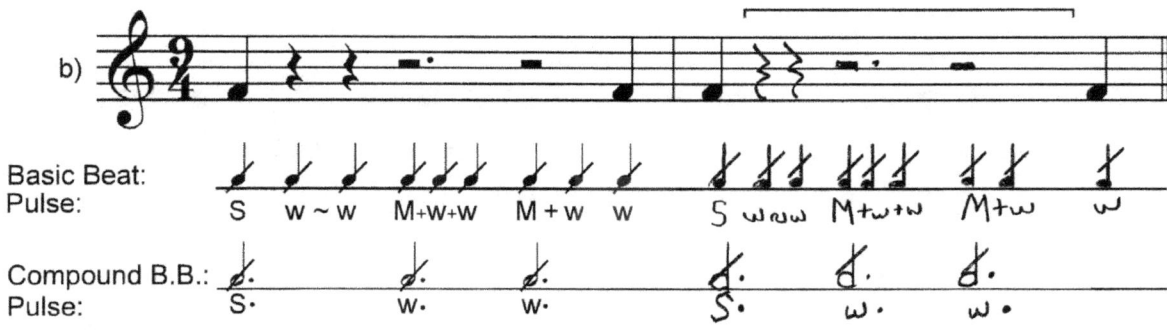

ADDING RESTS in COMPOUND TIME

When combining **COMPOUND BASIC BEATS** using **RESTS**:	
A Strong dotted pulse joins a weak dotted pulse into one rest.	S• + w•
A Medium dotted pulse joins a weak dotted pulse into one rest.	M• + w•
A weak dotted pulse can NOT be joined to a Medium or a weak pulse.	w• ~ M• or w• ~ w•

♪ **Note:** Plus (+) sign: **join** the **S•+w•** and **M•+w•**   Tilde (~) sign: do **NOT** join the **w•~M•** or **w•~w•**

1. Add rests below each bracket to complete the measure. Cross off the Basic Beat and the Compound Basic Beat as each beat is completed.

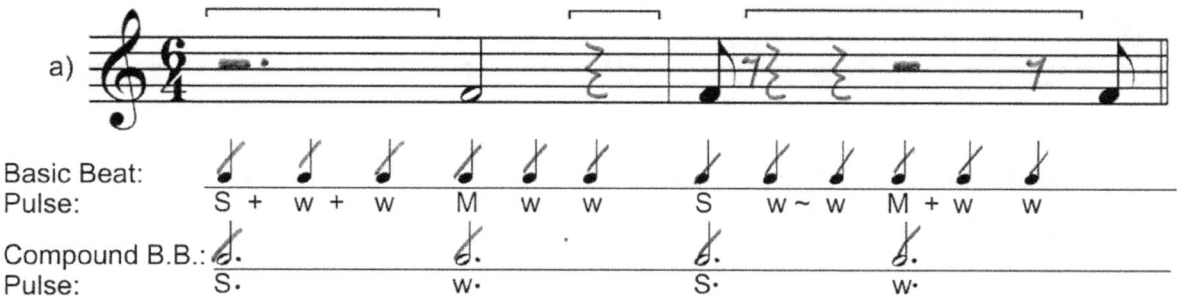

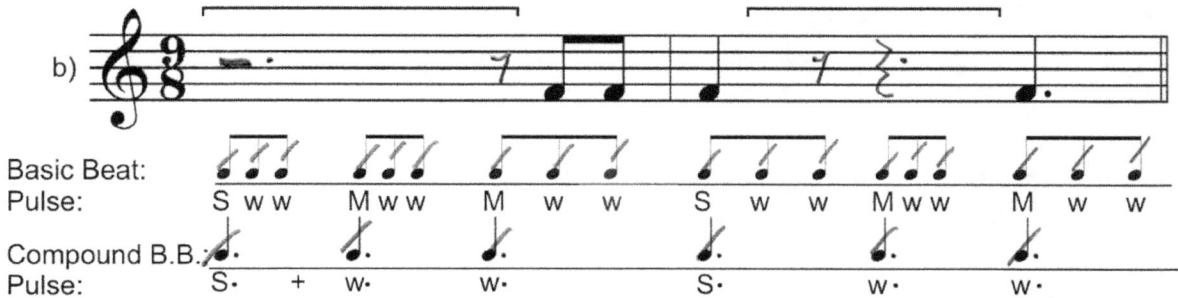

DOTTED WHOLE REST in COMPOUND TIME

A **DOTTED WHOLE REST** is ONLY used in $\frac{9}{4}$ or $\frac{12}{4}$ time to combine S• + w• or M• + w•

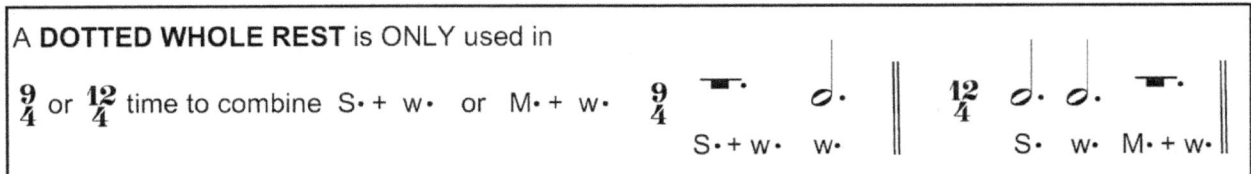

♪ Note: A **REST** for a **STRONG** beat or **MEDIUM** beat is combined with a **weak** beat. A rest for a **weak** beat stands alone. The dot after a dotted rest always goes in space three.

1. Add rests below each bracket to complete the measure. Cross off the Basic Beat and the Compound Basic Beat as each beat is completed.

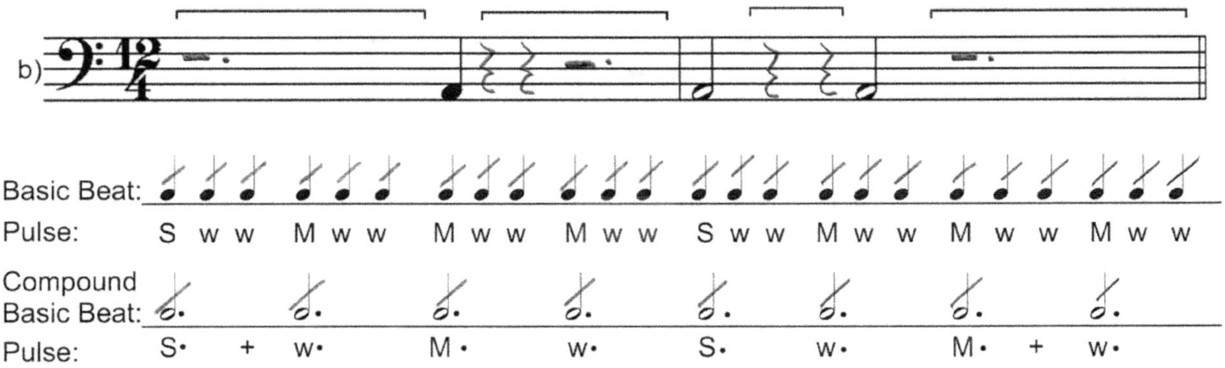

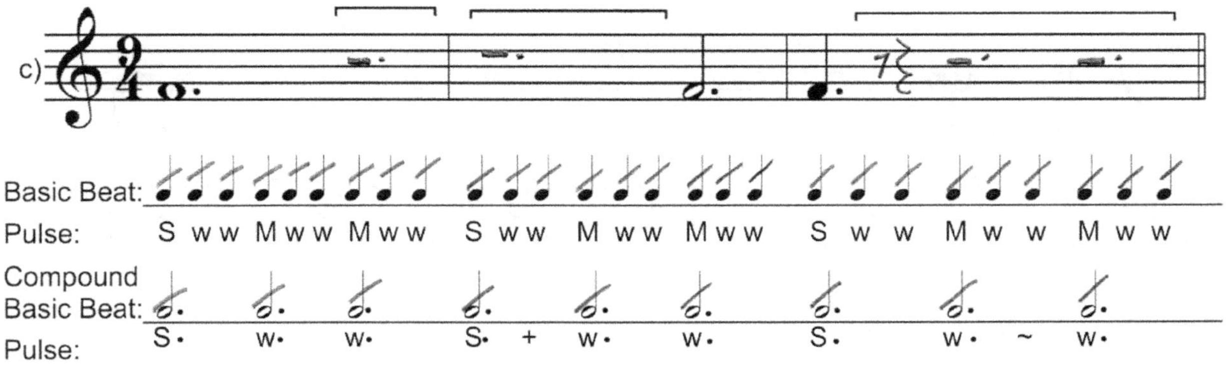

WHOLE REST in COMPOUND TIME

A **WHOLE REST** fills any measure with silence in Compound Time.

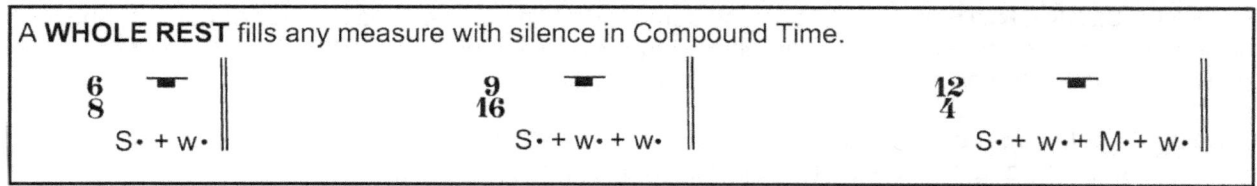

♪ **Note:** A **WHOLE REST** combines a **STRONG** beat with all the other beats. The top number of the Compound Time Signature indicates the number of beats the whole rest receives.

1. Add rests below each bracket to complete the measure. Cross off the Basic Beat and the Compound Basic Beat as each beat is completed.

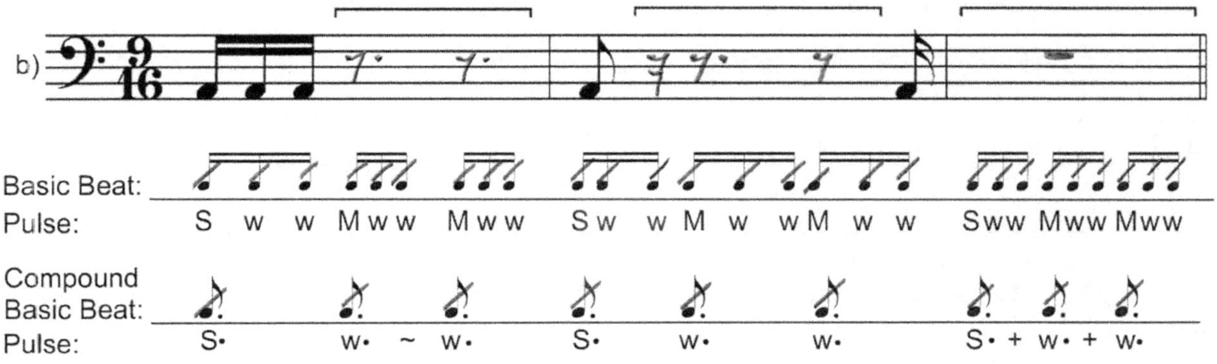

IRREGULAR GROUPS in SIMPLE TIME and COMPOUND TIME

An **IRREGULAR GROUP** in Simple Time or Compound Time is identified by a small number above or below a group of notes. The number indicates how many notes are in the group. An irregular group is played in the time of a regular group of the SAME note value.

♪ **Note:** Simple Time regular groups are 2 or 4. Compound Time regular groups are 3 or 6.
An irregular group is equal to one regular group (one complete beat).

Irregular Groups in Simple Time
A Quintuplet (group of 5), a Sextuplet (group of 6) and a Septuplet (group of 7) are played in the time of 4 notes of the same value.

 or  or

1. a) Write the number of regular notes that equal each irregular group in Simple Time.
   b) Write the regular group of notes that equal each irregular group of notes in Simple Time.

   Quintuplet
   a) 5 notes played in the time of = __4__ notes   b)

   Sextuplet
   a) 6 notes played in the time of = __4__ notes   b)

   Septuplet
   a) 7 notes played in the time of = __4__ notes   b)

Irregular Groups in Compound Time
A Duplet (group of 2) and a Quadruplet (group of 4) are played in the time of 3 notes of the same value.

 or =

2. a) Write the number of regular notes that equal each irregular group in Compound Time.
   b) Write the regular group of notes that equal each irregular group of notes in Compound Time.

   Duplet
   a) 2 notes played in the time of = __3__ notes   b)

   Quadruplet
   a) 4 notes played in the time of = __3__ notes   b)

IRREGULAR GROUPS with DIFFERENT REGULAR GROUPS

1. a) Write the number of regular notes that equal each irregular group in Compound Time.
   b) Write the regular group of notes that equal each irregular group of notes in Compound Time.

   Quintuplet
   a) 5 notes played in the time of = __3__ notes   b) [quintuplet of sixteenths] = [three eighths]

   OR

   Quintuplet
   a) 5 notes played in the time of = __6__ notes   b) [quintuplet of sixteenths] = [six sixteenths]

   Septuplet
   a) 7 notes played in the time of = __3__ notes   b) [septuplet of sixteenths] = [three eighths]

   OR

   Septuplet
   a) 7 notes played in the time of = __6__ notes   b) [septuplet of sixteenths] = [six sixteenths]

2. Add the correct Time Signature below each bracket.

DOUBLE DOTTED NOTES

A **DOUBLE DOTTED NOTE** has 2 dots. The first dot equals half the value of the note. The second dot equals half the value of the first dot.

1. Write the note value of the dotted note and the note value of each dot.

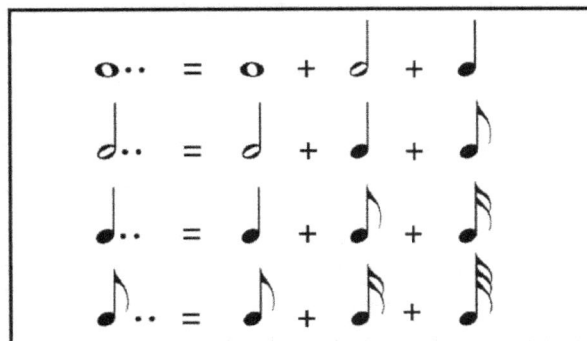
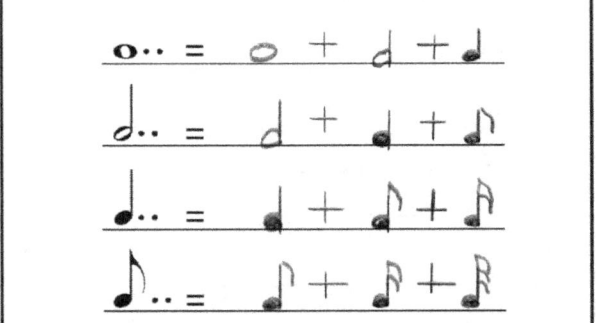

2. Add bar lines to complete the following rhythms.

3. Add the correct Time Signature below each bracket.

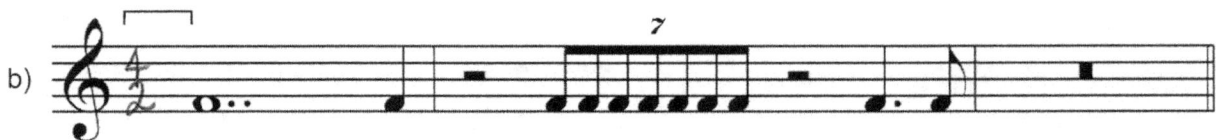

Lesson 5 — Review Test

Total Score: ____ / 100

Write the Circle of Fifths on a blank piece of paper. Use it as a reference when doing the review test.

1. Name the following intervals.

/10

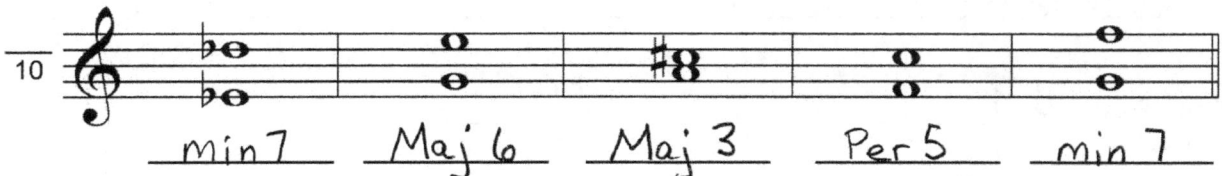

min 7   Maj 6   Maj 3   Per 5   min 7

2. Add the correct Time Signature below each bracket.

/10

3. Match each musical term with the English definition. (Not all definitions will be used.)

/10

Term		Definition
larghetto	g	a) slowing down
Tempo primo, Tempo I	c	b) smooth
Compound Time Signature	k	c) return to the original tempo
rallentando, rall.	a	d) moderate tempo
Simple Time Signature	f	e) very fast
presto	e	f) top number is **2**, **3** or **4**
legato	b	g) not as slow as *largo*
mano destra, M.D.	j	h) from the sign
dal segno, D.S., 𝄋	h	i) a stressed note
moderato	d	j) right hand
		k) top number is **6**, **9** or **12**

69

4. Write the **BASIC BEAT** and the **PULSE** below each measure. Add rests below each bracket to complete the measure. Cross off the Basic Beat as each beat is completed.

5. Add **BAR LINES** to complete the following rhythms.

6. Name the key of the following melody. Rewrite it at the **SAME PITCH** in the Bass Clef using the correct Key Signature.

Key: E♭ Major

7. Write the following scales, ascending and descending, using the correct **KEY SIGNATURE**. Use whole notes.

___
10

a) relative Major of c minor in the Treble Clef
b) g sharp minor melodic in the Bass Clef
c) enharmonic Tonic minor, harmonic form, of g sharp minor in the Treble Clef
d) d minor natural in the Bass Clef
e) chromatic scale beginning on C (any standard notation) in the Bass Clef

a)

b)

c)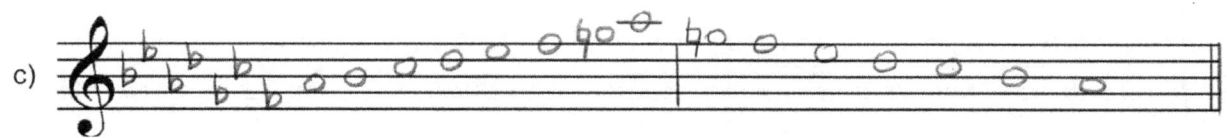

d)

e)

8. Write the following solid triads in **ROOT POSITION** in the Bass Clef, using accidentals. Use whole notes.

___
10

a) the **SUBMEDIANT** triad of C sharp Major
b) the **SUBDOMINANT** triad of g minor harmonic
c) the **SUPERTONIC** triad of B Major
d) the **DOMINANT** triad of f minor harmonic
e) the **MEDIANT** triad of E Major

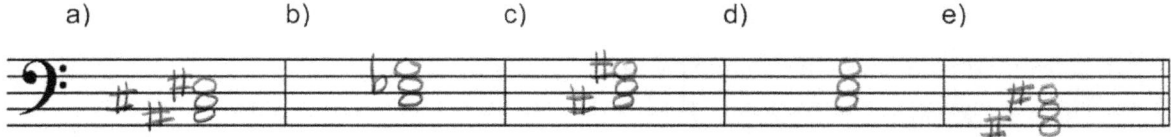

9. Give the **TECHNICAL DEGREE NAME** for each note. (Tonic, Supertonic, etc.)

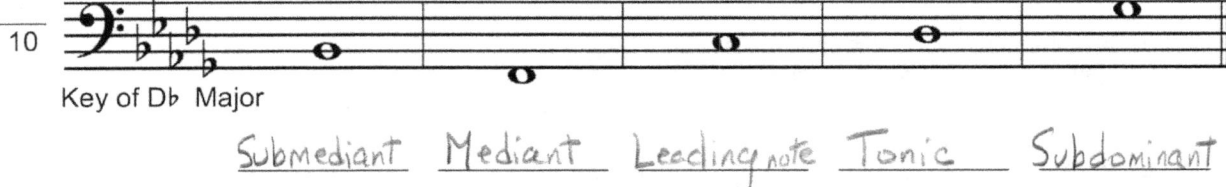

Key of D♭ Major

Submediant Mediant Leading note Tonic Subdominant

10. Analyze the following piece of music by answering the questions below.

Sarabande

Louis Couperin
(1626 - 1661)

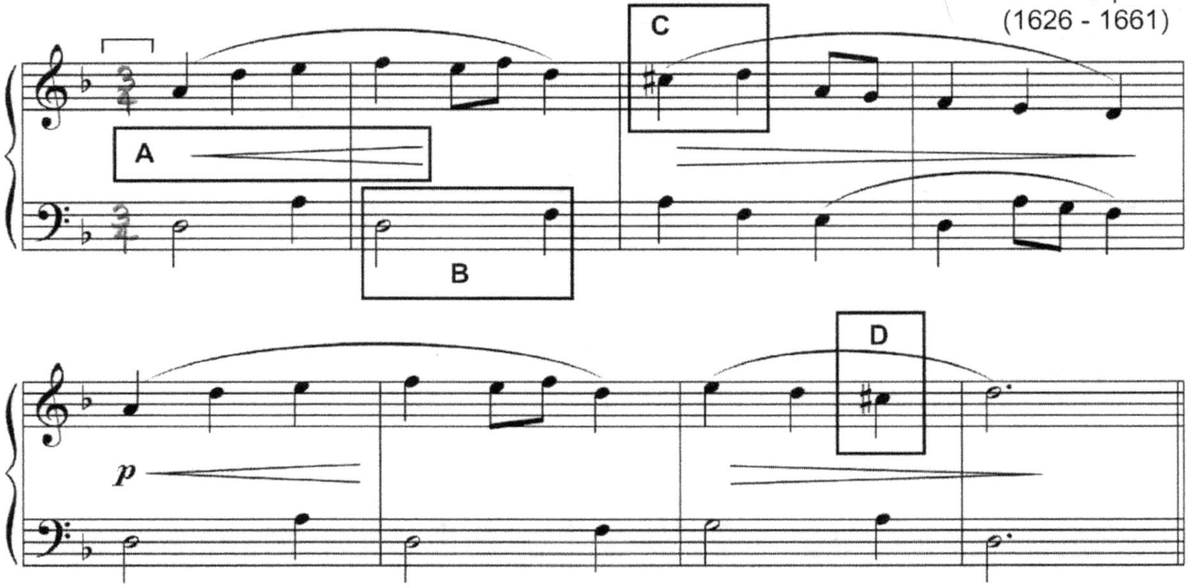

a) Add the correct Time Signature directly on the music.
b) Name the key of this piece. ___d minor___
c) Name the composer. ___Louis Couperin___
d) Explain the meaning of the sign at the letter **A**. ___crescendo - becoming louder___
e) Name the interval at the letter **B**. ___minor 3___
f) Name the interval at the letter **C**. ___minor 2___
g) Explain the sharp at the letter **D**. ___C# is the raised 7th note of d minor harmonic___
h) Name the title of this piece. ___Sarabande___
i) How many measures are in this piece? ___8___
j) How many slurs are in this piece? ___5___

Lesson 6   Intervals - Augmented, Diminished and Inversions

AUGMENTED INTERVAL

An **Augmented interval** is one semitone LARGER than a Perfect or Major interval.

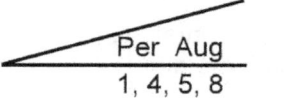
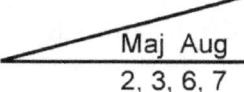

♪ **Note:** To change a Perfect or Major interval into an AUGMENTED interval: raise the top note one chromatic semitone (half step), or lower the bottom note one chromatic semitone (half step).

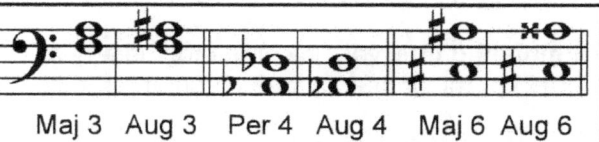

Augmented interval: raise the top note of a Perfect or Major interval one chromatic semitone.

♪ **Note:** Abbreviations: Major = **Maj**; Perfect = **Per**; Augmented = **Aug**.

1. Change these Perfect or Major intervals into Augmented intervals by raising the top note one chromatic semitone (half step). Use whole notes. Name the intervals.

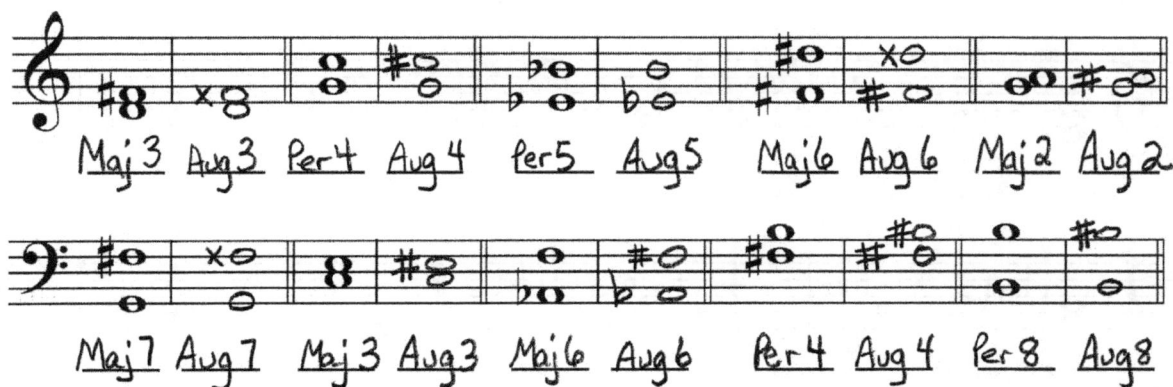

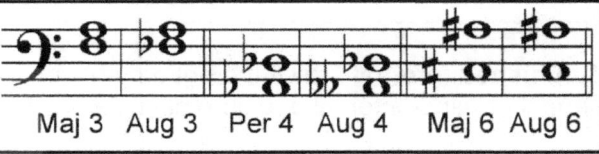

Augmented interval: lower the bottom note of a Perfect or Major interval one chromatic semitone.

2. Change these Perfect or Major intervals into Augmented intervals by lowering the bottom note one chromatic semitone (half step). Use whole notes. Name the intervals.

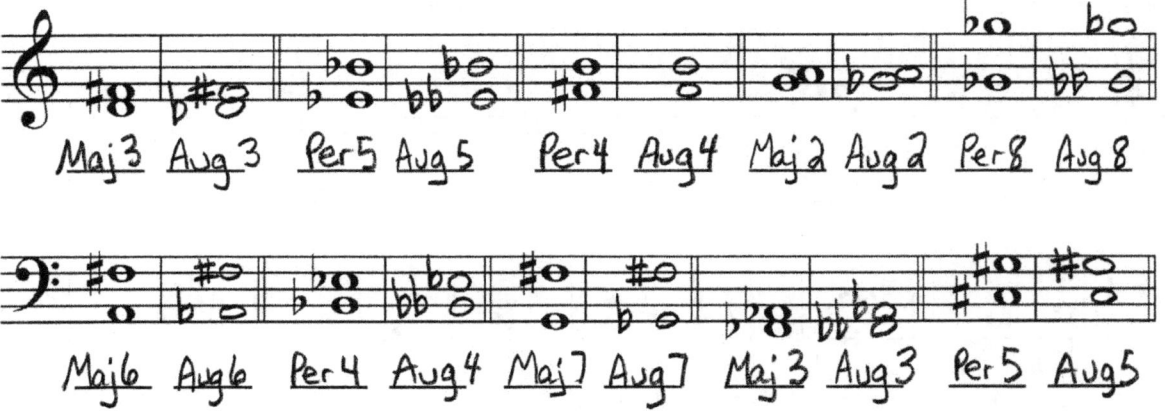

DIMINISHED INTERVAL

A **diminished interval** is one semitone **SMALLER** than a Perfect or minor interval.
A Perfect 1 (unison) cannot become diminished.

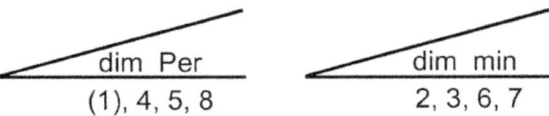

♪ Note: To change a Perfect or minor interval into a DIMINISHED interval: lower the top note one chromatic semitone (half step), or raise the bottom note one chromatic semitone (half step).

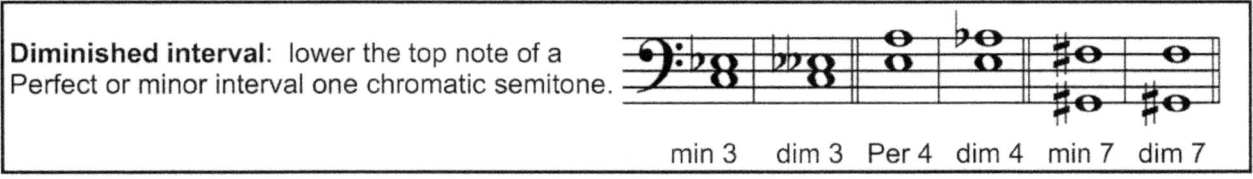

Diminished interval: lower the top note of a Perfect or minor interval one chromatic semitone.

♪ Note: Abbreviations: Perfect = **Per**; minor = **min**; diminished = **dim**.

1. Change these Perfect or minor intervals into diminished intervals by lowering the top note one chromatic semitone (half step). Use whole notes. Name the intervals.

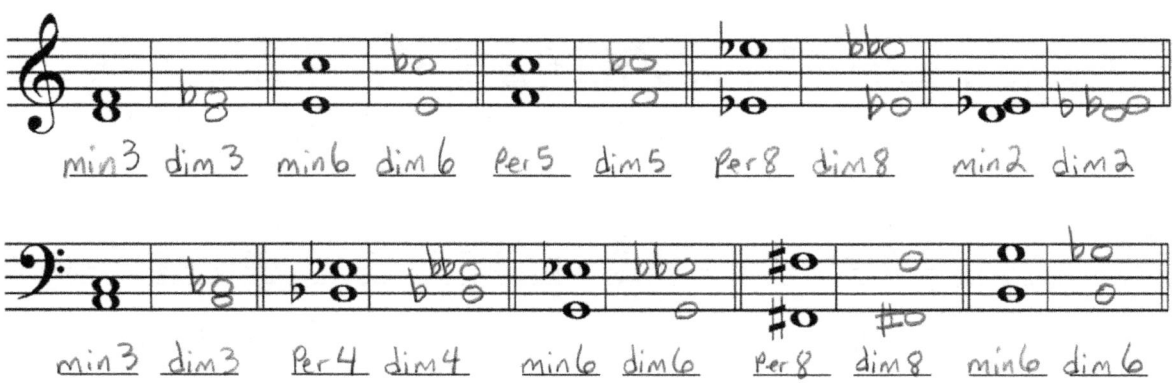

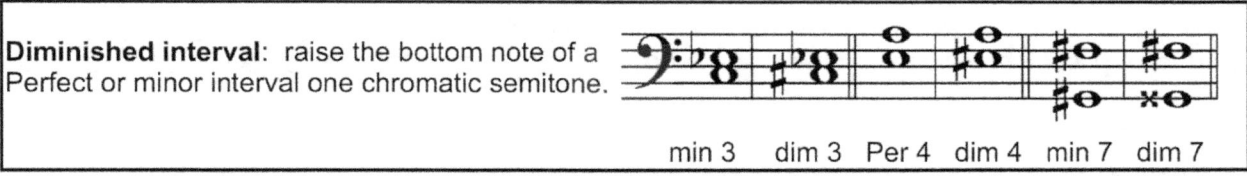

Diminished interval: raise the bottom note of a Perfect or minor interval one chromatic semitone.

2. Change these Perfect or minor intervals into diminished intervals by raising the bottom note one chromatic semitone (half step). Use whole notes. Name the intervals.

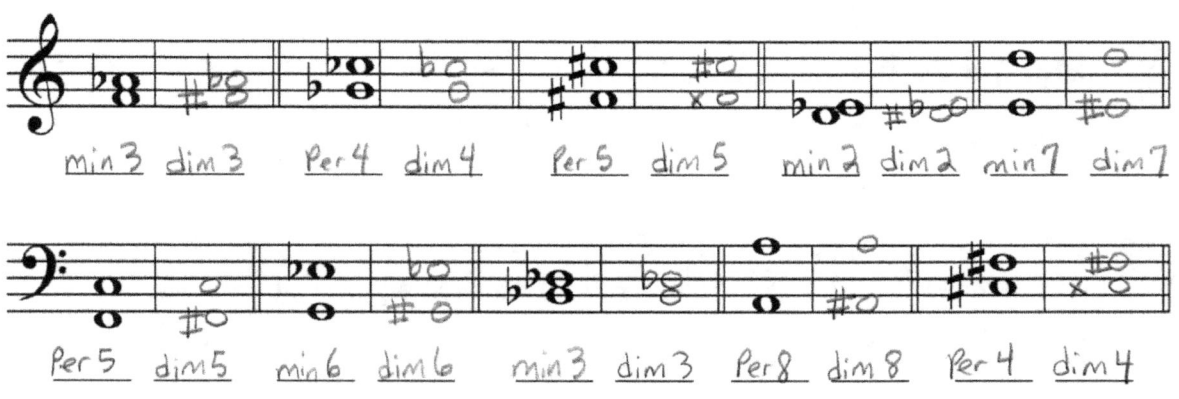

DIMINISHED INTERVAL to AUGMENTED INTERVAL

DIMINISHED (semitone larger→) **PERFECT** (semitone larger→) **AUGMENTED**

A Perfect interval - one chromatic semitone LARGER becomes Augmented.
A Perfect interval - one chromatic semitone SMALLER becomes diminished.

dim Per Aug
1, 4, 5, 8

♪ **Note:** An interval of a Perfect 1 (unison) may become Augmented but NOT diminished.

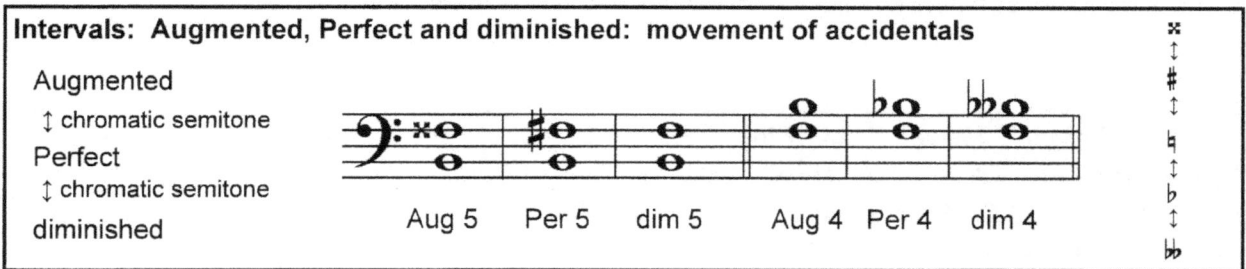

1. Change the following Perfect intervals into Augmented intervals and then into diminished intervals by changing the top note one chromatic semitone (half step). Use whole notes.

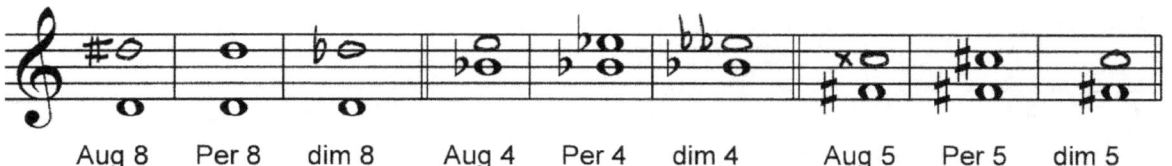

DIMINISHED (semitone larger→) **MINOR** (semitone larger→) **MAJOR** (semitone larger→) **AUGMENTED**

A Major interval - one chromatic semitone LARGER becomes Augmented.
A Major interval - one chromatic semitone SMALLER becomes minor.
A Major interval - two chromatic semitones SMALLER becomes diminished.

dim min Maj Aug
2, 3, 6, 7

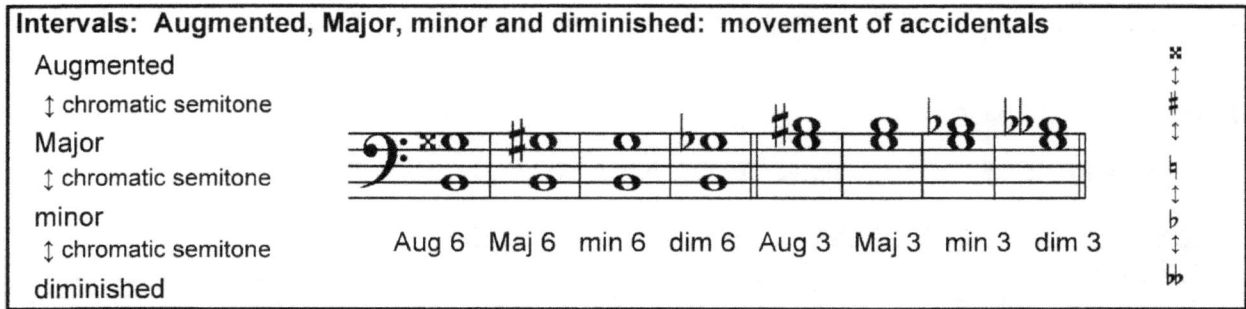

2. Change the following Major intervals into Augmented intervals, and then into minor intervals and diminished intervals by changing the top note one chromatic semitone. Use whole notes.

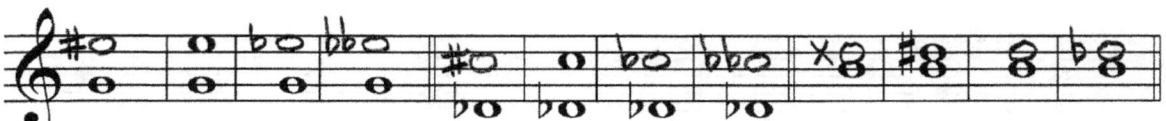

HARMONIC and MELODIC INTERVALS BELOW a GIVEN NOTE

To write an interval **BELOW a GIVEN NOTE**, follow these steps:
Step 1: Count down to determine the note that is the interval number below the given note. Write that note without an accidental.
Step 2: Determine the type/quality of the interval (Augmented, Perfect, Major, minor or diminished) based upon the Major Key Signature of the bottom note.
Step 3: Using accidentals (double sharp, sharp, flat or double flat), move one chromatic semitone (half step) at a time to adjust the bottom note until the correct interval is formed.

♪ **Note:** The **Type/Quality** of an interval is determined by the **Major** key of the lower note.

Harmonic interval - Major 3 BELOW the given note D.	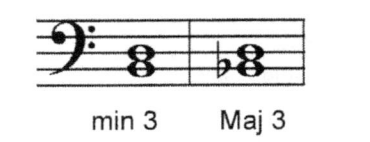
Down a 3rd from D is B. Key of B Major (F# C# G# D# A#).	
B to D is a min 3. **LOWER** the bottom note B to B♭.	
Key of B♭ Major (B♭ E♭). The interval of B♭ to D is a Maj 3.	min 3 Maj 3

♪ **Note:** Do NOT change the given note. Determine the Major or Perfect interval below the given note first. Raise or lower the bottom note to form the correct interval.

1. Write the following harmonic intervals BELOW the given notes.

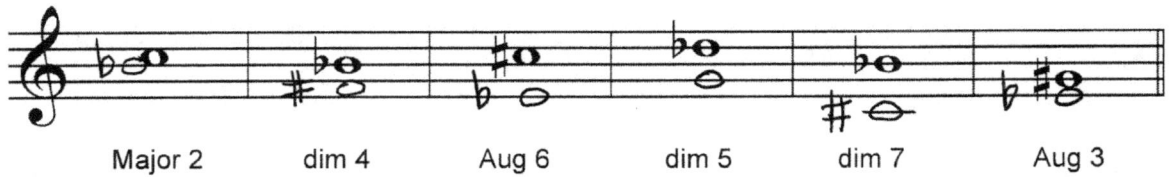

Major 2   dim 4   Aug 6   dim 5   dim 7   Aug 3

Melodic interval - minor 3 BELOW the given note E#.	
Down a 3rd from E# is C. Key of C Major. C to E is a Maj 3.	
C to E# is an Aug 3. **RAISE** the bottom note C to C#.	Aug. 3 Maj 3 min 3
Key of C# Major (F# C# G# D# A# E# B#). C# to E# is a Maj 3.	
Change the Maj 3 to a min 3. **RAISE** the bottom note C# to C𝄪. Interval C𝄪 to E# is a min 3.	

♪ **Note:** Do NOT change the given note. The bottom note may be a double flat or a double sharp.

2. Write the following melodic intervals BELOW the given notes.

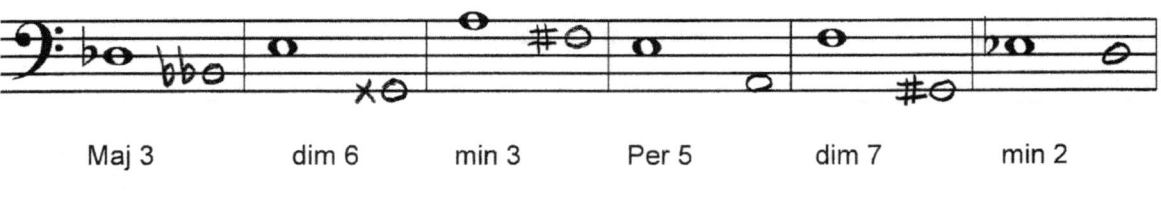

Maj 3   dim 6   min 3   Per 5   dim 7   min 2

dim 3   Aug 6   dim 3   dim 5   Aug 7   Maj 2

INTERVALS - DIMINISHED, MINOR, MAJOR, PERFECT and AUGMENTED

Major or **Perfect** intervals are identified by the Major key of the BOTTOM note. **Augmented, minor** and **diminished** intervals are raised or lowered in pitch based on the Key Signature of the Major key.

Type/Quality of intervals are one chromatic semitone (half step) apart.
Intervals 2, 3, 6, 7   **Diminished** *semitone* **minor** *semitone* **Major** *semitone* **Augmented**   dim   min   Maj   Aug
Intervals 1, 4, 5, 8   **Diminished** *semitone* **Perfect** *semitone* **Augmented**   dim   Per   Aug

1. Name the following melodic intervals.

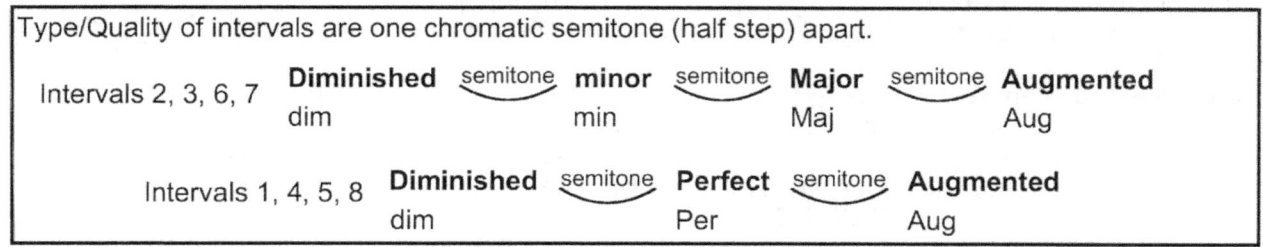

Per 4   dim 5   Aug 6   Maj 2   min 7

If the bottom note is NOT a Major key on the Circle of Fifths, change the accidental to a Major key. Determine the interval based on the Major key. Ex: F♭♭ becomes F Major.

Move the lower note, one semitone at a time, back to the original pitch to determine the given interval.

                           F♭♭ to A♭   F - A♭   F♭ - A♭   F♭♭ - A♭
                       Key: F Major   min 3   Maj 3   Aug 3

♪ **Note:** When both notes move up or down the same distance, the interval name remains the same.
        Example: Perfect 4: D to G, D♯ to G♯, D♭ to G♭, D𝄪 to G𝄪, D♭♭ to G♭♭

2. Name the following melodic intervals.

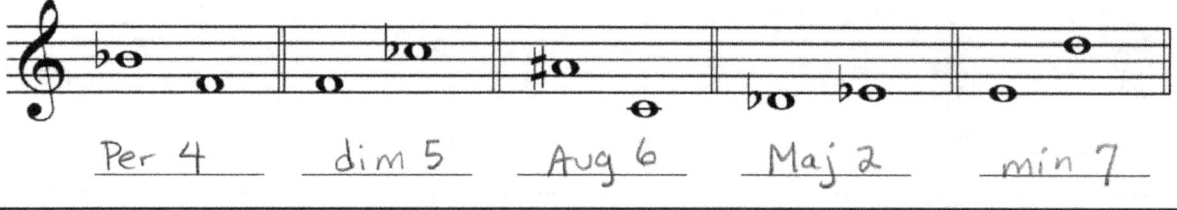

dim 6   Aug 8   Maj 3   min 7   dim 2

♪ **Note:** When writing a harmonic second below a given note, the lower note is written to the left.
        When there is **no room** for correct placement, it may be written to the right of the given note.

3. Write the following harmonic intervals BELOW the given note.

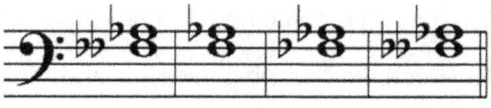

dim 3   Aug 5   min 2   Maj 7   Aug 6

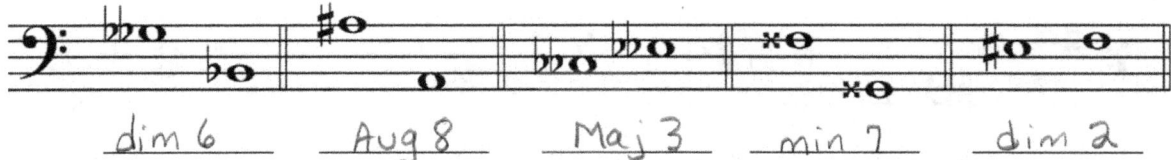

dim 4   Aug 8   dim 3   Maj 2   dim 5

INVERSIONS of INTERVALS

An **inversion** of an interval is turning it upside down.

To invert: The bottom note moves to the top. 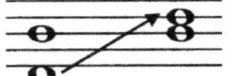 or The top note moves to the bottom.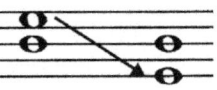

When inverting intervals:
MAJOR becomes MINOR
MINOR becomes MAJOR
AUGMENTED becomes DIMINISHED
DIMINISHED becomes AUGMENTED
PERFECT stays PERFECT

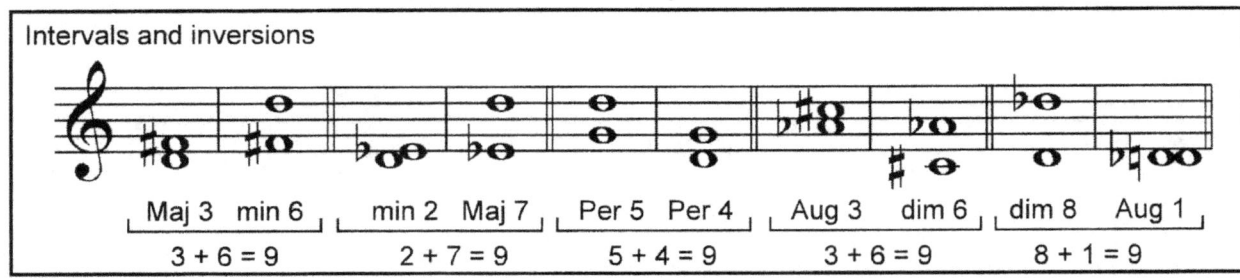

♫ **Note:** The combined number of the interval and its inversion ALWAYS equals NINE.

1. Name the following intervals and their inversions. Add the interval numbers to equal 9.

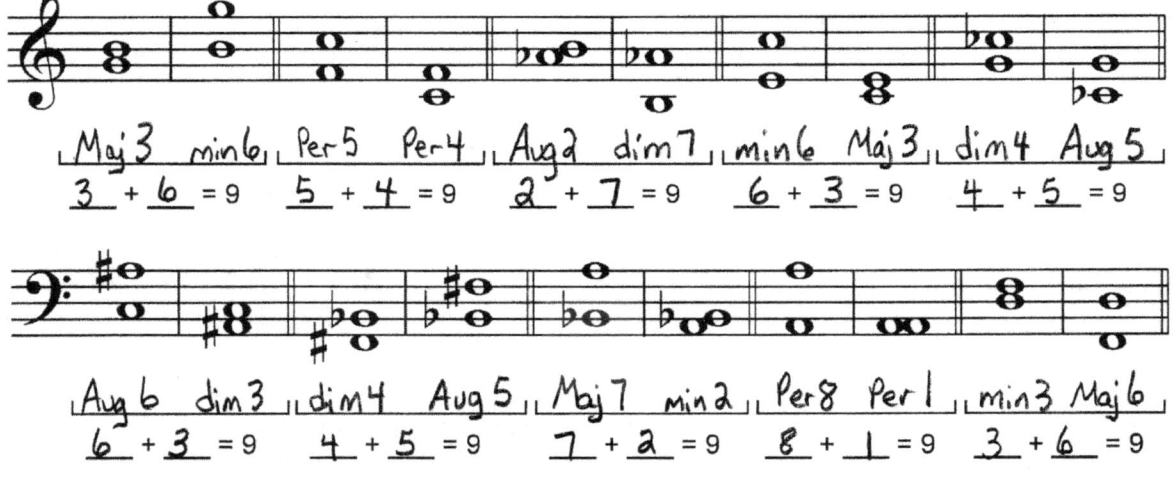

2. Name the following intervals. Invert each interval in the same clef. Name the inversions.

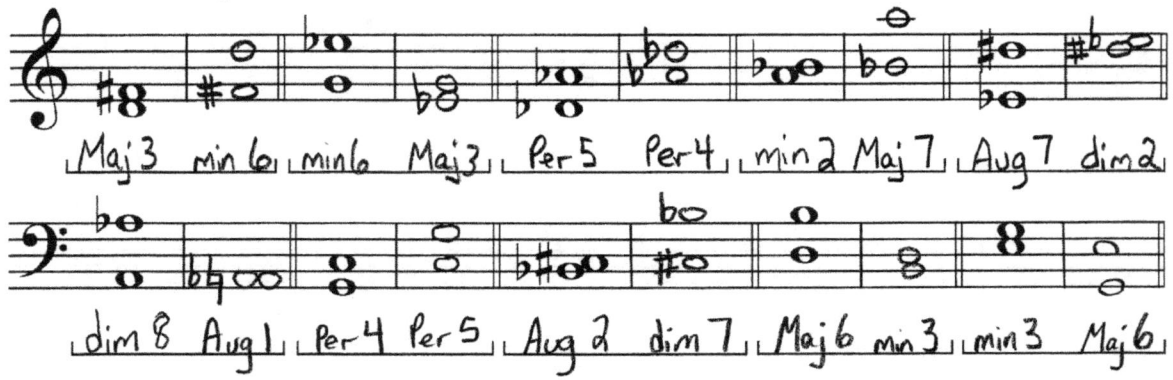

Lesson 6 — Review Test

Total Score: ____ / 100

Write the Circle of Fifths on a blank piece of paper. Use it as a reference when doing the review test.

1. Write the following harmonic intervals **ABOVE** the given notes. Invert the intervals. Use whole notes. Use accidentals. Name the inversions.

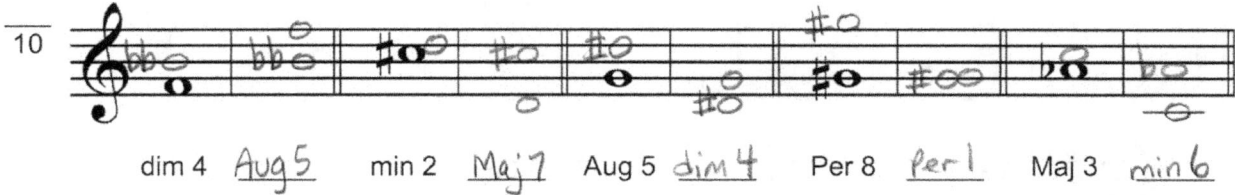

dim 4 Aug 5   min 2 Maj 7   Aug 5 dim 4   Per 8 Per 1   Maj 3 min 6

2. Add the correct Time Signature below each bracket.

3. Match each musical term with the English definition. (Not all definitions will be used.)

Term		Definition
fermata, 𝄐	j	a) moderately slow; at a walking pace
8va- - - - - ⌐	f	b) repeat the music within the double bar lines
⌊_____⌋, Ped.	i	c) marked or stressed
adagio	e	d) loud, then suddenly soft
fortepiano, *fp*	d	e) slower than *andante*, but not as slow as *largo*
8va- - - - - ⌟	g	f) play one octave above the written pitch
marcato, marc.	c	g) play one octave below the written pitch
a tempo	h	h) return to the original tempo
andante	a	i) pedal marking
𝄇	b	j) pause; hold the note or rest longer than its written value
		k) soft

79

4. Write the **BASIC BEAT** and the **PULSE** below each measure. Add rests below each bracket to complete the measure. Cross off the Basic Beat as each beat is completed.

5. Write the following harmonic intervals **BELOW** the given notes. Invert the intervals. Use accidentals. Use whole notes. Name the inversions.

min 6 Maj 3   Aug 7 dim 2   Maj 2 min 7   Per 5 Per 4   dim 4 Aug 5

6. Name the key of the following melody. Transpose it **UP** one octave in the Treble Clef using the correct Key Signature.

Key: D Major

7. For each of the following **MINOR** keys, identify the **technical degree name** of the root for each broken triad as **T** (Tonic), **SD** (Subdominant) or **D** (Dominant).

    a) c minor harmonic
    b) c sharp minor harmonic
    c) g minor harmonic
    d) f minor harmonic
    e) e flat minor harmonic

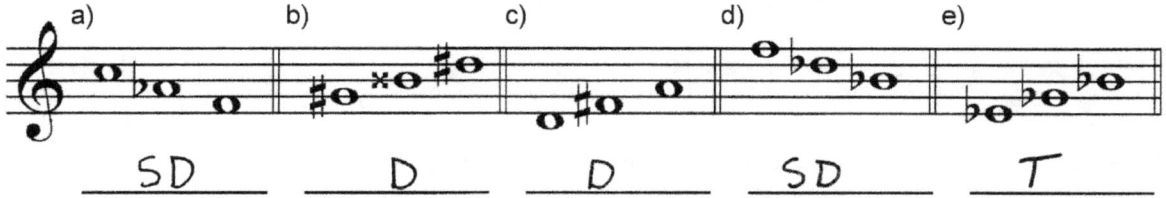

8. Write the following scales, ascending and descending, using the correct **KEY SIGNATURE**. Use whole notes.

    a) g minor harmonic in the Treble Clef
    b) Tonic minor, melodic form, of A flat Major in the Bass Clef
    c) enharmonic Tonic Major of B Major in the Treble Clef
    d) c sharp minor natural in the Bass Clef
    e) chromatic scale beginning on E (any standard notation) in the Bass Clef

9. a) Name the **MINOR** key for each of the following Key Signatures.
   b) Give the **TECHNICAL DEGREE NAME** for each note. (Tonic, Supertonic, etc.)

a) f# minor   f minor   a# minor   b minor   g# minor
b) Submediant Leading note Supertonic Submediant Mediant

10. Analyze the following piece of music by answering the questions below.

Allemande

Johann Hermann Schein
(1586 - 1630)

Allegretto

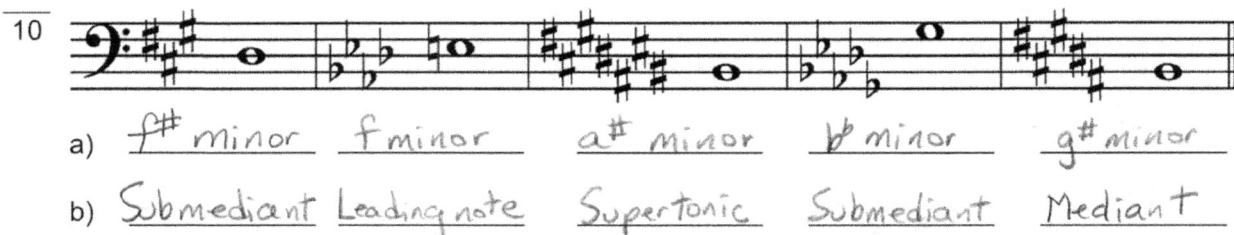

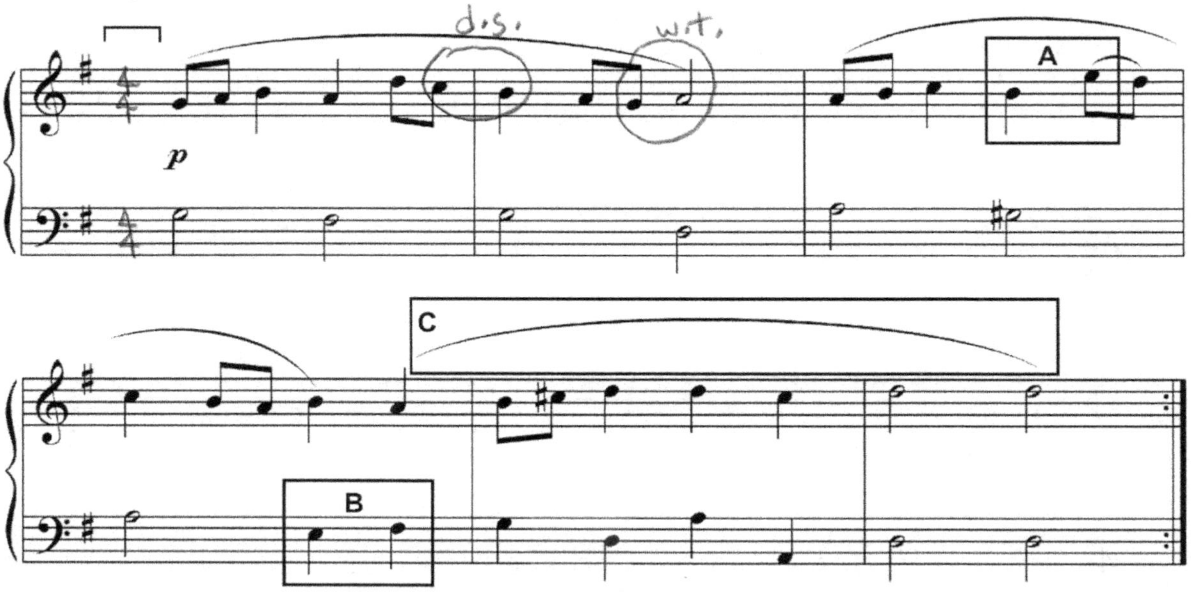

a) Add the correct Time Signature directly on the music.
b) Name the title of this piece. ___Allemande___
c) Name the composer of this piece. ___Johann Hermann Schein___
d) When did the composer live? ___1586 - 1630___
e) Explain the meaning of **Allegretto**. ___fairly fast; not as fast as allegro___
f) Name the interval at the letter **A**. ___Perfect 4___
g) Name the interval at the letter **B**. ___Major 2___
h) Locate and circle a diatonic semitone in this piece. Label it d.s.
i) Locate and circle a whole tone in this piece. Label it w.t.
j) Explain the sign at the letter **C**. ___slur - play the notes legato (smooth)___

Lesson 7 Triads - Inversions, Close and Open Position

An **INVERSION** of a triad occurs when the Root (Key note) of the triad is moved to a new position. A root position triad is all LINES or all SPACES. The Root of a root position triad is the lowest note. In **ANY INVERSION**, the position of a triad is always determined by the LOWEST note.

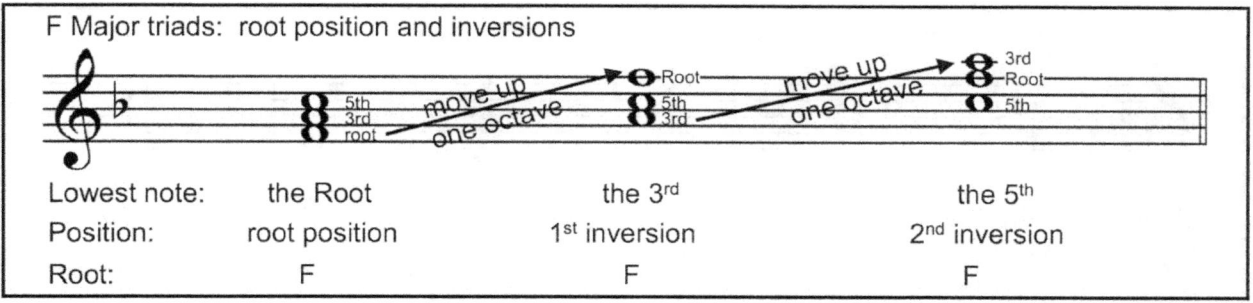

♪ **Note:** The name of the Root of the triad remains the same in root position, 1st inv. and 2nd inv.

Proper placement of accidentals in triads and inversions are as follows:
1 - closest to the top note, 2 - further away from the bottom note, 3 - furthest away from the middle note.

1. Write the following root position triads in 1st inversion (inv) and 2nd inversion (inv) by moving the lowest note up one octave. Use whole notes. Use accidentals. Name the Root.

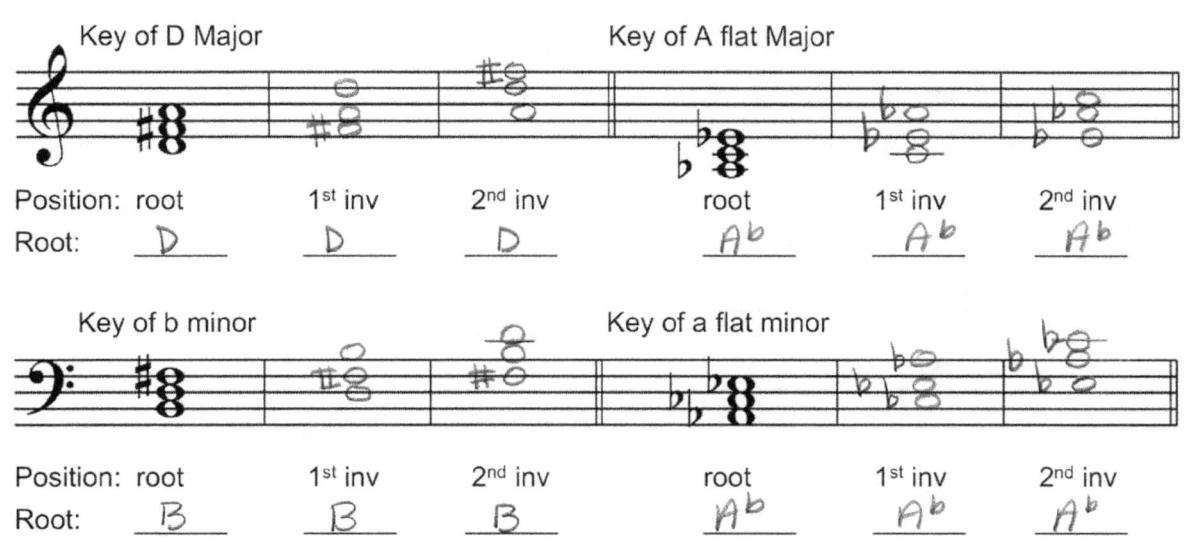

2. Invert the following triads. Use whole notes. a) Name the position. b) Name the Root.

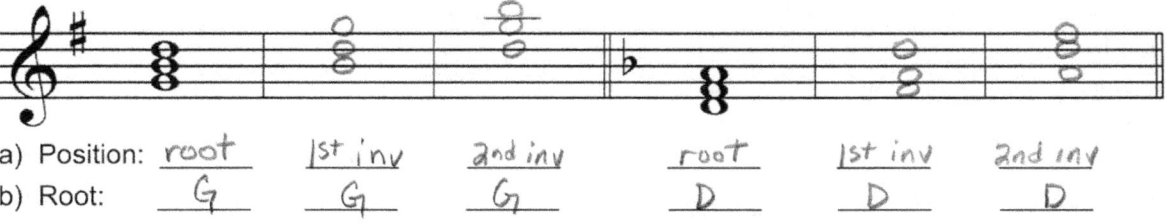

MAJOR and MINOR TRIADS

A root position Major triad consists of the Root, Major 3rd and Perfect 5th.
A root position minor triad consists of the Root, minor 3rd and Perfect 5th.

F Major triads — d minor triads

Root:	F	F	F	D	D	D
Type:	Major	Major	Major	minor	minor	minor
Position:	root	1st inv	2nd inv	root	1st inv	2nd inv

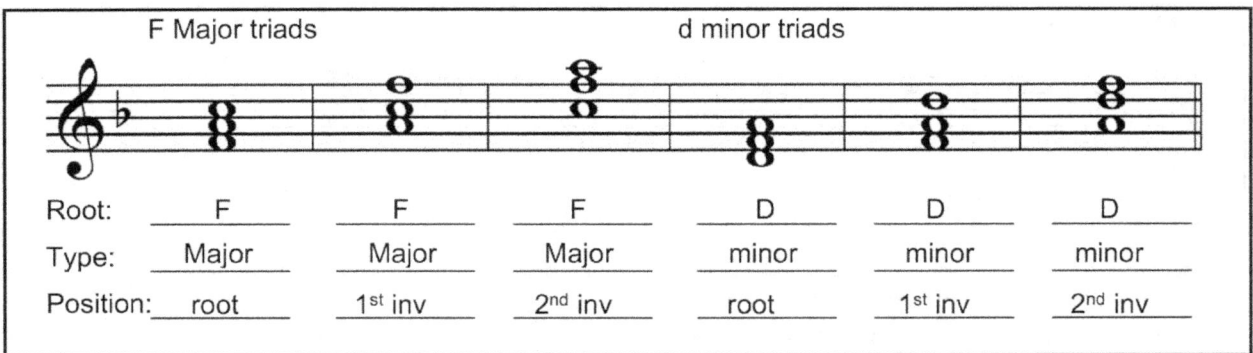

1. Invert the following triads. Use whole notes. For each triad, name:
   a) the Root (Key note).
   b) the type/quality (Major or minor).
   c) the position (root, 1st inv or 2nd inv).

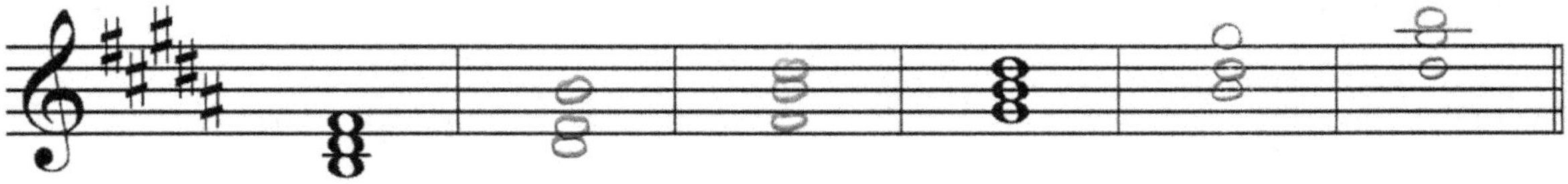

a) Root:	B	B	B	G#	G#	G#
b) Type:	Major	Major	Major	minor	minor	minor
c) Position:	root	1st inv	2nd inv	root	1st inv	2nd inv

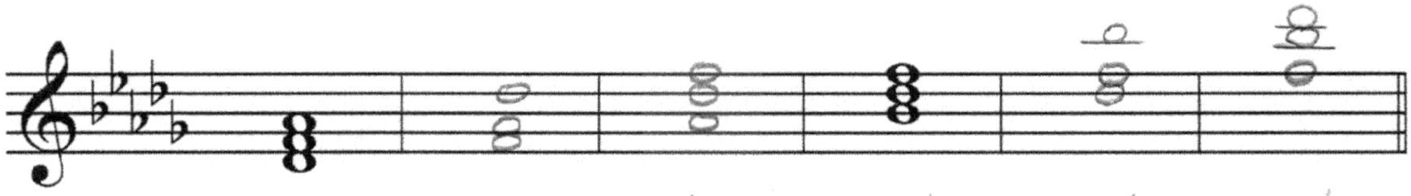

a) Root:	Db	Db	Db	Bb	Bb	Bb
b) Type:	Major	Major	Major	minor	minor	minor
c) Position:	root	1st inv	2nd inv	root	1st inv	2nd inv

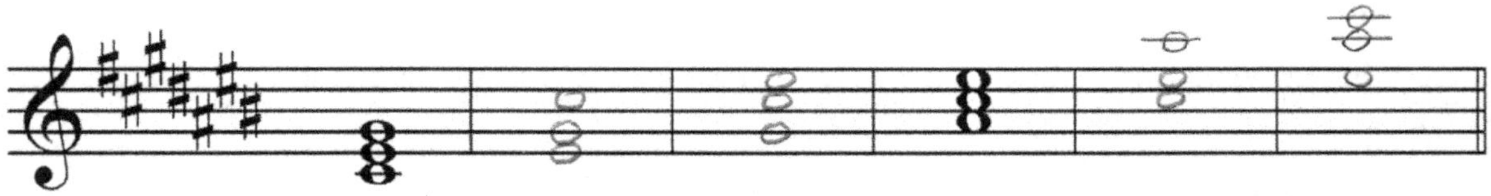

a) Root:	C#	C#	C#	A#	A#	A#
b) Type:	Major	Major	Major	minor	minor	minor
c) Position:	root	1st inv	2nd inv	root	1st inv	2nd inv

INVERSIONS of TONIC TRIADS

When writing an inversion of a triad, write it in root position first and then write the inversion.

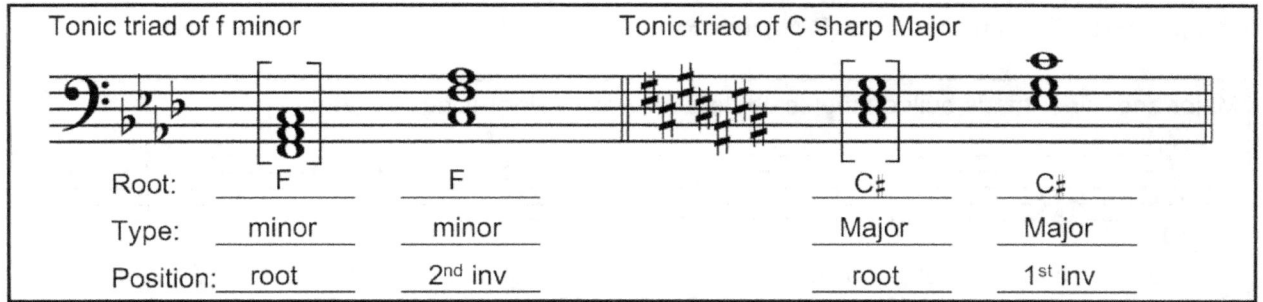

Root:	F	F	C#	C#
Type:	minor	minor	Major	Major
Position:	root	2nd inv	root	1st inv

1. Write the following triads in the Bass Clef, using a Key Signature. Write the triad in root position in the [square bracket], then write the correct inversion. Use whole notes. Name the Root (Key note).

    a) the **TONIC** triad of E flat Major in second inversion
    b) the **TONIC** triad of d minor in first inversion
    c) the **TONIC** triad of c sharp minor in second inversion
    d) the **TONIC** triad of B flat Major in first inversion
    e) the **TONIC** triad of f sharp minor in root position
    f) the **TONIC** triad of A Major in second inversion

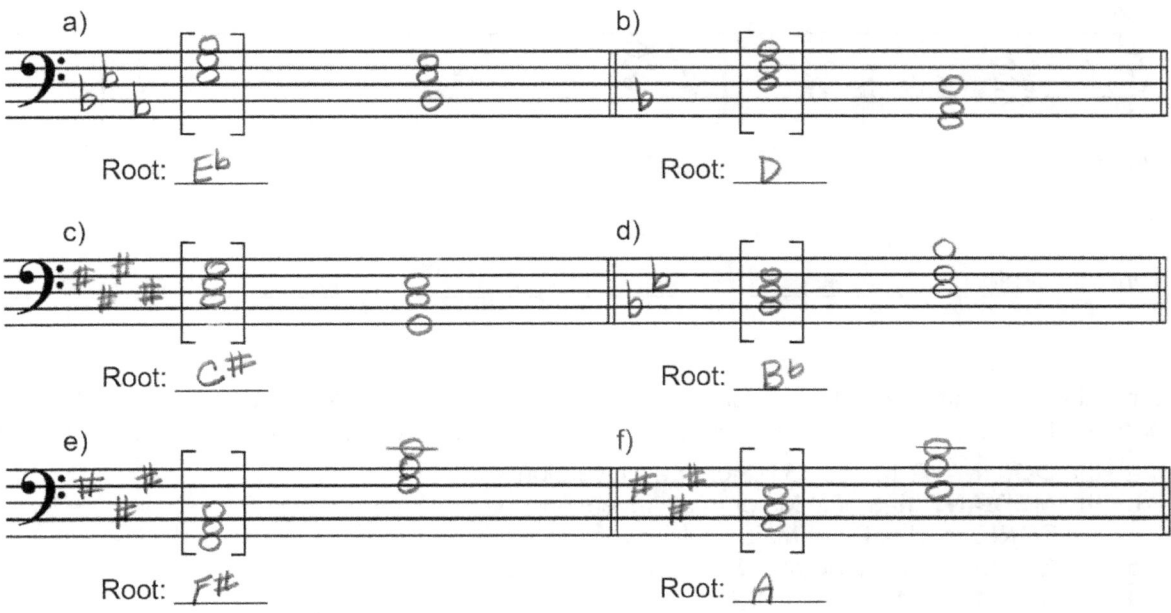

Root: Eb   Root: D
Root: C#   Root: Bb
Root: F#   Root: A

2. For each triad, name: a) the Root; b) the type/quality; c) the position.

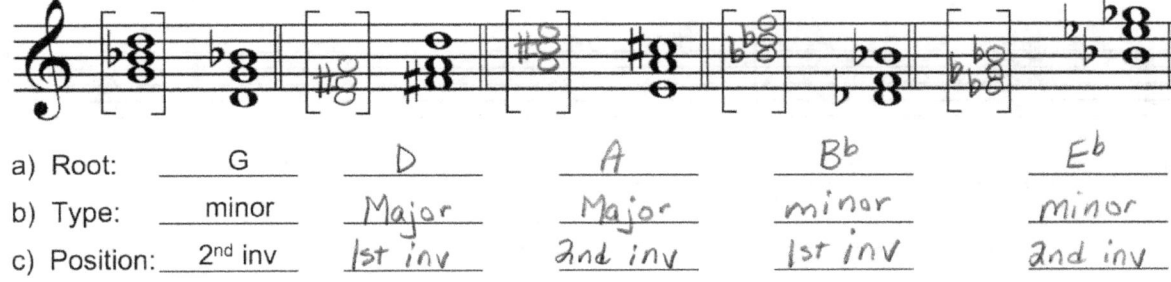

a) Root:	G	D	A	Bb	Eb
b) Type:	minor	Major	Major	minor	minor
c) Position:	2nd inv	1st inv	2nd inv	1st inv	2nd inv

TRIADS BUILT on MAJOR SCALE DEGREES

TRIADS are built on any degree of a **MAJOR** scale. Roman Numerals are used to indicate the scale degree of the Root note of the triad. Roman Numerals (R.N.) in **UPPER** case indicate the type as a **Major triad**. Roman Numerals (R.N.) in **lower case** indicate the type as a **minor triad**.

Major and minor triads built on the scale degrees of D Major (using accidentals).

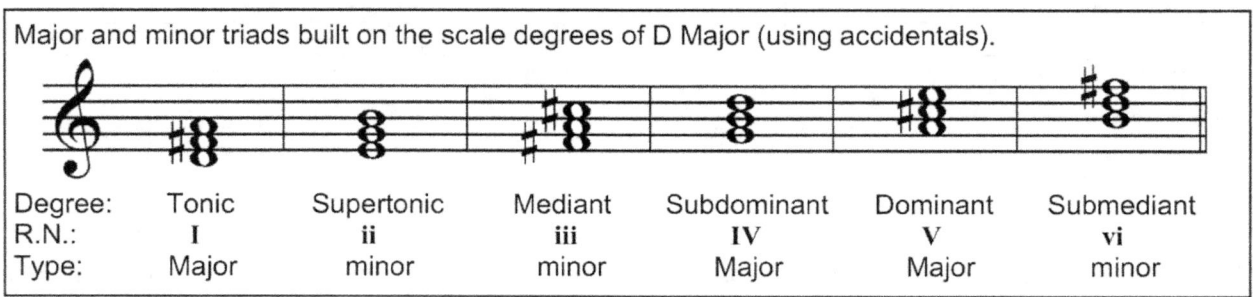

Degree:	Tonic	Supertonic	Mediant	Subdominant	Dominant	Submediant
R.N.:	I	ii	iii	IV	V	vi
Type:	Major	minor	minor	Major	Major	minor

♪ **Note:** In the **MAJOR** scale, only triads built on the Tonic, Supertonic, Mediant, Subdominant, Dominant and Submediant are Major or minor triads.

1. Write a root position triad above each of the following notes using the E Major Scale. Use whole notes. Use accidentals. For each triad, name: a) the technical degree (lowest note); b) the Roman Numeral (R.N.) for each degree; c) the type/quality (Major or minor).

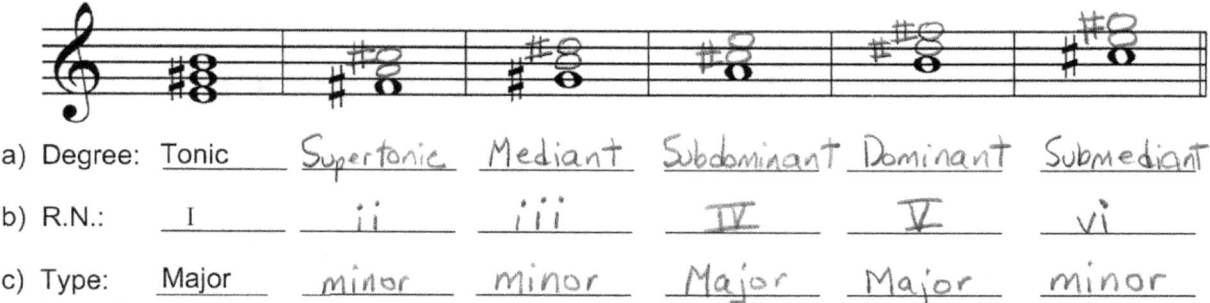

a) Degree:	Tonic	Supertonic	Mediant	Subdominant	Dominant	Submediant
b) R.N.:	I	ii	iii	IV	V	vi
c) Type:	Major	minor	minor	Major	Major	minor

2. Write the following triads. Use whole notes. Use accidentals. Write the degree of each Major or minor triad using Roman Numerals (R.N.). Name the type/quality of the triad as Major or minor.
    a) the **DOMINANT** triad of G Major in 2nd inversion
    b) the **MEDIANT** triad of D Major in 2nd inversion
    c) the **TONIC** triad of B flat Major in 1st inversion
    d) the **SUPERTONIC** triad of C Major in root position
    e) the **SUBMEDIANT** triad of A flat Major in 1st inversion
    f) the **SUBDOMINANT** triad of F Major in root position

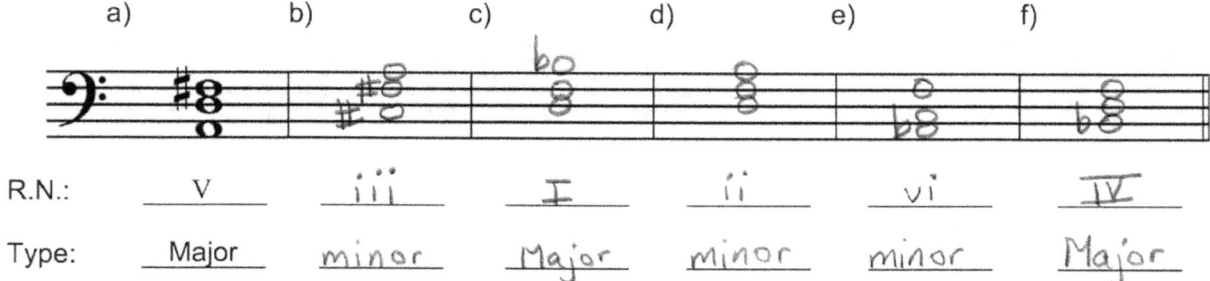

	a)	b)	c)	d)	e)	f)
R.N.:	V	iii	I	ii	vi	IV
Type:	Major	minor	Major	minor	minor	Major

TRIADS BUILT on HARMONIC MINOR SCALE DEGREES

TRIADS are built on any degree of a harmonic **MINOR** scale. Roman Numerals are used to indicate the scale degree of the Root note of the triad. Roman Numerals (R.N.) in **UPPER** case indicate the type as a **Major triad**. Roman Numerals (R.N.) in **lower** case indicate the type as a **minor triad**.

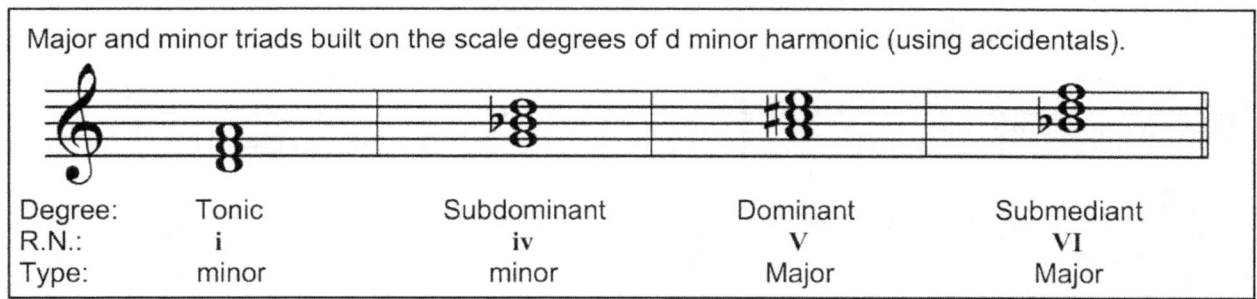

Major and minor triads built on the scale degrees of d minor harmonic (using accidentals).

Degree:	Tonic	Subdominant	Dominant	Submediant
R.N.:	i	iv	V	VI
Type:	minor	minor	Major	Major

♪ **Note:** In the **HARMONIC MINOR** scale, only triads built on the Tonic, Subdominant, Dominant and Submediant are Major or minor triads.

1. Write a root position triad above each of the following notes using the e minor harmonic scale. Use whole notes. Use accidentals. For each triad, name: a) the technical degree (lowest note); b) the Roman Numeral for each degree; c) the type/quality (Major or minor).

a) Degree: Tonic   Subdominant   Dominant   Submediant
b) R.N.:   i   iv   V   VI
c) Type: minor   minor   Major   Major

♪ **Note:** Use proper placement of accidentals when writing triads using accidentals.

2. Write the following triads. Use whole notes. Use accidentals. Write the degree of each Major or minor triad using Roman Numerals (R.N.). Name the type/quality of the triad as Major or minor.

   a) the **SUBDOMINANT** triad of b flat minor harmonic in 1st inversion
   b) the **DOMINANT** triad of f sharp minor harmonic in 2nd inversion
   c) the **TONIC** triad of e flat minor harmonic in 1st inversion
   d) the **SUBMEDIANT** triad of a sharp minor harmonic in 2nd inversion

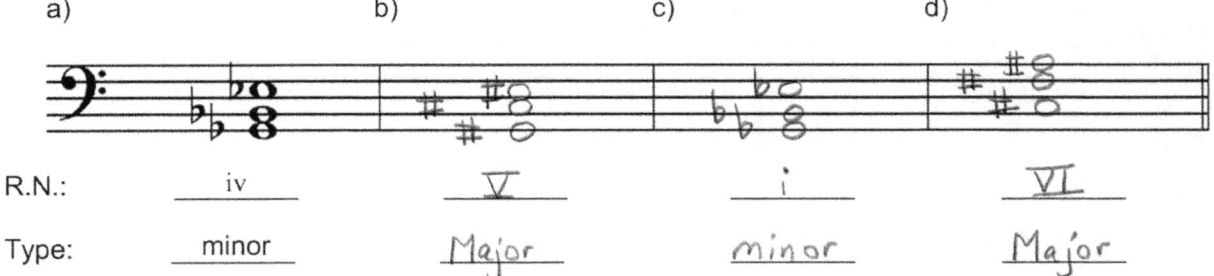

	a)	b)	c)	d)
R.N.:	iv	V	i	VI
Type:	minor	Major	minor	Major

TRIADS in CLOSE POSITION

A triad in **CLOSE POSITION** is written as close together as possible. NO interval is larger than a 6th. A triad in close position may be written as broken or solid; and in root position or an inversion.

♪ **Note:** The POSITION of a triad is ALWAYS determined by the LOWEST note.

Lowest note:	Root (Key note)	3rd above the Root	5th above the Root
Position:	root position	1st inversion	2nd inversion

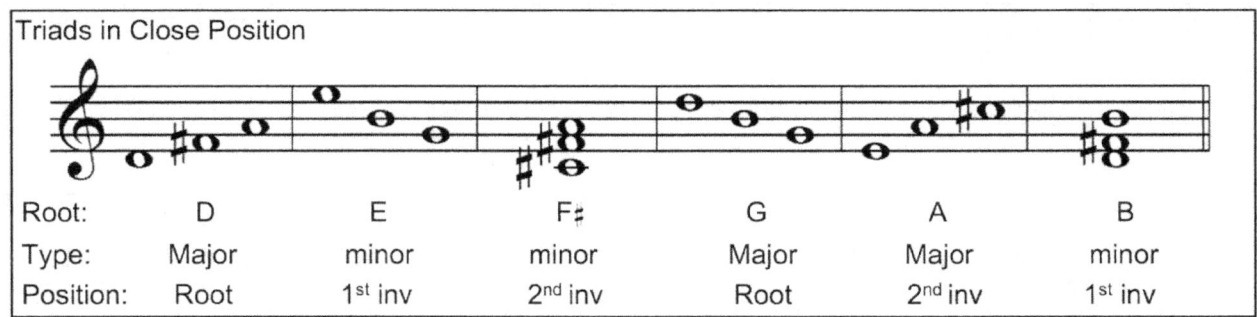

Root:	D	E	F♯	G	A	B
Type:	Major	minor	minor	Major	Major	minor
Position:	Root	1st inv	2nd inv	Root	2nd inv	1st inv

1. For each triad in close position, name: a) the Root; b) the type/quality; c) the position.

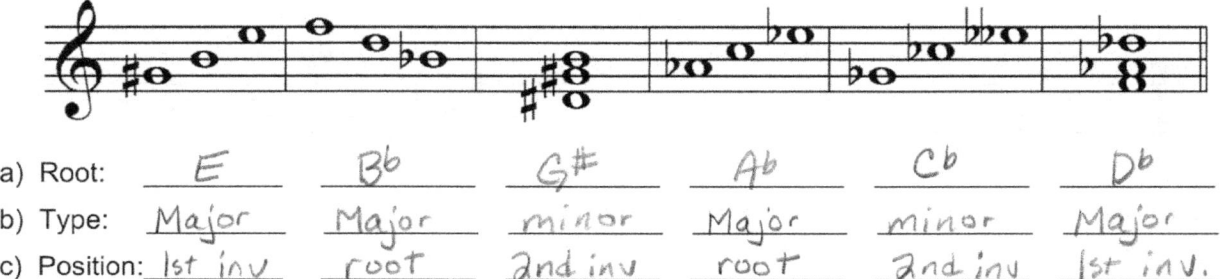

a) Root:	E	B♭	G♯	A♭	C♭	D♭
b) Type:	Major	Major	minor	Major	minor	Major
c) Position:	1st inv	root	2nd inv	root	2nd inv	1st inv.

♪ **Note:** A triad in CLOSE position may be written on the Grand Staff, divided between the Treble Clef and the Bass Clef, as long as the distance from the lowest to highest note is no larger than a 6th.

2. Rewrite the given triad in close root position in the [square] brackets. For each of the following triads name: a) the Root; b) the type/quality; c) the position of the given triad.

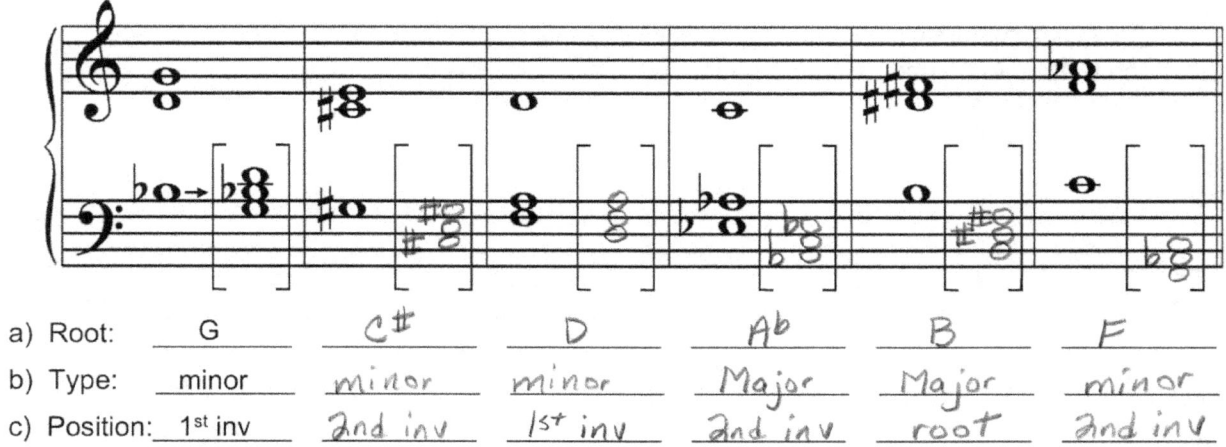

a) Root:	G	C♯	D	A♭	B	F
b) Type:	minor	minor	minor	Major	Major	minor
c) Position:	1st inv	2nd inv	1st inv	2nd inv	root	2nd inv

TRIADS in OPEN POSITION

A triad in **OPEN POSITION** is written with intervals larger than a 6th. An OPEN position triad may be written on a single staff or on the Grand Staff. One of the notes (usually the Root) may be doubled. A triad in open position may be written as broken or solid; and in root position or an inversion.

♪ **Note:** The position of a triad is ALWAYS determined by the LOWEST note.

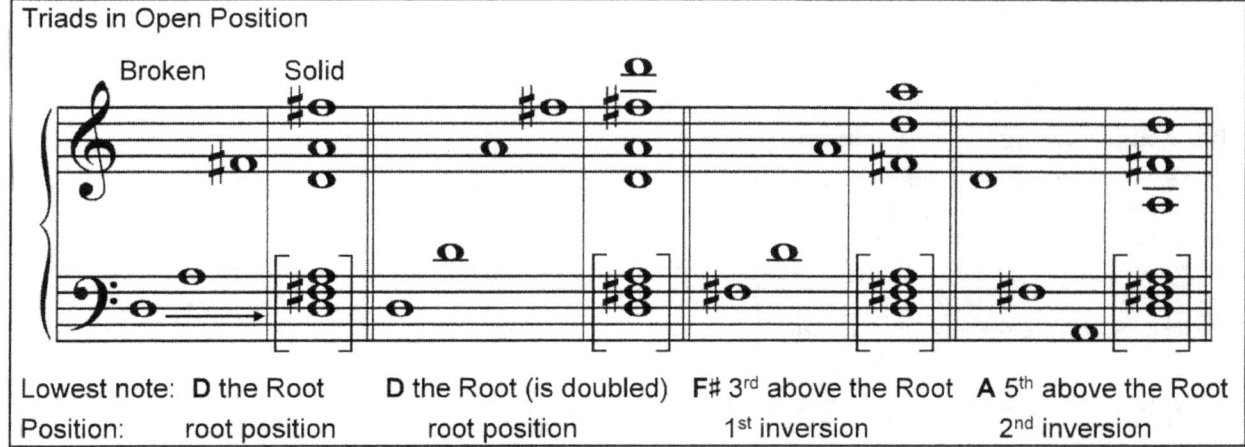

1. Rewrite the given triad in close root position in the [square] brackets. For each of the following triads name: a) the Root; b) the type/quality; c) the position of the given triad.

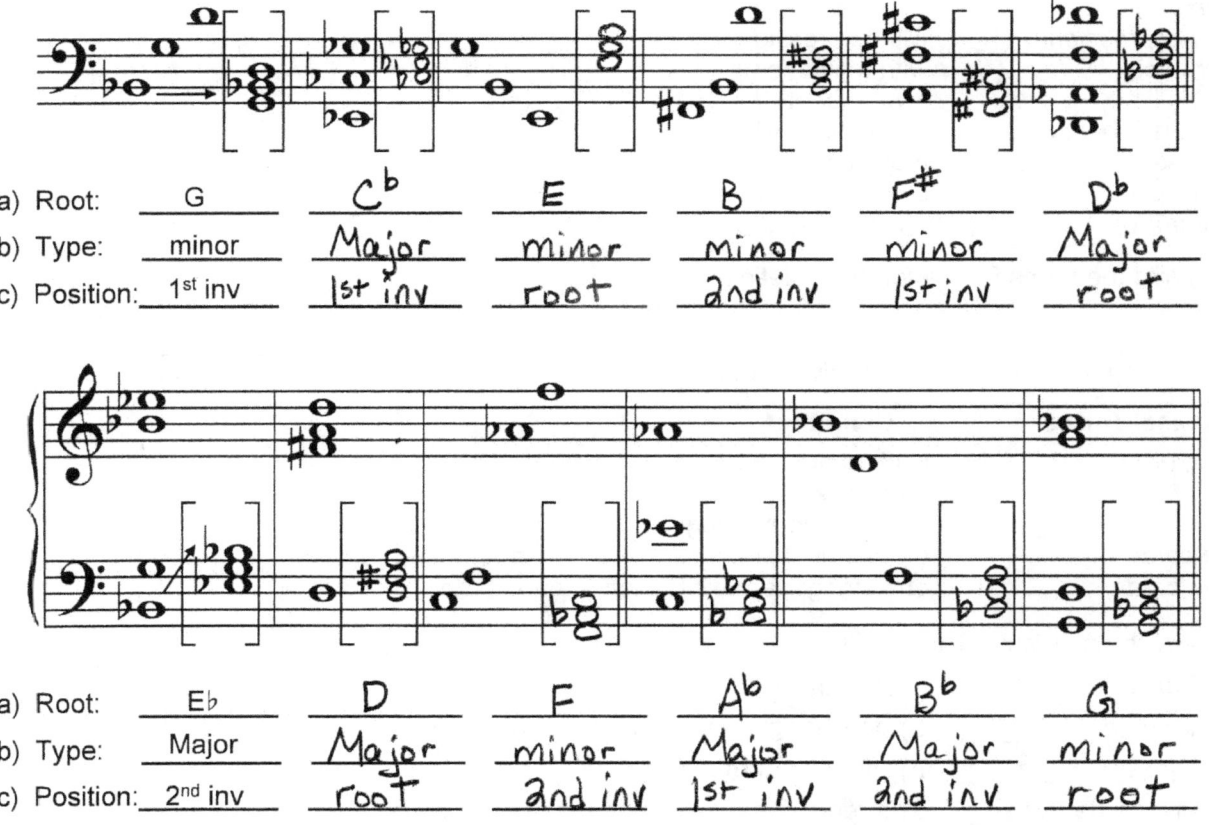

TEMPO, CHANGES in TEMPO, STYLE in PERFORMANCE and MUSICAL TERMS

Tempo	Definition
grave	slow and solemn
vivace	lively, brisk

1. Write the definition for the following terms.

   vivace — **lively, brisk**

   grave — **slow and solemn**

Changes in Tempo	Definition
accelerando, accel.	becoming quicker
meno mosso	less movement, slower
più mosso	more movement, quicker
rubato	with some freedom of tempo (flexible tempo) to enhance musical expression

2. Write the terms for the following definitions.

   più mosso — more movement

   accelerando — becoming quicker

   rubato — flexible tempo

   meno mosso — less movement

Style in Performance	Definition
animato	lively, animated
brillante	brilliant
cantabile	in a singing style
con brio	with vigor, spirit
con espressione	with expression
con moto	with movement
dolce	sweet, gentle
espressivo, espress.	expressive, with expression
maestoso	majestic
spiritoso	spirited
tranquillo	quiet, tranquil

3. Write the terms for the following definitions.

   spiritoso — spirited

   animato — lively, animated

   con brio — with vigor, spirit

   Tranquillo — quiet, tranquil

Musical Terms	Definition
leggiero	light, nimble, quick
M. M.	Maelzel's metronome
loco	return to normal register
tre corde	three strings; release the left (piano) pedal
una corda	one string; depress the left (piano) pedal

4. Match each musical term with the English definition.

Term		Definition
tre corde	**c**	a) one string; depress the left (piano) pedal
leggiero	**d**	b) return to normal register
una corda	**a**	c) three strings; release the left (piano pedal)
loco	**b**	d) light, nimble, quick

Lesson 7   Review Test

Total Score: ____ / 100

Write the Circle of Fifths on a blank piece of paper. Use it as a reference when doing the review test.

1. Write the following harmonic intervals **BELOW** the given notes. Invert the intervals. Use whole notes. Use accidentals. Name the inversions.

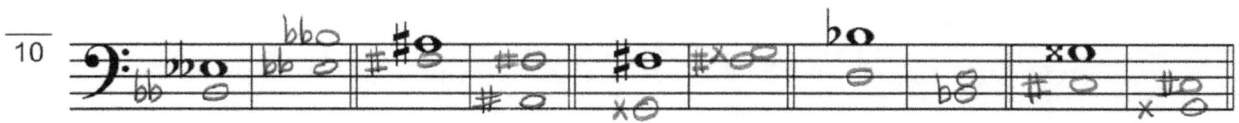

Per 4   _Per 5_   Maj 3   _min 6_   dim 7   _Aug 2_   min 6   _Maj 3_   Aug 5   _dim 4_

2. Add the correct Time Signature below each bracket.

3. Match each musical term with the English definition. (Not all definitions will be used.)

Term		Definition
meno mosso	_d_	a) lively, animated
espressivo, espress.	_f_	b) slow and solemn
animato	_a_	c) light, nimble, quick
una corda	_h_	d) less movement, slower
brillante	_i_	e) Maelzel's metronome
tre corde	_g_	f) expressive, with expression
con brio	_k_	g) three strings; release the left (piano) pedal
M.M.	_e_	h) one string; depress the left (piano) pedal
leggiero	_c_	i) brilliant
grave	_b_	j) right hand
		k) with vigor, spirit

4. Write the **BASIC BEAT** and the **PULSE** below each measure. Add rests below each bracket to complete the measure. Cross off the Basic Beat as each beat is completed.

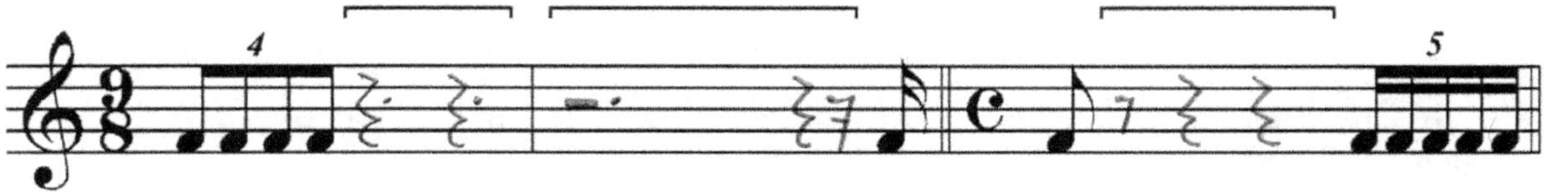

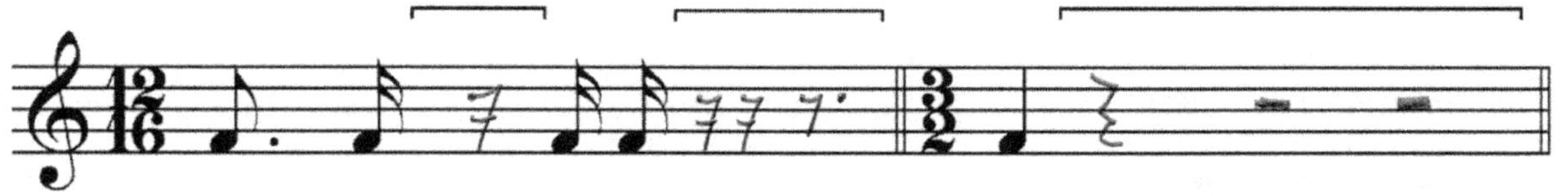

5. Name the key of the following melody. Transpose it **UP** one octave into the Treble Clef using the correct Key Signature.

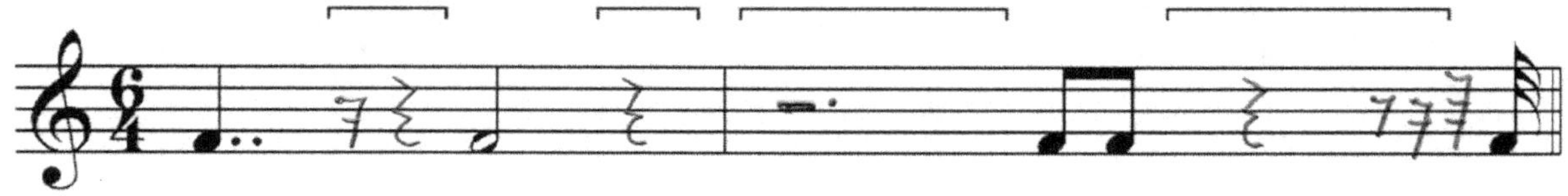

Key: Gb Major

6. Rewrite the open position triad in CLOSE root position below each bracket.
   For each of the given triads, name: a) the Root; b) the type/quality; c) the position.

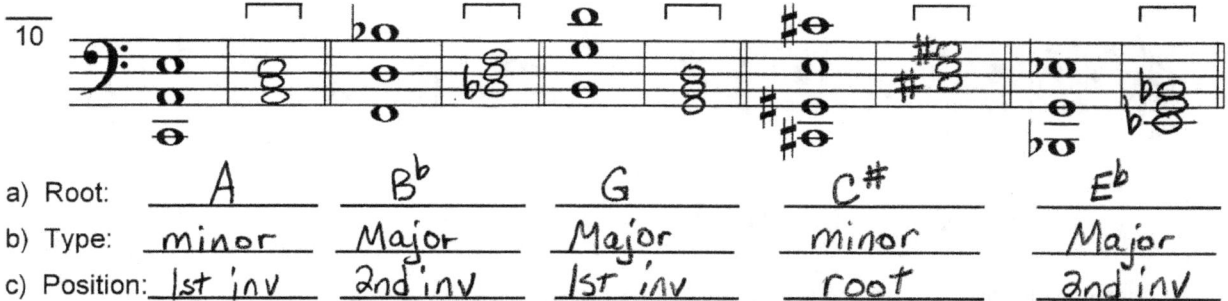

a) Root:	A	B♭	G	C#	E♭
b) Type:	minor	Major	Major	minor	Major
c) Position:	1st inv	2nd inv	1st inv	root	2nd inv

7. Use Roman Numerals to identify the type/quality of triad built on the following scale degrees.

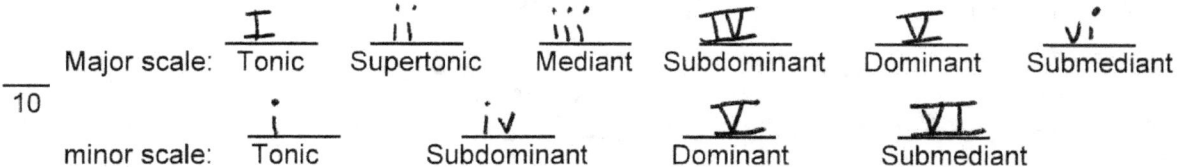

Major scale: I (Tonic), ii (Supertonic), iii (Mediant), IV (Subdominant), V (Dominant), vi (Submediant)

minor scale: i (Tonic), iv (Subdominant), V (Dominant), VI (Submediant)

8. Write the following scales, ascending and descending, using **ACCIDENTALS** instead of a Key Signature. Use whole notes.

   a) G flat Major in the Treble Clef
   b) b minor natural in the Bass Clef
   c) enharmonic Tonic Major of D flat Major in the Treble Clef
   d) Tonic minor, melodic form, of A Major in the Bass Clef
   e) chromatic scale beginning on B flat (any standard notation) in the Bass Clef

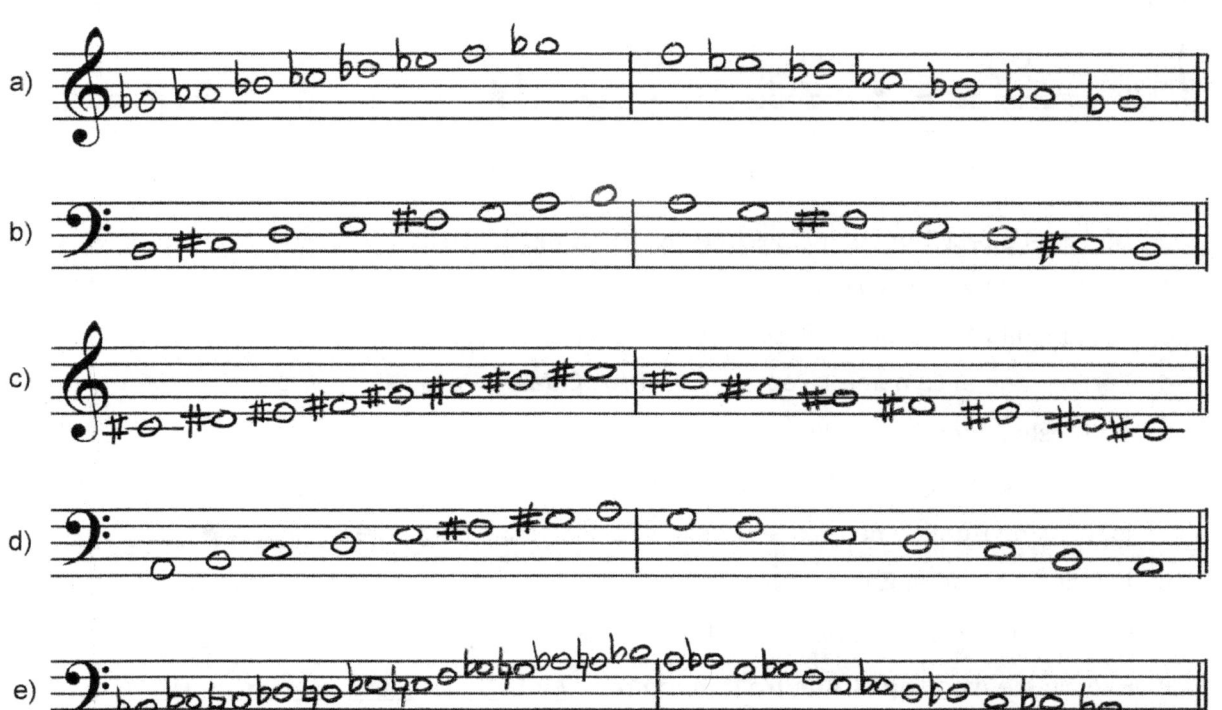

9. a) Name the **MINOR** key for each of the following Key Signatures.
b) Give the **TECHNICAL DEGREE NAME** for each note. (Tonic, Supertonic, etc.)

10

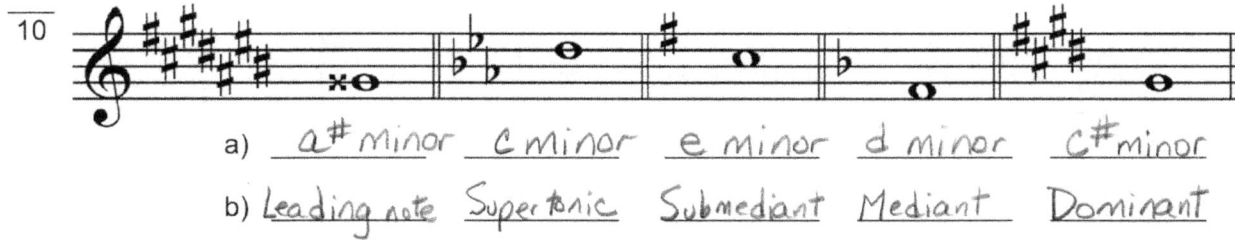

a) a# minor c minor e minor d minor c# minor

b) Leading note Supertonic Submediant Mediant Dominant

10. Analyze the following piece of music by answering the questions below.

10

Allegro con moto

Temper Tantrum

S. McKibbon

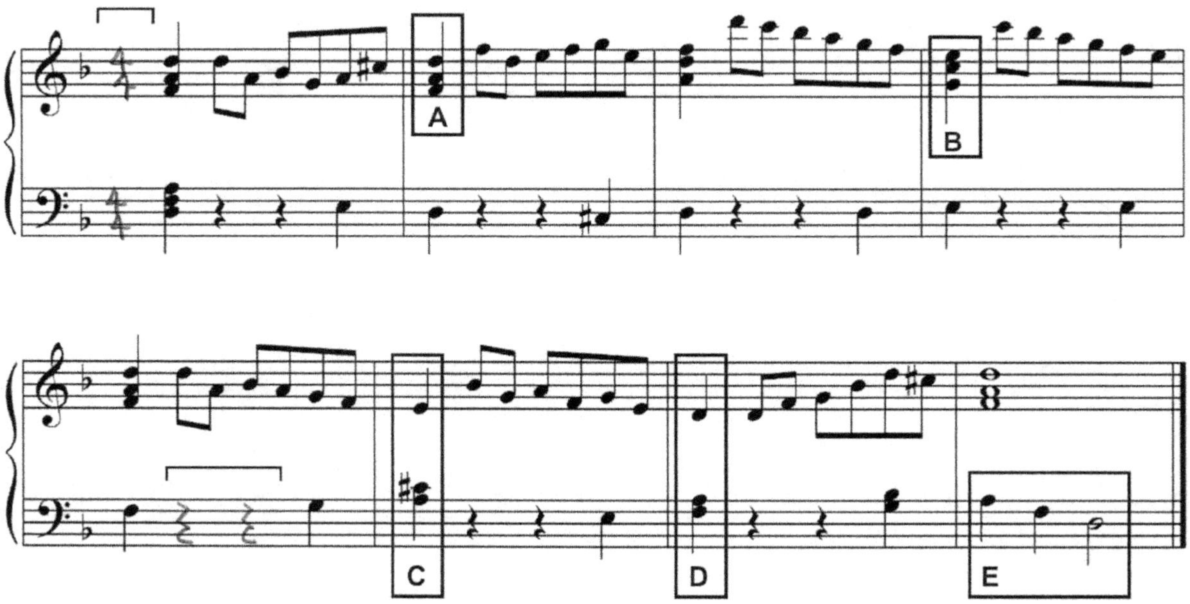

a) Add the correct Time Signature directly on the music.

b) Name the key of this piece. d minor

c) For the triad at **A**, name: Root: D Type/Quality: minor Position: 1st inv

d) For the triad at **B**, name: Root: C Type/Quality: Major Position: 2nd inv

e) Add rests under the bracket in Measure 5 to complete the measure.

f) Identify the Root of the triad at **C** as the Tonic or Dominant note. Dominant

g) Identify the Root of the triad at **D** as the Tonic or Dominant note. Tonic

h) Identify the triad at **E** as solid or broken. broken Name the Root: D

i) How many times is C sharp played in this piece? 4

j) Explain the meaning of ***Allegro con moto.*** fast with movement

Lesson 8 Whole Tone, Pentatonic, Blues and Octatonic Scales

20th CENTURY SCALES include **Whole Tone, Pentatonic, Blues** and **Octatonic** scales.

A **Whole Tone** scale is a series of seven notes made up of six consecutive whole tones (six different letter names), beginning and ending on the same letter name. There are only two ways of writing the whole tone scale: using the group of 3 black keys or the group of 2 black keys.

♪ **Note:** A whole tone scale uses the same notes and accidentals ascending and descending. Use all sharps or all flats. One letter name will be omitted creating a dim 3.

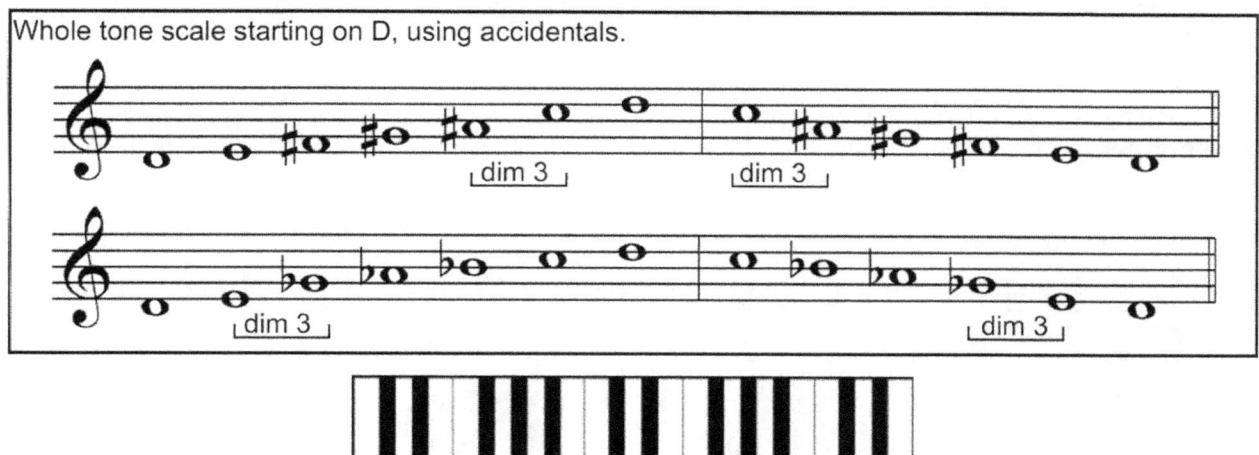

1. Write the following whole tone scales, ascending and descending, using accidentals. Use whole notes.

   a) whole tone scale starting on C in the Treble Clef
   b) whole tone scale starting on F sharp in the Bass Clef
   c) whole tone scale starting on D flat in the Treble Clef
   d) whole tone scale starting on A in the Bass Clef

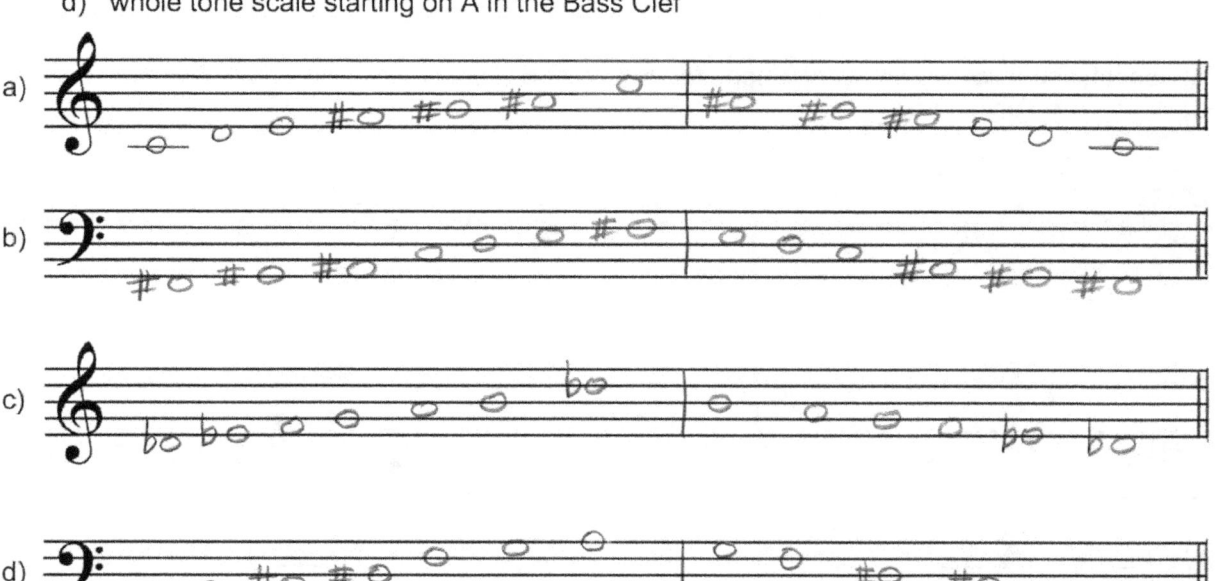

MAJOR and MINOR PENTATONIC SCALES

A **PENTATONIC** scale (penta means 5) consists of 5 notes plus the upper Tonic, for a total of 6 notes. A **Major pentatonic** scale may be formed by taking a Major scale and omitting the 4th and 7th degrees. The distance between the first 2 notes of a Major pentatonic scale is a Major 2nd.

A **minor pentatonic** scale may be formed by taking a natural minor scale and omitting the 2nd and 6th degrees. The distance between the first 2 notes of a minor pentatonic scale is a minor 3rd.

♪ **Note:** A Major pentatonic scale and its relative minor pentatonic scale use the SAME notes.

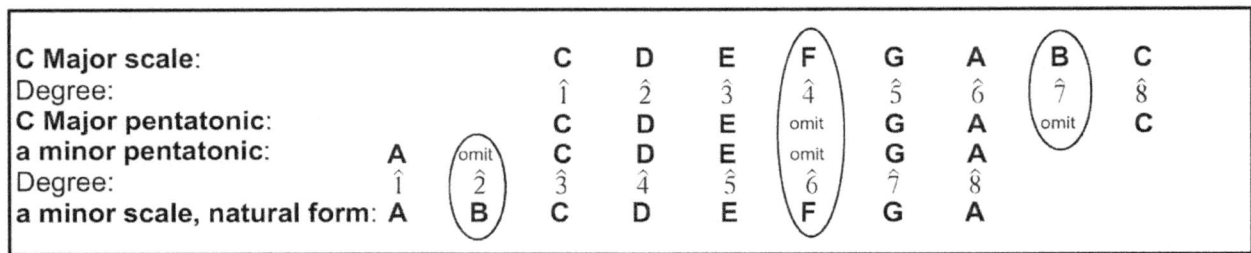

1. a) Identify the following as a Major pentatonic or a minor pentatonic scale.
   b) Name the Tonic note.

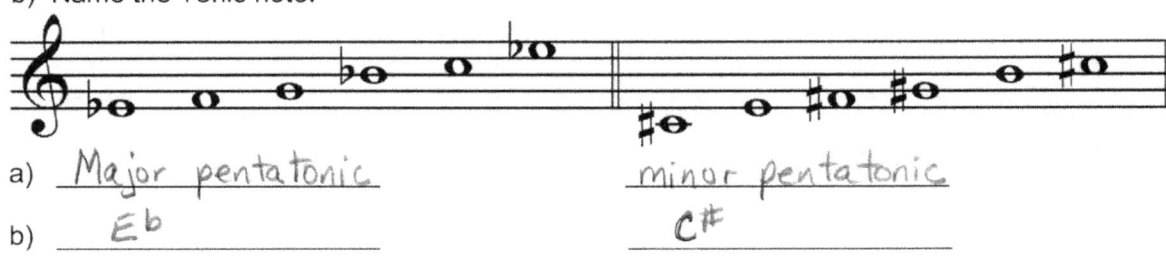

a) __Major pentatonic__   __minor pentatonic__
b) __Eb__   __C#__

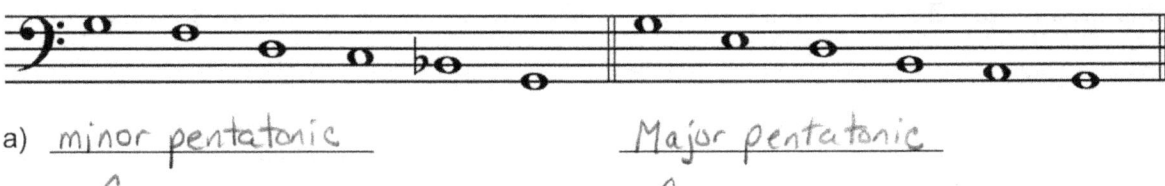

a) __minor pentatonic__   __Major pentatonic__
b) __G__   __G__

BLUES SCALES and OCTATONIC SCALES

A **BLUES** scale may be formed by taking a Major scale, omitting the 2nd and 6th degrees, lowering the 3rd and 7th degrees and creating the "blue note" by repeating the 5th one chromatic semitone lower or repeating the 4th one chromatic semitone higher.

♪ **Note:** A blues scale may be written with a lowered 5th degree or a raised 4th degree.

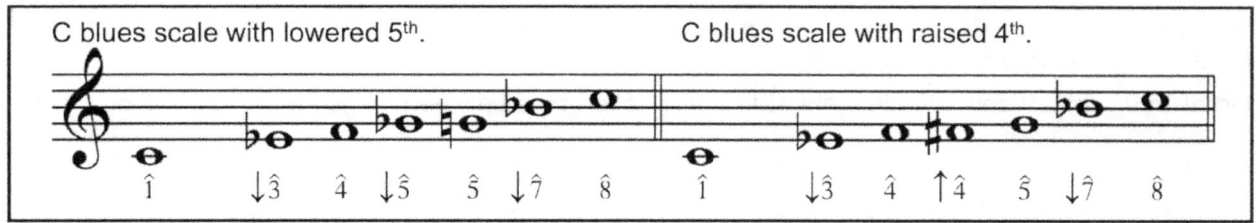

A **blues** scale may also be formed by taking the natural minor scale, omitting the 2nd and 6th degrees (minor pentatonic scale), and adding the "blue note" of the raised 4th or lowered 5th degree.

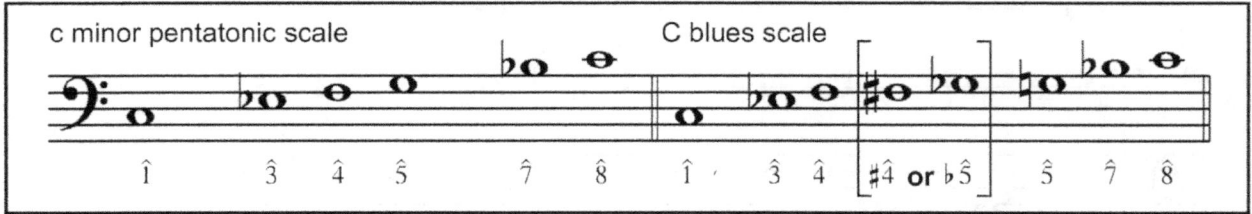

An **OCTATONIC** scale (octave means 8) consists of 8 notes plus the upper Tonic, for a total of 9 notes. An octatonic scale may be formed by alternating whole tone (whole step) and semitone (half step) OR semitone (half step) and whole tone (whole step). **WT** (whole tone) **ST** (semitone)

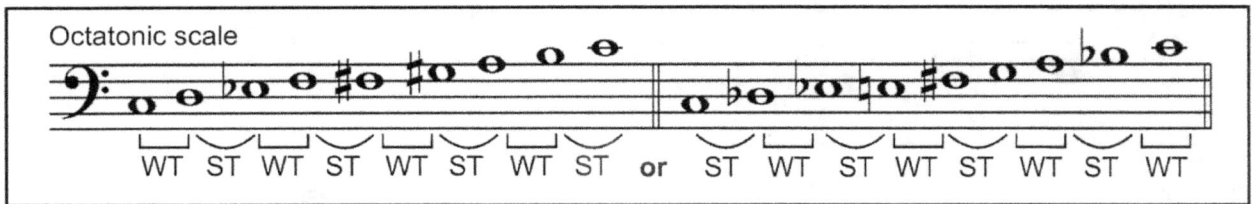

1. Identify the following as a blues scale or an octatonic scale.

octatonic   Blues

Blues   octatonic

SCALES - WHOLE TONE, PENTATONIC, BLUES and OCTATONIC

Whole Tone scale: (7 notes - 6 whole tones), beginning and ending on the same letter name.

Major pentatonic scale: 6 notes (5 plus repeated Tonic), Major scale omitting the 4th and 7th degrees.

Minor pentatonic scale: 6 notes (5 plus repeated Tonic), natural minor scale omitting the 2nd and 6th degrees.

Blues scale: 7 notes (6 plus repeated Tonic), minor pentatonic scale adding the "blue note" of the raised 4th or lowered 5th degree.

Octatonic scale: 9 notes (8 plus repeated Tonic), alternates between tones and semitones or semitones and tones.

1. Name the following scales as: whole tone, blues, Major pentatonic, minor pentatonic or octatonic.

a) Major pentatonic

b) octatonic

c) Blues

d) whole tone

e) minor pentatonic

f) Blues

MUSICAL TERMS USED WITH OTHER MUSICAL TERMS and DEFINITIONS

A **Musical term** may be written in front of another term to alter the meaning of the term.
For example, the Italian term **con** means with and **senza** means without. When used in front of the term *pedale* the meaning is altered to **con pedale**, with pedal and **senza pedale**, without pedal.

♪ **Note:** More than one term may be written in front of another term.
For example, the Italian terms **poco a poco accelerando ma non troppo** mean little by little becoming quicker but not too much.

Term	Definition
alla, all'	in the manner of
assai	much, very much (example: *allegro assai*, very fast)
ben, bene	well (example: *ben marcato*, well marked)
col, coll', colla, colle	with (example: *coll' ottava*, with an added octave)
con	with
e, ed	and
ma	but (example: *ma non troppo*, but not too much)
meno	less
molto	much, very
non	not
non troppo	not too much
più	more
poco	little
poco a poco	little by little
quasi	as if
sempre	always, continuously
senza	without
troppo	too much

1. Write the term that has the opposite meaning for each of the following terms.

    senza   meno   molto

    con   *più*   *non troppo*

2. Write the definition for the following terms.

    molto espressivo   ben marcato   coll' ottava   allegro assai

    much expression   *well marked*   *with an added octave*   *very fast*

3. Write the terms for the following definitions.

    little less movement   as if graceful   fast but not too much   not with freedom of tempo

    poco meno mosso   *quasi grazioso*   *allegro ma non troppo*   *non rubato (or) non con rubato*

4. Match each musical term with the English definition.

Term		Definition
dolce ed piano	b	a) more majestic
con spiritoso	d	b) sweet and soft
più maestoso	a	c) in the manner of a singing style
alla cantabile	c	d) with spirit

Lesson 8   Review Test

Total Score: ____ / 100

Write the Circle of Fifths on a blank piece of paper. Use it as a reference when doing the review test.

1. Write the following harmonic intervals **ABOVE** the given notes. Invert the intervals.
   Use whole notes. Use accidentals. Name the inversions.

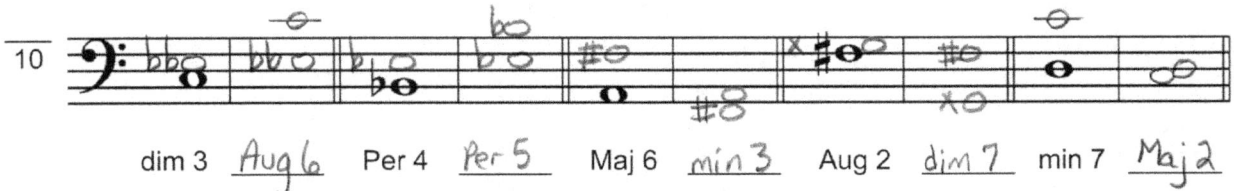

   dim 3 Aug 6   Per 4 Per 5   Maj 6 min 3   Aug 2 dim 7   min 7 Maj 2

2. Add the correct Time Signature below each bracket.

3. Match each musical term with the English definition. (Not all definitions will be used.)

Term		Definition
più mosso	d	a) quiet, tranquil
con espressione	j	b) with movement
tranquillo	a	c) return to normal register
senza rubato	k	d) more movement, quicker
vivace	i	e) as if graceful
con moto	b	f) very spirited
loco	c	g) always sweet, gentle
spiritoso assai	f	h) little by little becoming quicker
poco a poco accelerando	h	i) lively, brisk
sempre dolce	g	j) with expression
		k) without a flexible tempo

4. Write the **BASIC BEAT** and the **PULSE** below each measure. Add rests below the bracket to complete each measure. Cross off the Basic Beat as each beat is completed.

5. Name the **HARMONIC MINOR KEY** for each of the following Key Signatures. Write the following triads. Use whole notes.

   a) the **SUBDOMINANT** triad in first inversion
   b) the **TONIC** triad in second inversion
   c) the **DOMINANT** triad in root position
   d) the **SUBMEDIANT** triad in first inversion
   e) the **DOMINANT** triad in second inversion

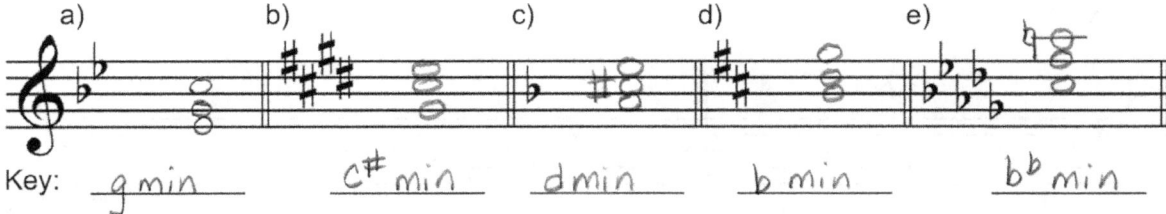

6. Name the key of the following melody. Rewrite it at the **SAME PITCH** in the Treble Clef using the correct Key Signature.

7. Write the following **NOTES** in the Bass Clef. Use the correct **KEY SIGNATURE** for each. Use whole notes.

10 a) the **LEADING NOTE** of g minor harmonic
b) the **SUBMEDIANT** of A flat Major
c) the **MEDIANT** of D Major
d) the **SUBDOMINANT** of f sharp minor harmonic
e) the **SUPERTONIC** of b flat minor harmonic

8. Write the following scales, ascending and descending, using **ACCIDENTALS** instead of a Key Signature. Use whole notes.

10 a) whole tone scale beginning on G in the Treble Clef
b) chromatic scale beginning on D flat (any standard notation) in the Bass Clef
c) C Major in the Treble Clef
d) e minor harmonic in the Bass Clef
e) enharmonic Tonic minor, melodic form, of a sharp minor in the Bass Clef

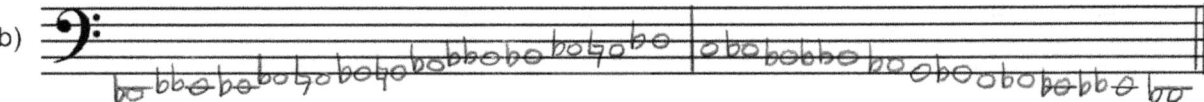

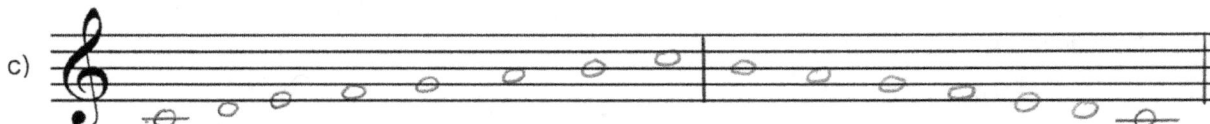

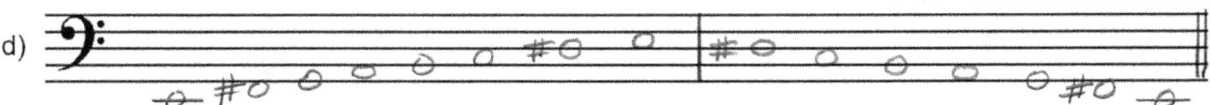

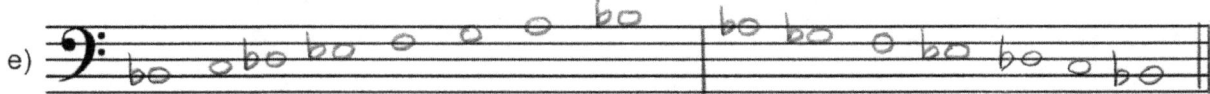

9. Name the following scales as whole tone, octatonic, Major pentatonic, minor pentatonic or blues.

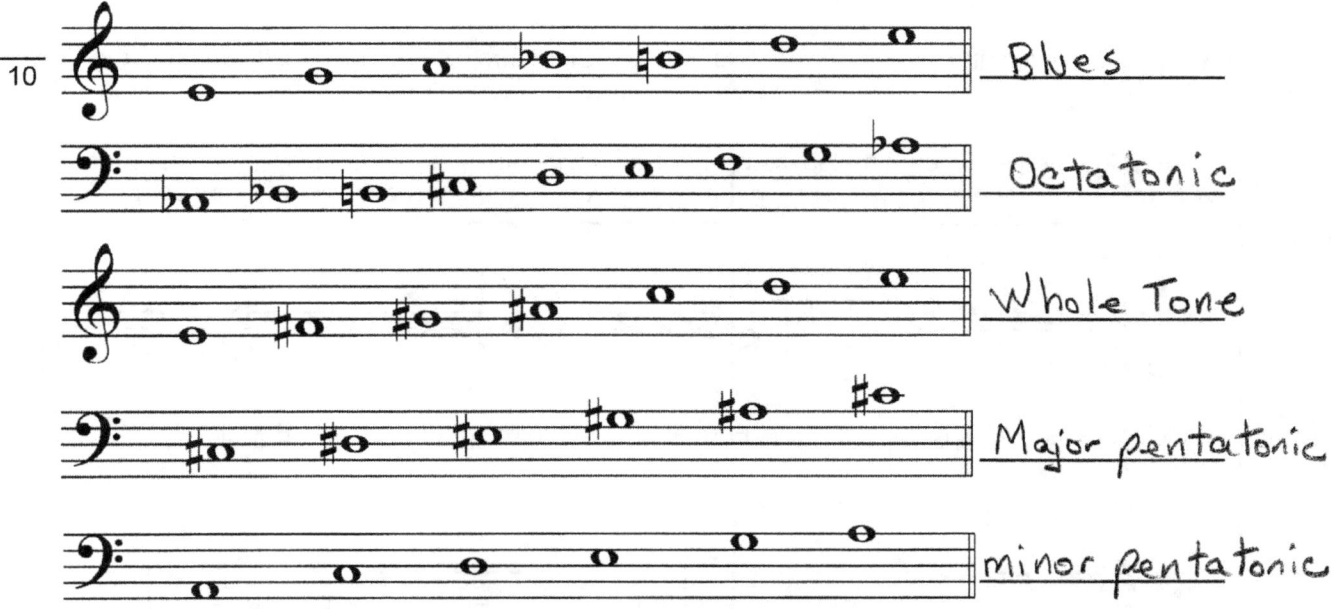

Blues
Octatonic
Whole Tone
Major pentatonic
minor pentatonic

10. Analyze the following piece of music by answering the questions below.

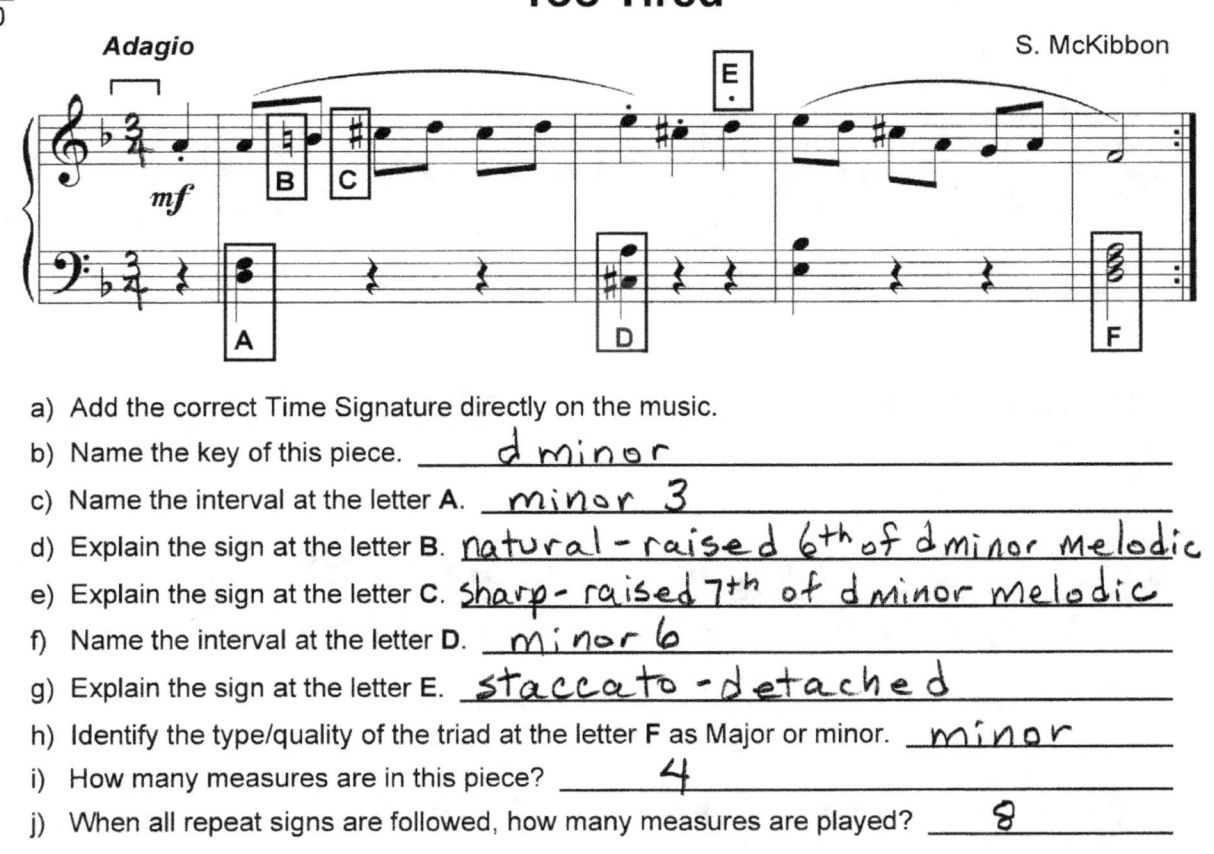

a) Add the correct Time Signature directly on the music.
b) Name the key of this piece. __d minor__
c) Name the interval at the letter A. __minor 3__
d) Explain the sign at the letter B. __natural - raised 6th of d minor melodic__
e) Explain the sign at the letter C. __sharp - raised 7th of d minor melodic__
f) Name the interval at the letter D. __minor 6__
g) Explain the sign at the letter E. __staccato - detached__
h) Identify the type/quality of the triad at the letter F as Major or minor. __minor__
i) How many measures are in this piece? __4__
j) When all repeat signs are followed, how many measures are played? __8__

Lesson 9   Rewriting a Melody using a Key Signature

A **Melody** may be written using accidentals or a Key Signature. A melody usually ends on the Tonic.

REWRITING a MAJOR KEY MELODY

To determine the key when a melody is written with accidentals, name the accidentals in order of the Key Signature. When accidentals are in the correct Key Signature order, the key is usually Major.

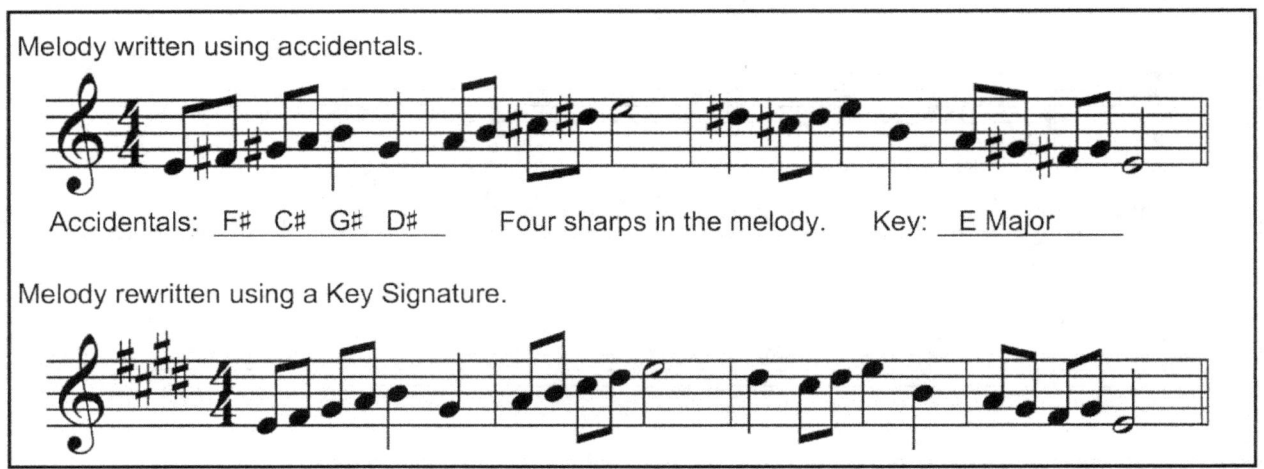

♪ **Note:** When rewriting a melody in a Major key using a Key Signature, accidentals are not used. The Key Signature is written directly after the clef and before the Time Signature.

1. Name the accidentals in the order of the Key Signature. Name the key. Rewrite the following melodies using a Key Signature.

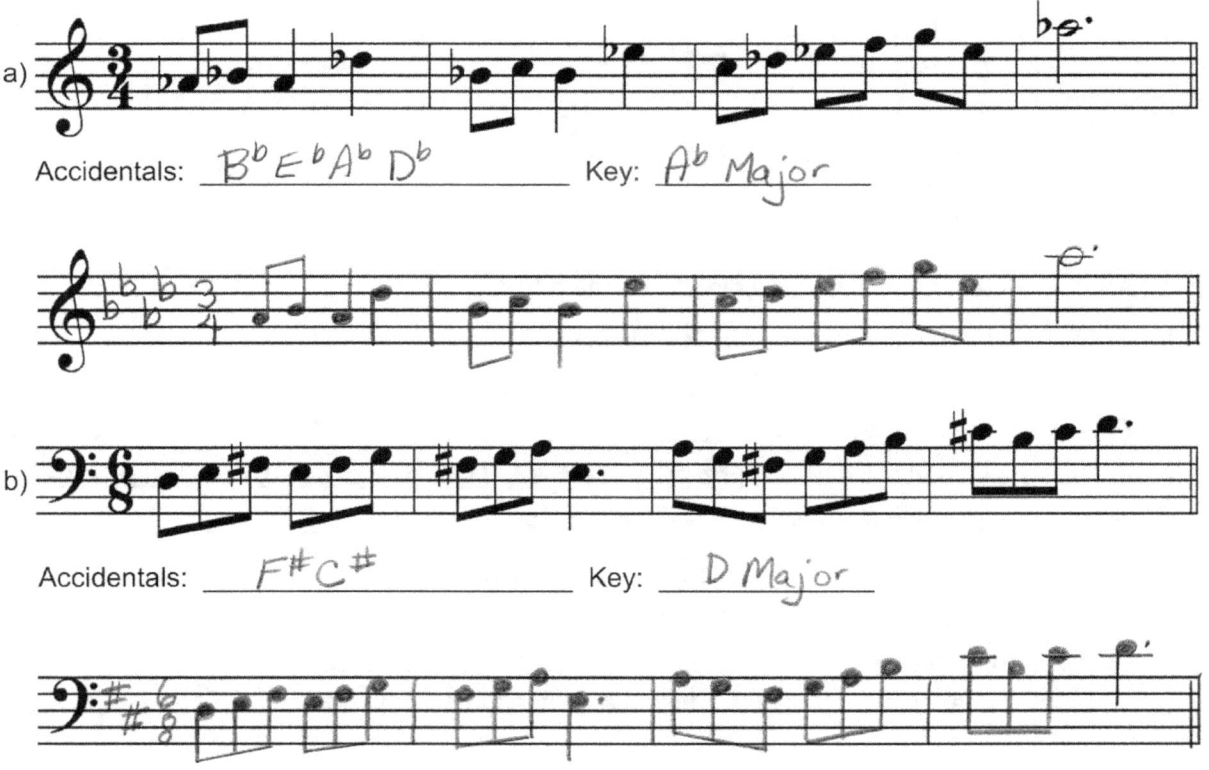

104

REWRITING a HARMONIC MINOR MELODY USING FLATS

A **Melody** written using accidentals with flats may NOT have all the flats in order of the Key Signature. The melody below is written using accidentals of flats. To determine the key, name the accidentals in the order of the Key Signature with flats. The missing flat indicates the raised 7th note of the harmonic minor key.

♪ **Note:** An accidental (natural) is used for the raised 7th note of the harmonic minor key.

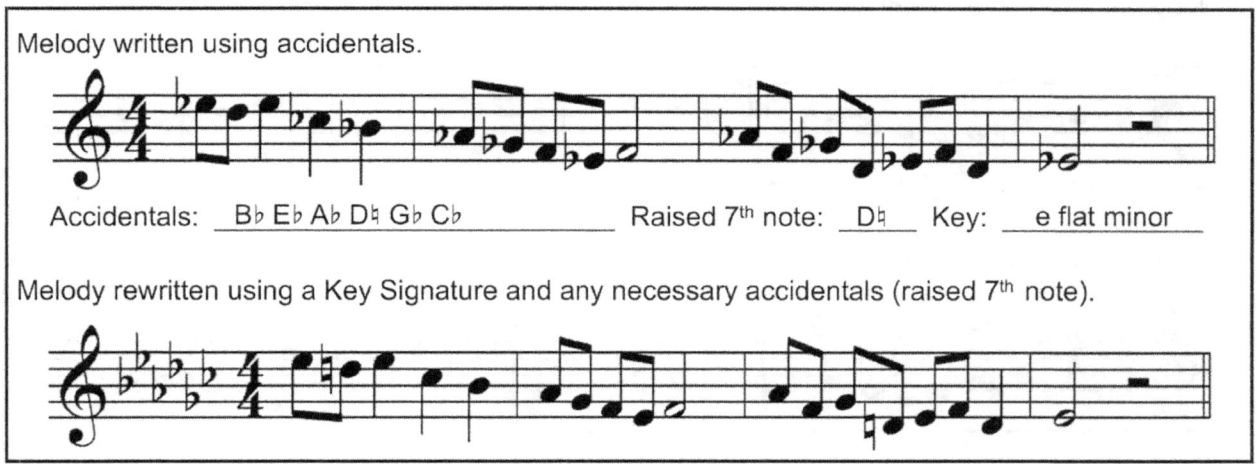

♪ **Note:** When rewriting a melody in a minor key, the flats are written in the Key Signature. An accidental (natural) is used for the raised 7th note of the harmonic minor key.

1. Name the accidentals in the order of the Key Signature. Name the raised 7th note. Name the key. Rewrite the following melodies using a Key Signature and any necessary accidentals.

REWRITING a HARMONIC MINOR MELODY USING FLATS and a SHARP

A **Melody** written using accidentals may have flats AND a sharp. The melody below is written using accidentals of flats and a sharp. To determine the key, name the accidentals in the order of the Key Signature with flats. The sharp indicates the raised 7th note of the harmonic minor key.

♪ **Note:** There are only two harmonic minor keys that contain flats and a sharp; g minor and d minor.

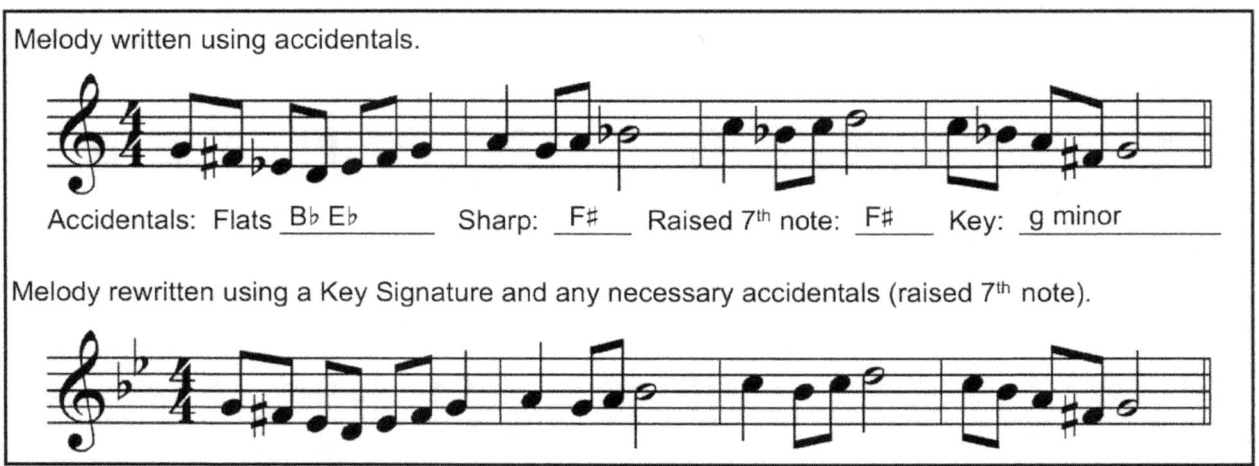

♪ **Note:** When rewriting a melody in a minor key, the flats are written in the Key Signature. An accidental (sharp) is used for the raised 7th note of the harmonic minor key.

1. Name the accidentals in the order of the Key Signature. Name the raised 7th note. Name the key. Rewrite the following melodies using a Key Signature and any necessary accidentals.

106

REWRITING a HARMONIC MINOR MELODY USING SHARPS

A **Melody** written using accidentals with sharps may contain an extra sharp that is NOT in the Key Signature. The melody below is written using accidentals of sharps. To determine the key, name the accidentals in the order of the Key Signature with sharps. The extra sharp indicates the raised 7th note of the harmonic minor key.

♪ **Note:** An accidental (sharp) is used for the raised 7th note of the harmonic minor key.

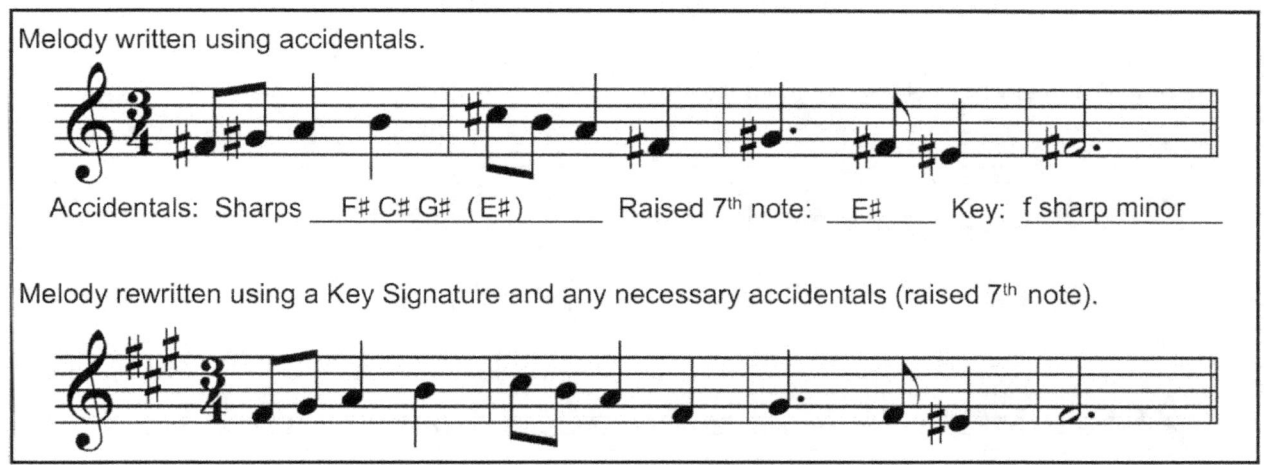

1. Name the accidentals in the order of the Key Signature. Name the raised 7th note. Name the key. Rewrite the following melodies using a Key Signature and any necessary accidentals.

107

REWRITING a HARMONIC MINOR MELODY USING SHARPS and a DOUBLE SHARP

A **Melody** written using accidentals may have sharps AND a double sharp. The melody below is written using accidentals of sharps and a double sharp. To determine the key, name the accidentals in the order of the Key Signature with sharps. The double sharp indicates the raised 7th note of the harmonic minor key.

♪ **Note:** There are only three harmonic minor keys that contain a double sharp as the raised 7th note: g sharp minor (F𝄪); d sharp minor (C𝄪); and a sharp minor (G𝄪).

1. Name the accidentals in the order of the Key Signature. Name the raised 7th note. Name the key. Rewrite the following melodies using a Key Signature and any necessary accidentals.

REWRITING a MELODIC MINOR MELODY

A **Melody** written using accidentals may contain two accidentals NOT in the Key Signature. The melody below is written using accidentals. To determine the key, name the accidentals in the order of the Key Signature. The two extra accidentals indicate the raised 6th and 7th notes of the melodic minor key.

♪ **Note:** In the melodic minor form, the 6th and 7th notes are raised in the ascending melody and may be lowered in the descending melody.

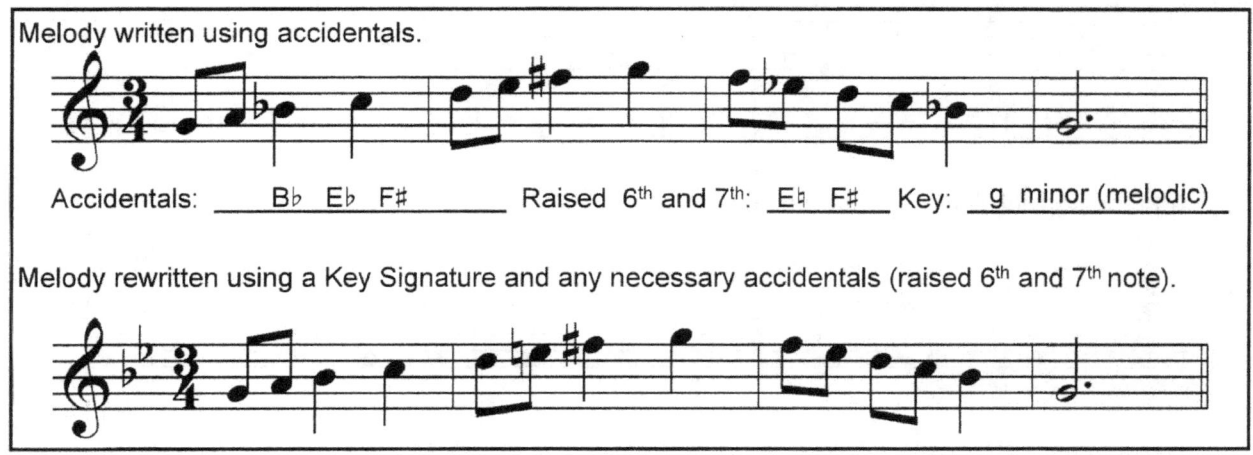

1. Name the accidentals in the order of the Key Signature. Name the raised 6th and 7th notes. Name the key. Rewrite the following melodies using a Key Signature and any necessary accidentals.

109

Lesson 9 — Review Test

Total Score: ____ / 100

Write the Circle of Fifths on a blank piece of paper. Use it as a reference when doing the review test.

1. Name the following harmonic intervals. Invert the intervals. Name the inversions.

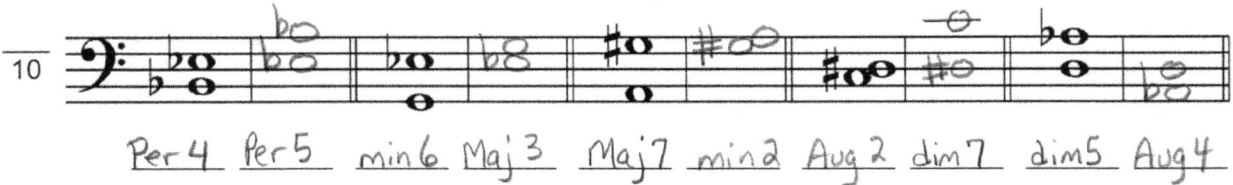

Per 4   Per 5   min 6   Maj 3   Maj 7   min 2   Aug 2   dim 7   dim 5   Aug 4

2. Add the correct Time Signature below each bracket.

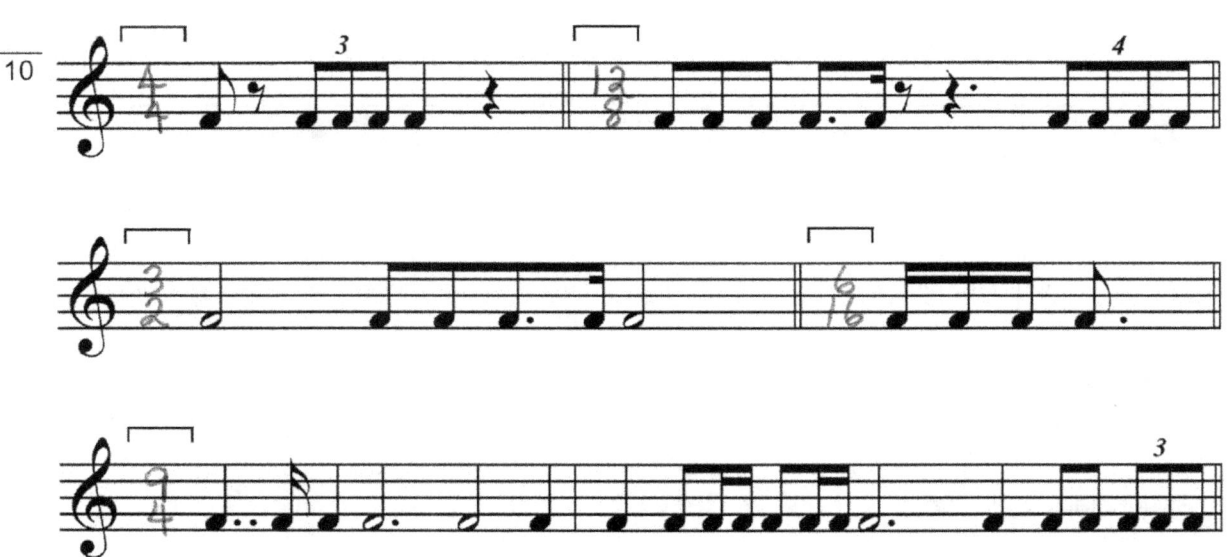

3. Match each musical term with the English definition. (Not all definitions will be used.)

Term		Definition
ben marcato	f	a) but not too much
con pedale	k	b) soft and sweet
ma non troppo	a	c) slowing down gradually a little
poco rit.	c	d) not smooth
alla	h	e) as if much expression
coll' ottava	j	f) well marked
piano ed dolce	b	g) fast
non legato	d	h) in the manner of
quasi molto expressivo	e	i) slow
allegro	g	j) with an added octave
		k) with pedal

110

4. Write the **BASIC BEAT** and the **PULSE** below each measure. Add rests below each bracket to complete the measure. Cross off the Basic Beat as each beat is completed.

5. Name the key. Rewrite the following melody in the Treble Clef using the correct Key Signature.

Key: f minor

6. Name the key. Rewrite the following melody in the Bass Clef using the correct Key Signature.

Key: a minor

7. Write the following triads in the Treble Clef, using the correct **KEY SIGNATURE** for each.

 10
- a) the **SUPERTONIC** (ii) triad of E Major in root position
- b) the **DOMINANT** (V) triad of d sharp minor harmonic in second inversion
- c) the **SUBMEDIANT** (VI) triad of g minor harmonic in second inversion
- d) the **SUBDOMINANT** (iv) triad of d minor harmonic in first inversion
- e) the **MEDIANT** (iii) triad of A flat Major in second inversion

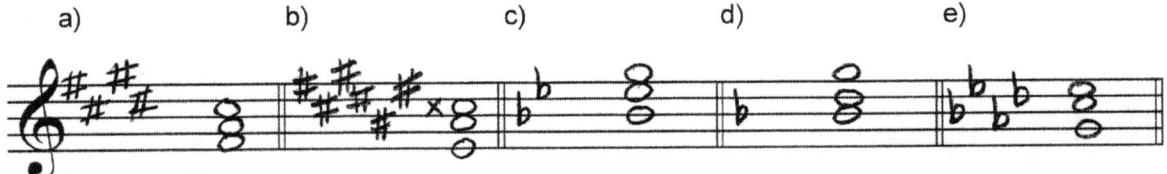

8. Write the following scales, ascending and descending. Use whole notes.

 10
- a) enharmonic Tonic Major of C flat Major in the Treble Clef, using the Key Signature
- b) c sharp minor harmonic in the Bass Clef, using the Key Signature
- c) D Major in the Treble Clef, using accidentals
- d) Tonic minor, melodic form, of G Major in the Bass Clef, using accidentals
- e) whole tone scale beginning on E in the Bass Clef, using accidentals

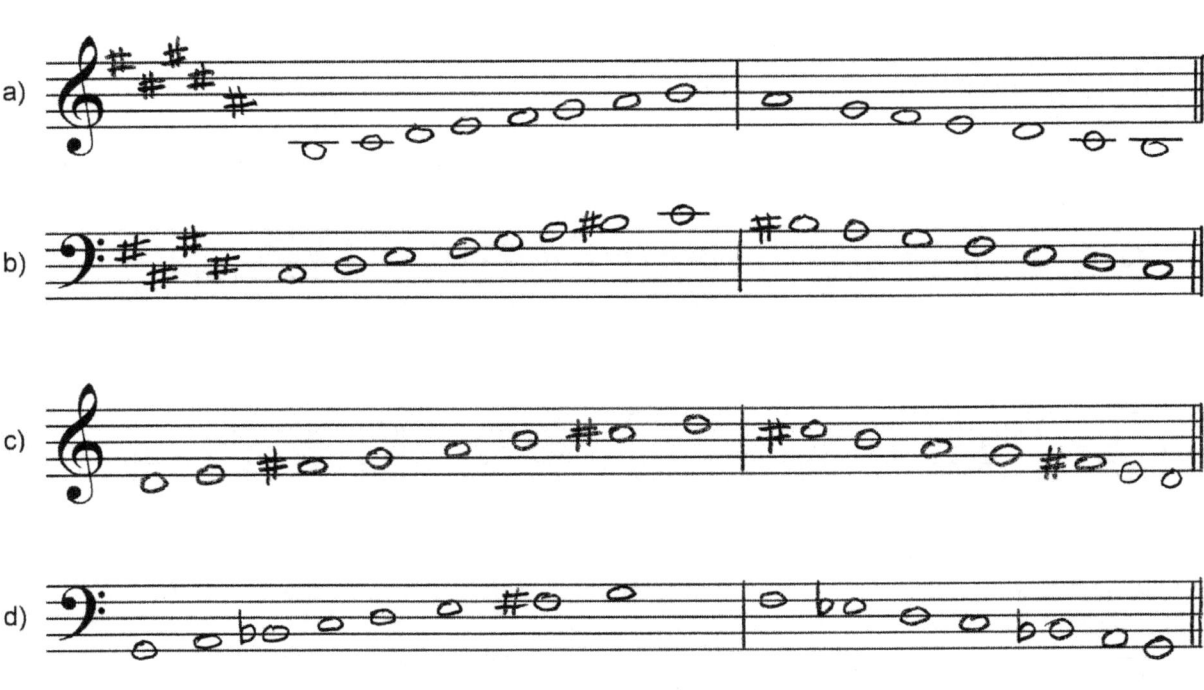

9. a) Name the **MINOR** key for each of the following Key Signatures.
    b) Give the **TECHNICAL DEGREE NAME** for each note. (Tonic, Supertonic, etc.)

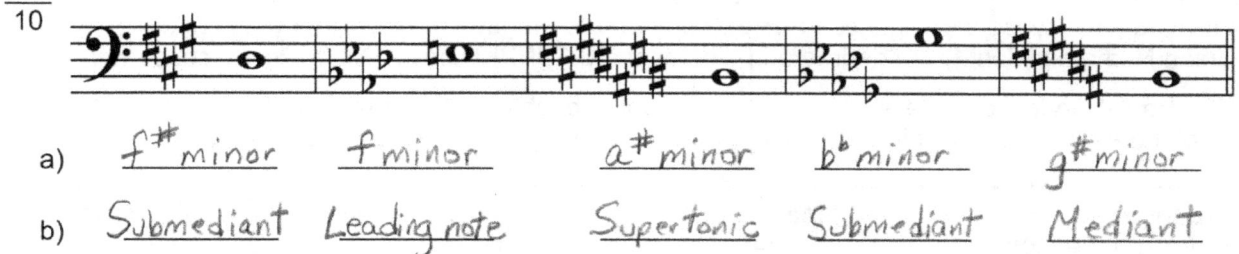

a) f#minor   f minor   a#minor   b♭minor   g#minor
b) Submediant   Leading note   Supertonic   Submediant   Mediant

10. Analyze the following piece of music by answering the questions below.

Andante

a) Add the correct Time Signature directly on the music.
b) Name the key of this piece. __a minor__
c) Explain the meaning of **Andante**. __walking pace__
d) Name the scale at the letter **A**. __a minor melodic__
e) For the triad at **B**, name: Root: __A__ Type/Quality: __minor__ Position: __1st inv__
f) For the triad at **C**, name: Root: __F__ Type/Quality: __Major__ Position: __2nd inv__
g) For the triad at **D**, name: Root: __C__ Type/Quality: __Major__ Position: __root__
h) Explain the G sharp at the letter **E**. __raised 7th note of a minor melodic__
i) Name the scale at the letter **F**. __a minor natural (descending a minor melodic)__
j) For the triad at **G**, name: Root: __D__ Type/Quality: __minor__ Position: __root__

Lesson 10   Cadences - Perfect, Plagal and Imperfect

A **CADENCE** is a progression of two chords that ends a phrase or section of music.
There are three types of cadences: **Perfect** (authentic), **Plagal** and **Imperfect** (half cadence).
Roman Numerals identify the degree and type of chord: UPPER case - Major; lower case - minor.

A **Keyboard Style** Cadence is written with the Root of each chord in the Bass Clef and the Root, 3rd and 5th notes of each chord in the Treble Clef. A cadence is often written over 2 measures.

Cadence	Major keys	minor keys
Perfect (authentic):	V - I	V - i
Plagal:	IV - I	iv - i
Imperfect (half cadence):	I - V, IV - V	i - V, iv - V

IDENTIFYING PERFECT and PLAGAL CADENCES

Perfect and Plagal Cadences (final cadences) end on the Tonic. They are often found at the end of a piece of music. The last note in the Bass Clef is the Tonic note and identifies the key. The Key Signature determines if the key is Major or minor. The bass notes determine the type of cadence.

♪ **Note:** Count **UP** from the Tonic note in the last measure, to the bass note in the first measure, to determine the degree of the note and identify the cadence as Perfect or Plagal.

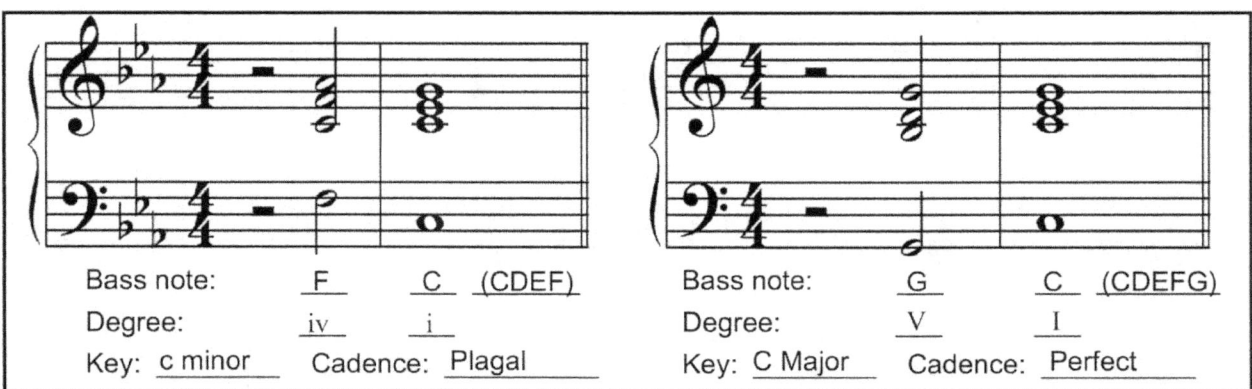

Bass note:	F C (CDEF)	Bass note: G C (CDEFG)
Degree:	iv i	Degree: V I
Key: c minor Cadence: Plagal		Key: C Major Cadence: Perfect

1. For each of the following cadences, name:
   a) the bass note in each measure; write the Tonic note UP to the next degree note (in brackets)
   b) the degree of each bass note (Use Roman Numerals: Upper case - Major; lower case - minor)
   c) the key (Major or minor)
   d) the cadence (Perfect or Plagal)

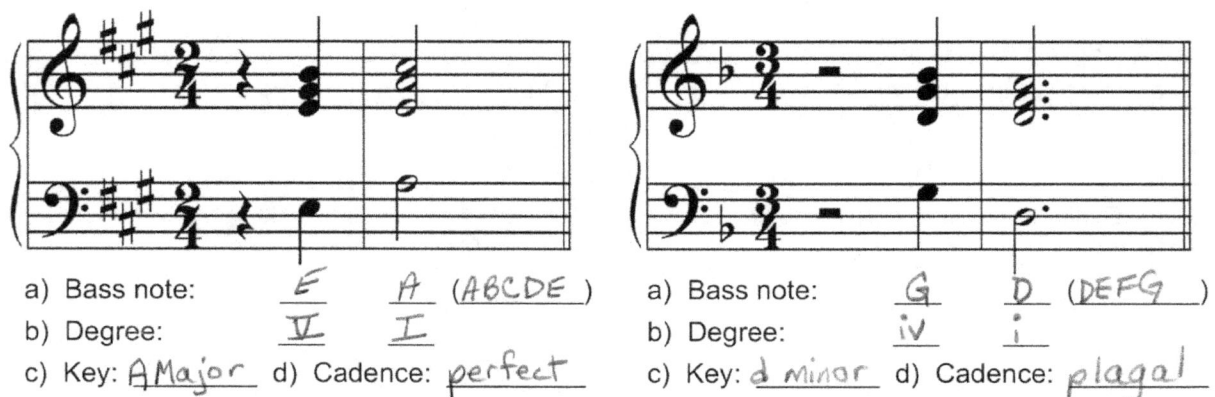

a) Bass note: E   A   (ABCDE)   a) Bass note: G   D   (DEFG)
b) Degree: V   I   b) Degree: iv i
c) Key: A Major   d) Cadence: perfect   c) Key: d minor   d) Cadence: plagal

IDENTIFYING KEYBOARD STYLE CADENCES - MAJOR KEYS

Keyboard Style Cadence	**Major keys**	**Cadence ending**
Perfect (authentic):	V - I	Tonic
Plagal:	IV - I	Tonic
Imperfect (half cadence):	I - V, IV - V	Dominant

♪ **Note:** An **Imperfect Cadence**, (**I - V**) or (**IV - V**), begins on the Tonic (**I**) or the Subdominant (**IV**) and ends on the Dominant (**V**). It is often found ending a phrase in the middle of a section.

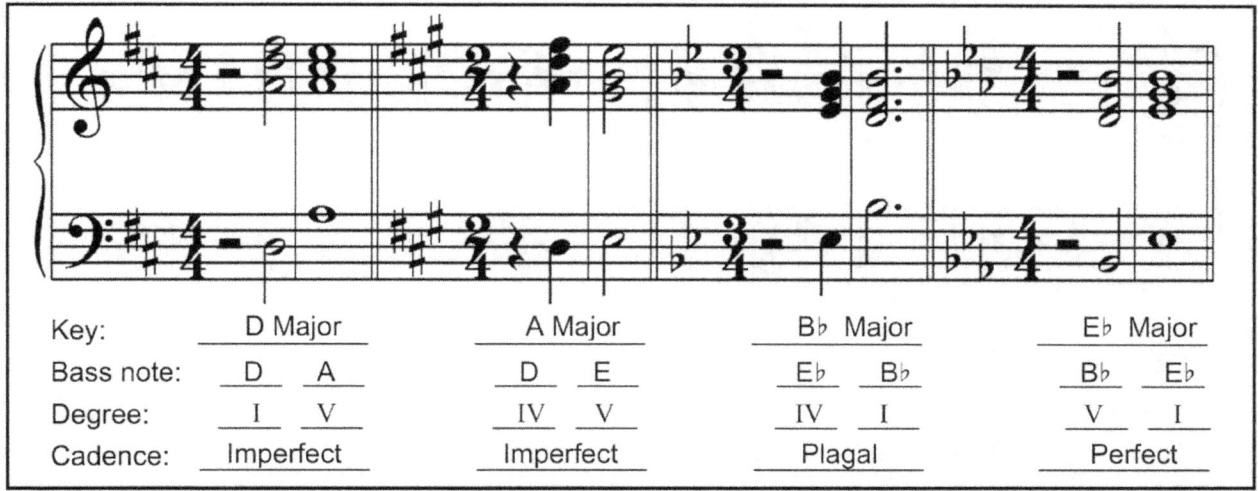

♪ **Note:** The notes in the Bass Clef determine if the cadence is Perfect, Plagal or Imperfect. Determine the key and the Tonic note. Count UP from the Tonic note to determine the degree of the notes in the Bass Clef.

1. For each of the following cadences, name:
   a) the Major key
   b) the bass note in each measure
   c) the degree of each bass note (Use Roman Numerals)
   d) the cadence (Perfect, Plagal or Imperfect)

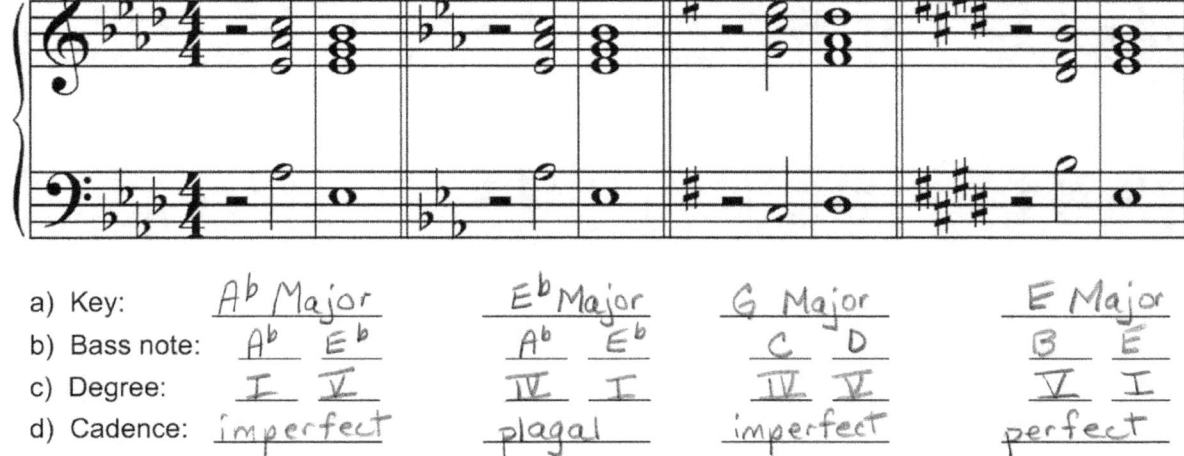

IDENTIFYING KEYBOARD STYLE CADENCES - MINOR KEYS

Keyboard Style Cadence minor keys   Cadence ending
Perfect (authentic):   V - i   Tonic
Plagal: iv - i   Tonic
Imperfect (half cadence): i - V, iv - V   Dominant

♫ **Note:** The Dominant (V) chord of the harmonic minor key ALWAYS contains the raised 7th note. The Dominant (V) chord is ALWAYS Major.

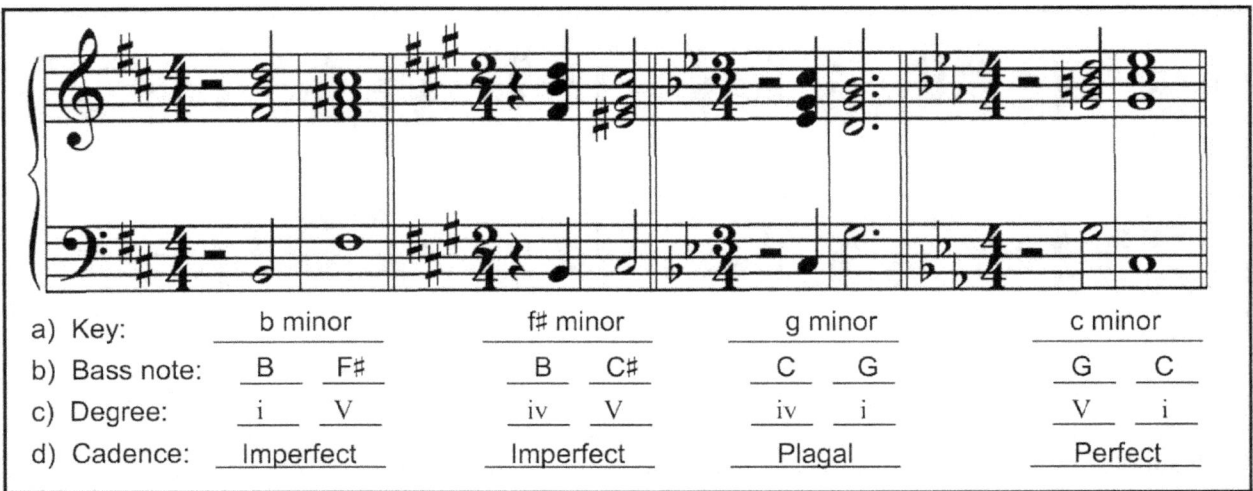

a) Key:	b minor	f# minor	g minor	c minor
b) Bass note:	B F#	B C#	C G	G C
c) Degree:	i V	iv V	iv i	V i
d) Cadence:	Imperfect	Imperfect	Plagal	Perfect

♫ **Note:** An accidental is used for the raised 7th note of the harmonic minor key. An UPPER case Roman Numeral is used for the Dominant (V) Major chord. Lower case Roman Numerals are used for the Subdominant (iv) and Tonic (i) minor chords.

1. For each of the following cadences, name:
   a) the minor key
   b) the bass note in each measure
   c) the degree of each bass note (Use Roman Numerals)
   d) the cadence (Perfect, Plagal or Imperfect)

a) Key:	f minor	c minor	e minor	c# minor
b) Bass note:	Bb F	C G	A B	G# C#
c) Degree:	iv i	i V	iv V	V i
d) Cadence:	plagal	imperfect	imperfect	perfect

IDENTIFYING the KEY for PERFECT and IMPERFECT CADENCES

When **IDENTIFYING the KEY for PERFECT and IMPERFECT CADENCES**, if the cadence contains an accidental (raised 7th note), the key is minor (Perfect V - i or Imperfect i - V, iv - V). If the cadence does NOT contain an accidental (raised 7th), the key is Major (Perfect V - I or Imperfect I - V, IV - V).

♪ **Note:** A Perfect Cadence ends on the Tonic. An Imperfect Cadence ends on the Dominant.

1. Identify the following cadences using Roman Numerals.

Cadence	Major keys	minor keys
Perfect (authentic):	V - I	V - i
Imperfect (half cadence):	IV - V OR I - V	iv - V OR i - V

2. For each of the following cadences, name:
   a) the key
   b) the bass note in each measure
   c) the degree of each bass note
   d) the cadence

a) Key:	b minor	B♭ Major	f# minor	D♭ Major
b) Bass note:	F# B	E♭ F	B C#	A♭ D♭
c) Degree:	V i	IV V	iv V	V I
d) Cadence:	Perfect	Imperfect	Imperfect	Perfect

a) Key:	C♭ Major	g# minor	D Major	a minor
b) Bass note:	F♭ G♭	D# G#	A D	D E
c) Degree:	IV V	V i	V I	iv V
d) Cadence:	Imperfect	Perfect	Perfect	Imperfect

IDENTIFYING the KEY for PLAGAL CADENCES

When **IDENTIFYING the KEY for PLAGAL CADENCES**, the cadence will NOT contain an accidental (raised 7th note) of the harmonic minor key. Plagal Cadence (minor) iv - i; (Major) IV - I.

♪ **Note:** To determine if the Plagal Cadence belongs to the Major key or the minor key, check the Key Signature. Determine if the Tonic note belongs to the Major key or the minor key.

1. Identify the following cadences using Roman Numerals.

Cadence	Major keys	minor keys
Plagal:	IV - I	iv - i

2. For each of the following cadences, name:
   a) the key
   b) the bass note in each measure
   c) the degree of each bass note
   d) the cadence

a) Key: E Major / g minor / d# minor / Gb Major
b) Bass note: A E / C G / G# D# / Cb Gb
c) Degree: IV I / iv i / iv i / IV I
d) Cadence: Plagal / Plagal / Plagal / Plagal

3. For each of the following cadences, name: a) the key; b) the type (Perfect, Plagal or Imperfect)

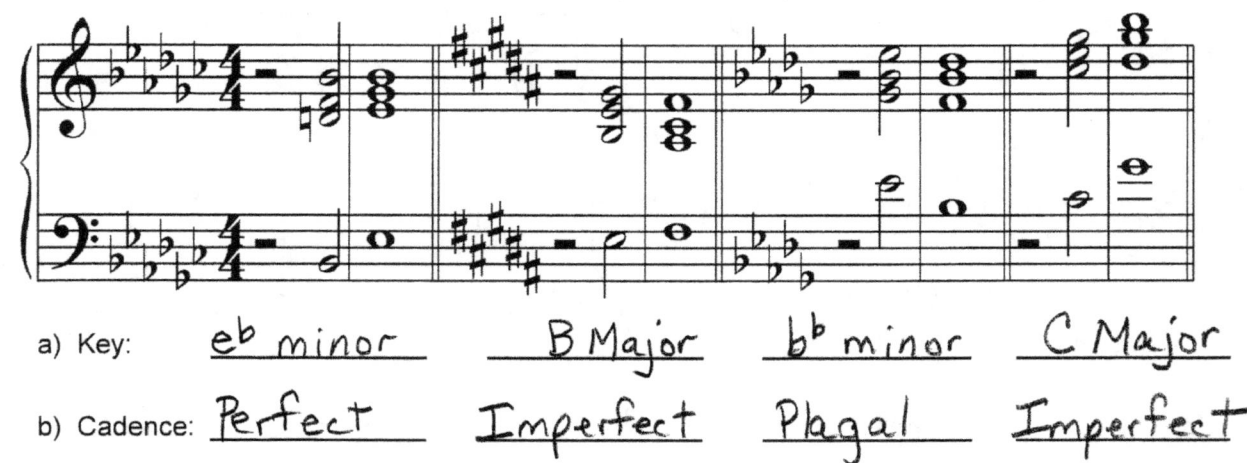

a) Key: eb minor / B Major / bb minor / C Major
b) Cadence: Perfect / Imperfect / Plagal / Imperfect

Lesson 10 — Review Test

Total Score: ____ / 100

Write the Circle of Fifths on a blank piece of paper. Use it as a reference when doing the review test.

1. Write the following harmonic intervals **BELOW** the given notes. Invert the intervals. Name the inversions.

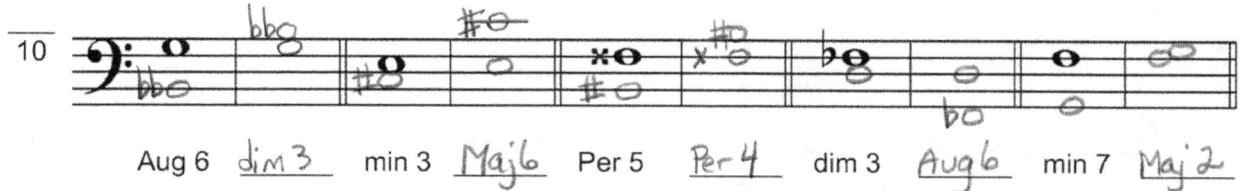

Aug 6 dim 3   min 3 Maj 6   Per 5 Per 4   dim 3 Aug 6   min 7 Maj 2

2. Add the correct Time Signature below each bracket.

3. Match each musical term with the English definition. (Not all definitions will be used.)

Term		Definition
animato	f	a) held, sustained
con brio	e	b) always one string; depress the left (piano) pedal
tenuto	a	c) fairly fast and detached
mano sinistra, M.S.	h	d) very slow
dal segno, D.S.	i	e) with vigor, spirit
largo	d	f) lively, animated
allegretto ed staccato	c	g) slow and solemn
quasi cantabile	k	h) left hand
grave	g	i) from the sign
sempre una corda	b	j) with an added octave
		k) almost, as if in a singing style

4. Write the **BASIC BEAT** and the **PULSE** below each measure. Add rests below each bracket to complete the measure. Cross off the Basic Beat as each beat is completed.

5. For each of the following cadences, name:
   a) the key; b) the type (Perfect, Plagal or Imperfect)

6. Write the following triads in the Bass Clef, using the correct KEY SIGNATURE for each.

   a) the **SUPERTONIC** (ii) triad of B Major in first inversion
   b) the **DOMINANT** (V) triad of c sharp minor harmonic in second inversion
   c) the **TONIC** (i) triad of a flat minor harmonic in root position
   d) the **SUBDOMINANT** (iv) triad of f minor harmonic in first inversion
   e) the **SUBMEDIANT** (vi) triad of F sharp Major in second inversion

10

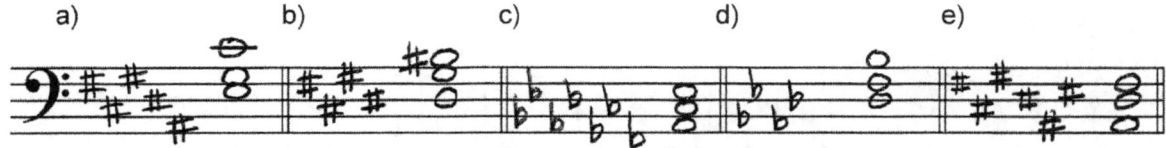

7. Write the following scales, ascending and descending. Use whole notes.

   a) enharmonic relative minor, melodic form, of C sharp Major in the Bass Clef, using the Key Signature
   b) Tonic Major of g minor in the Treble Clef, using the Key Signature
   c) e flat minor harmonic in the Bass Clef, using the Key Signature
   d) chromatic scale beginning on F (any standard version) in the Treble Clef, using accidentals
   e) whole tone scale beginning on C sharp in the Bass Clef, using accidentals

10

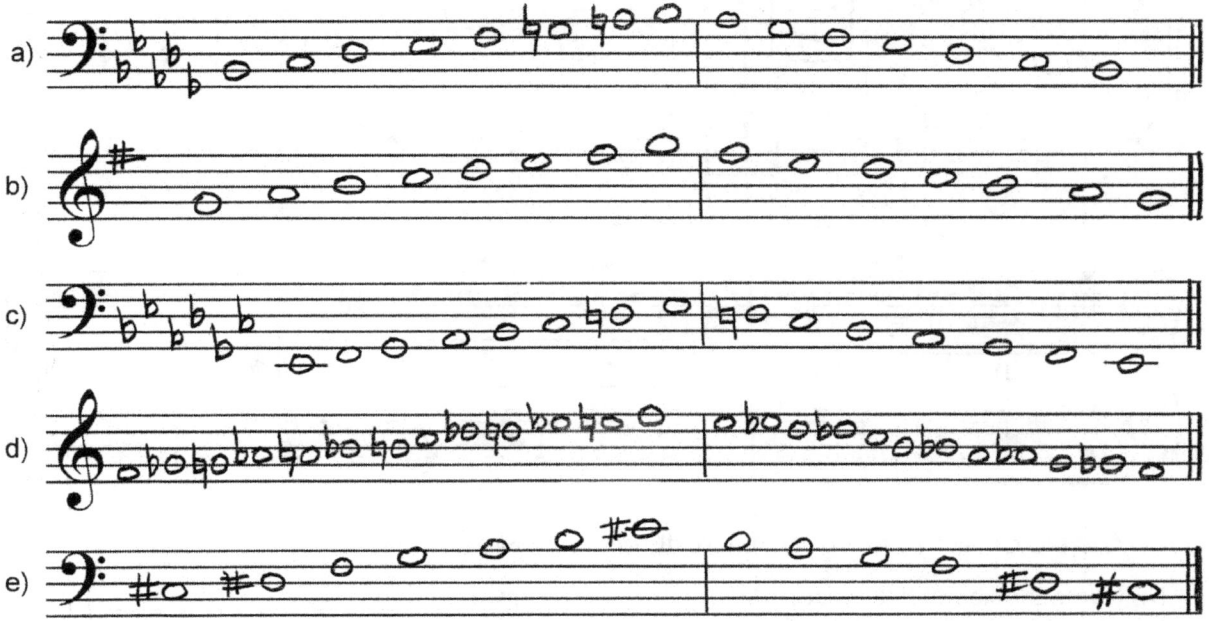

8. a) Name the **MINOR KEY** for each of the following key signatures.
   b) Give the **TECHNICAL DEGREE NAME** for each note. (Tonic, Supertonic, etc.)

10

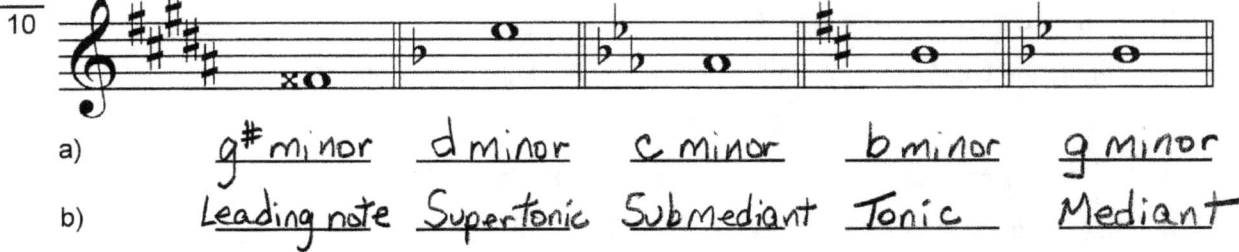

a) g# minor   d minor   c minor   b minor   g minor
b) Leading note Supertonic Submediant Tonic Mediant

9. Name the key. Rewrite the following melody in the Bass Clef using the correct Key Signature.

Key: g minor

10. Analyze the following piece of music by answering the questions below.

Minuet — George F. Handel (1685-1759)

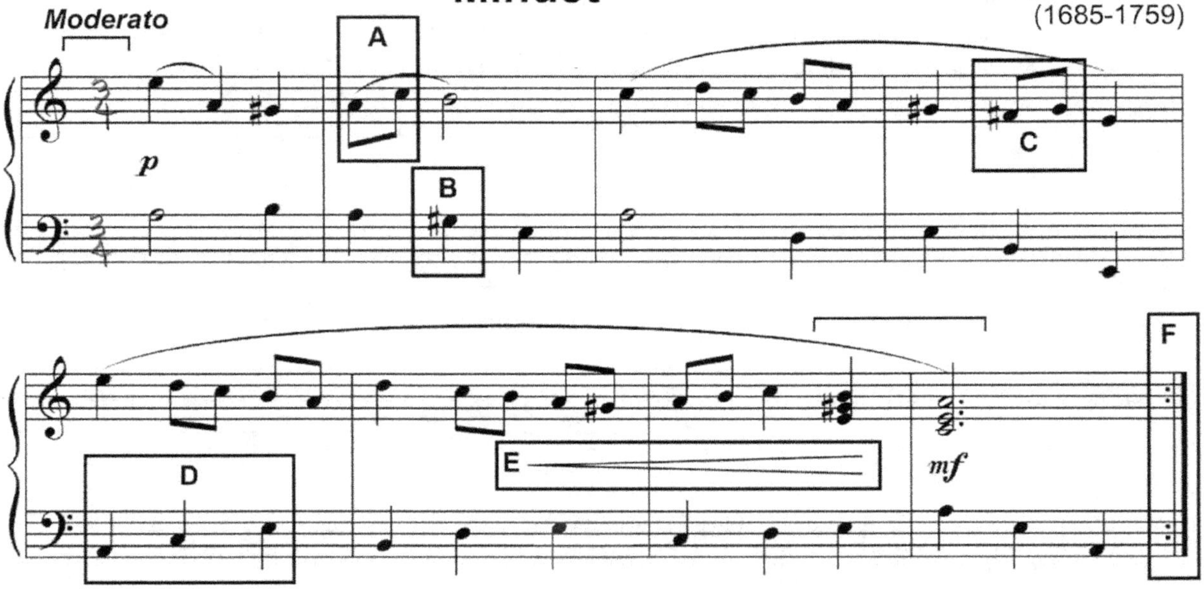

a) Add the correct Time Signature directly on the music.
b) Name the key of this piece. __a minor__
c) How many measures are in this piece? __8__
d) Name the interval at the letter **A**. __minor 3__
e) Give the technical degree name of the note at the letter **B**. __Leading note__
f) Name the interval at the letter **C**. __Major 2__
g) Identify the type/quality of the broken triad at the letter **D** as Major or minor. __minor__
h) Explain the sign at the letter **E**. __crescendo - becoming louder__
i) Identify the cadence at the end of the piece as Perfect or Plagal. __perfect__
j) Give the meaning of the sign at the letter **F**. __repeat the music__

Lesson 11   Transposition - Major Key to Major Key

TRANSPOSITION from MAJOR KEY to MAJOR KEY is when music is written or played at a different pitch. When **transposing** from a Major key to a Major key, name the **ORIGINAL** key first. Start at the Tonic note and count **UP** to determine the interval note name. The TOP note names the NEW Major key. All the notes must move up the same interval.

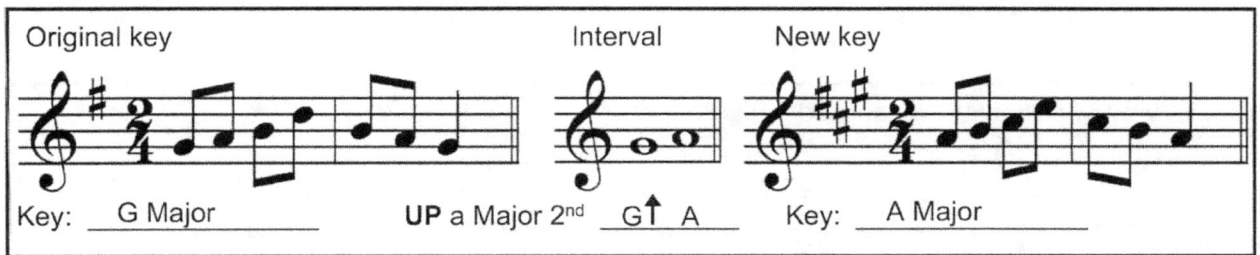

1. a) Name the key of the given melody.
    b) Write the interval of a melodic Major 2nd ABOVE the Tonic note (D). Name the note.
    c) Name the new key. Transpose the given melody **UP** a Major 2nd using the correct Key Signature.

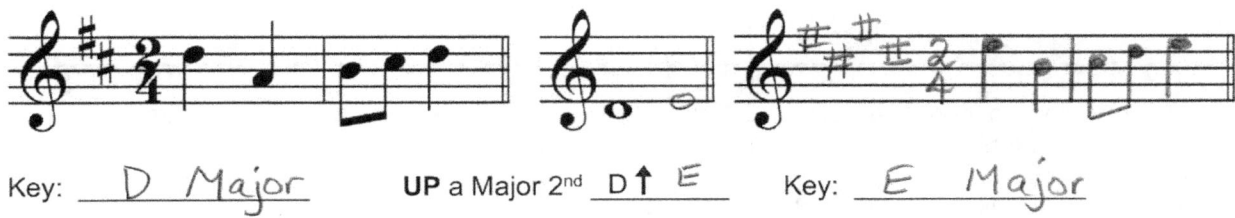

♪ **Note:** When a Major key is transposed to a new key, the key will ALWAYS remain MAJOR.

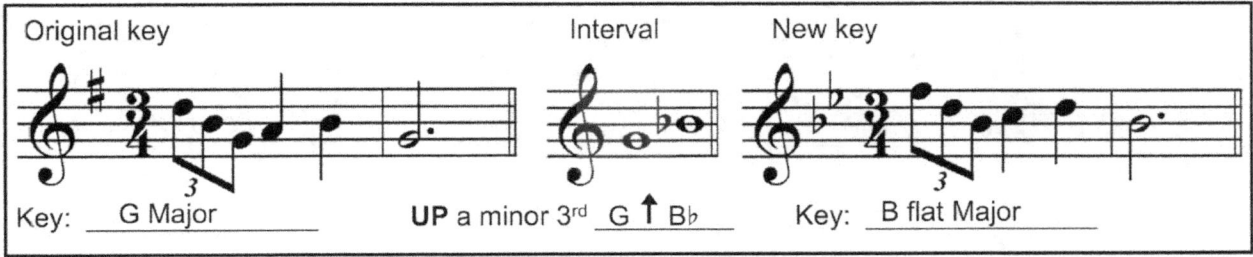

2. a) Name the key of the given melody.
    b) Write the interval of a melodic minor 3rd ABOVE the Tonic note (D). Name the note.
    c) Name the new key. Transpose the given melody **UP** a minor 3rd using the correct Key Signature.

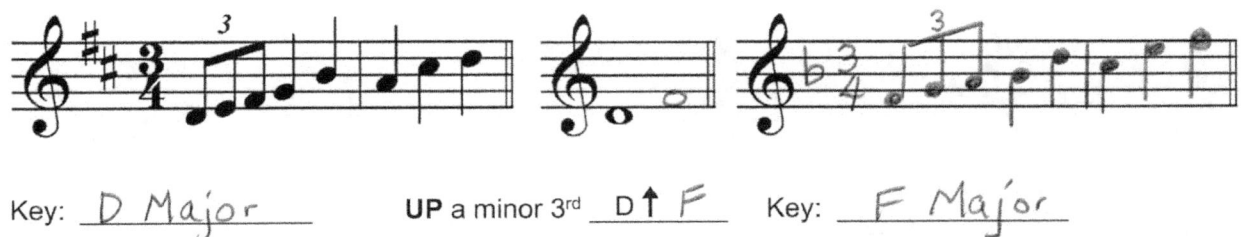

TRANSPOSING a MELODY with ACCIDENTALS

When **TRANSPOSING a MELODY with ACCIDENTALS**: if the original melody contains accidentals, the transposed melody will contain accidentals. If an accidental raises or lowers a note in the original melody, the transposed melody must contain an accidental to raise or lower the note as well.

♪ **Note:** When adding accidentals, observe the Key Signature. Example: Key of G Major, F sharp is lowered to F natural in the original key. Transposing to the new key of C Major, the same degree is the note B. B natural is lowered to B flat.

♪ **Note:** When transposing a melody UP to a new key, always determine the interval first. The bottom note names the original key. The top note names the new key.

1. The following melody is in the key of F Major.
    a) Transpose the given melody **UP** a Major 3rd, using the correct Key Signature. Name the key.
    b) Transpose the given melody **UP** a minor 2nd, using the correct Key Signature. Name the key.

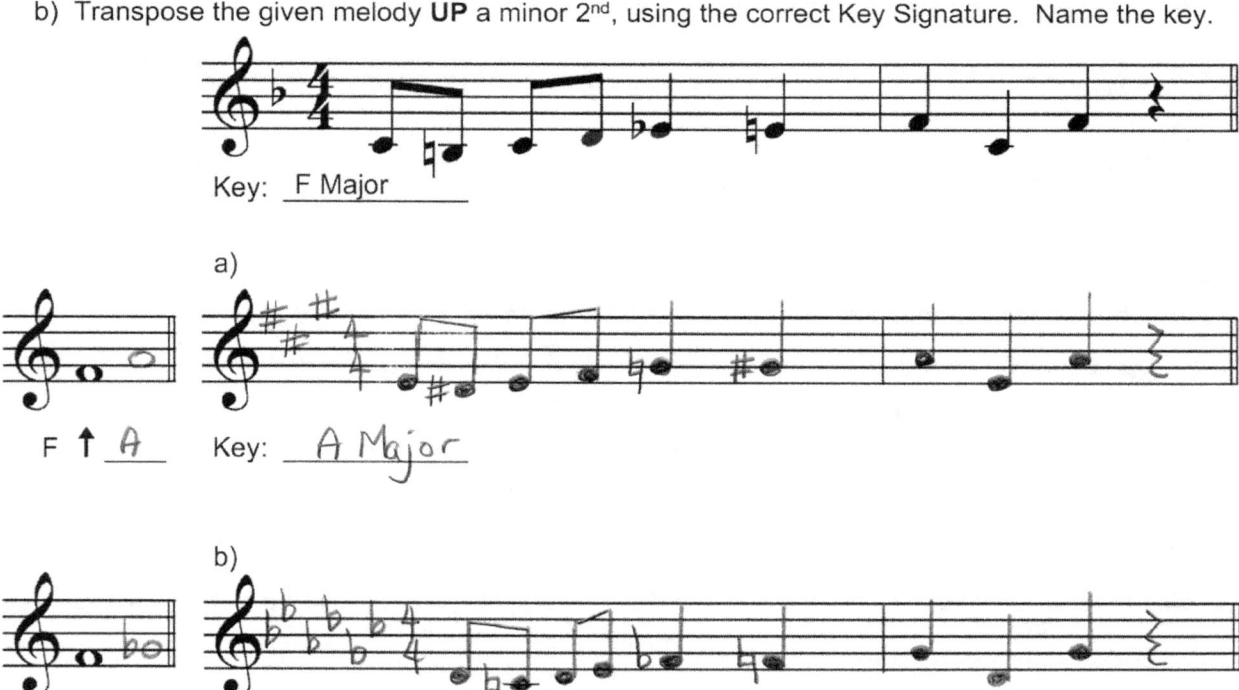

TRANSPOSING a MELODY UP an INTERVAL

When **TRANSPOSING a MELODY UP an INTERVAL**, write the interval ABOVE the Tonic note of the given melody. The TOP note determines the new key.

Key: E flat Major   UP a minor 3rd   New Key: G flat Major

1. For each of the following:
   a) Name the key of the given melody.
   b) Write the Tonic note and the given interval ABOVE the Tonic note.
   c) Name the new key. Transpose the melody UP by the given interval, using the correct Key Signature.

a) 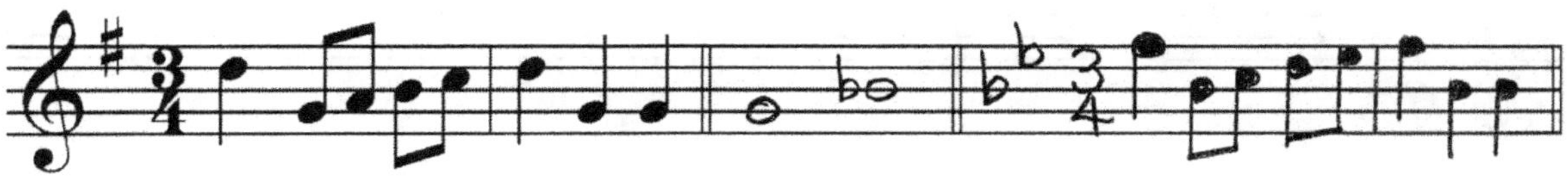 Key: G Major   UP a minor 3rd   New Key: B♭ Major

b) 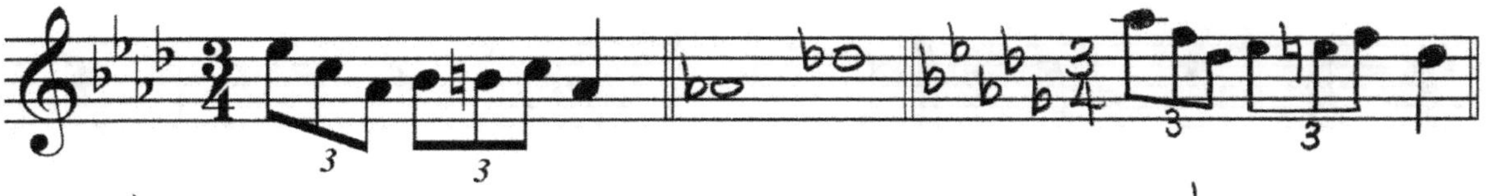 Key: A♭ Major   UP a Perfect 4th   New Key: D♭ Major

c) 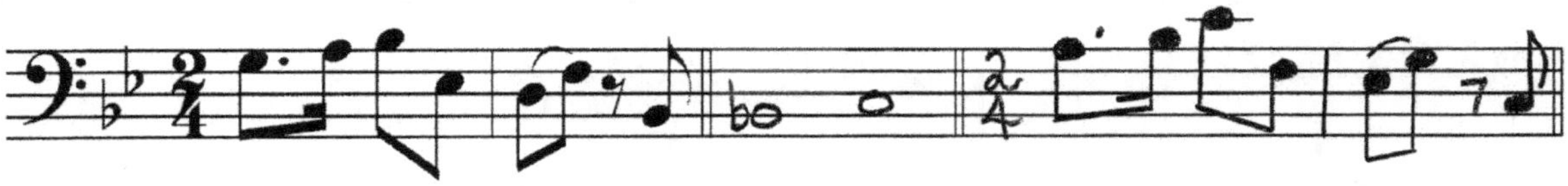 Key: B♭ Major   UP a Major 2nd   New Key: C Major

d) 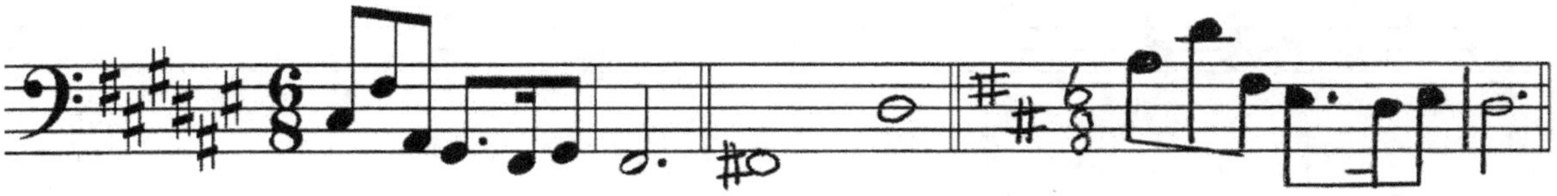 Key: F# Major   UP a minor 6th   New Key: D Major

TRANSPOSING a MELODY to a NEW KEY

When **TRANSPOSING a MELODY to a NEW KEY**, a Major key will ALWAYS remain a Major key. All the notes move UP the SAME interval.

♪ **Note:** Draw a staff in the margin. Write the interval above the Tonic note of the given melody. The top note names the new key.

1. The following melody is in the key of G flat Major. Transpose the given melody UP an Augmented 2nd using the correct Key Signature. Name the new key.

Key: A Major

2. The following melody is in the key of F Major. Transpose the given melody UP a minor 3rd using the correct Key Signature. Name the new key.

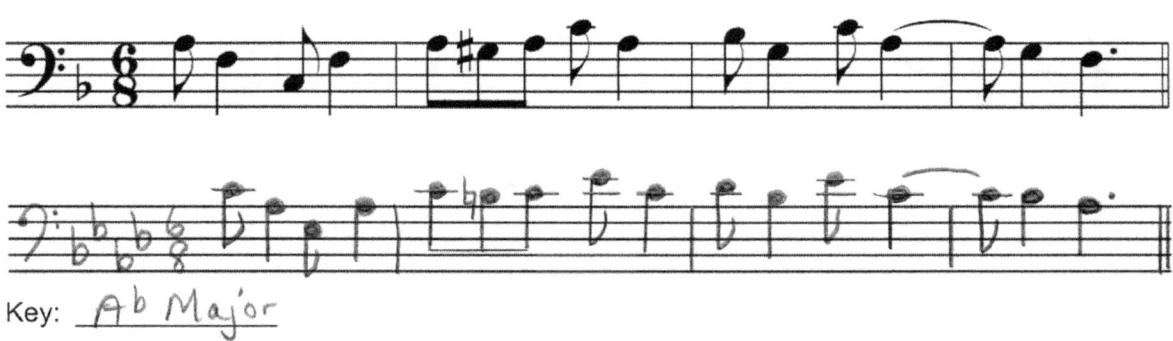

Key: Ab Major

3. The following melody is in the key of C sharp Major. Transpose the given melody UP a Perfect 4th using the correct Key Signature. Name the new key.

Key: F# Major

Lesson 11   Review Test

Total Score: ____
/100

Write the Circle of Fifths on a blank piece of paper. Use it as a reference when doing the review test.

1. a) Write the following melodic intervals **ABOVE** each of the given notes. Use whole notes.

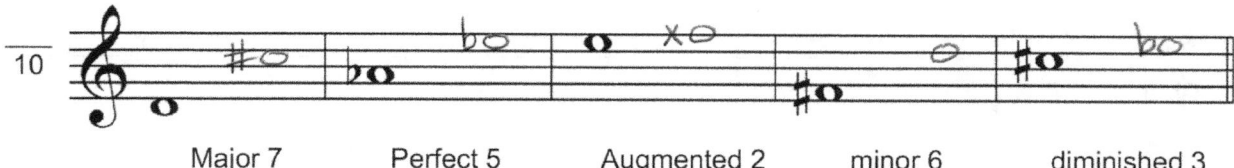

     Major 7   Perfect 5   Augmented 2   minor 6   diminished 3

b) Invert the above intervals in the same clef. Name the inversions.

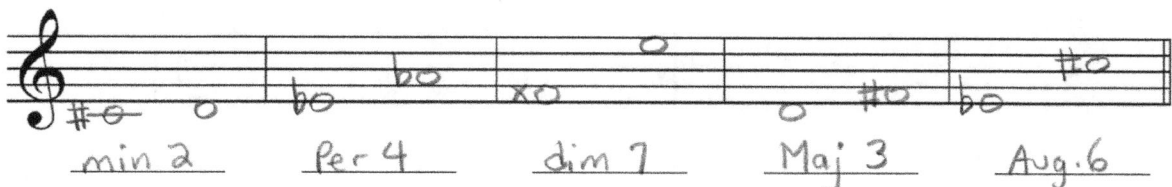

    min 2   Per 4   dim 7   Maj 3   Aug. 6

2. Write the **BASIC BEAT** and the **PULSE** below each measure. Add rests below each bracket to complete the measure. Cross off the Basic Beat as each beat is completed.

3. Rewrite the open position triad in CLOSE root position below each bracket.
   For each of the given triads name: a) the Root; b) the type/quality; c) the position.

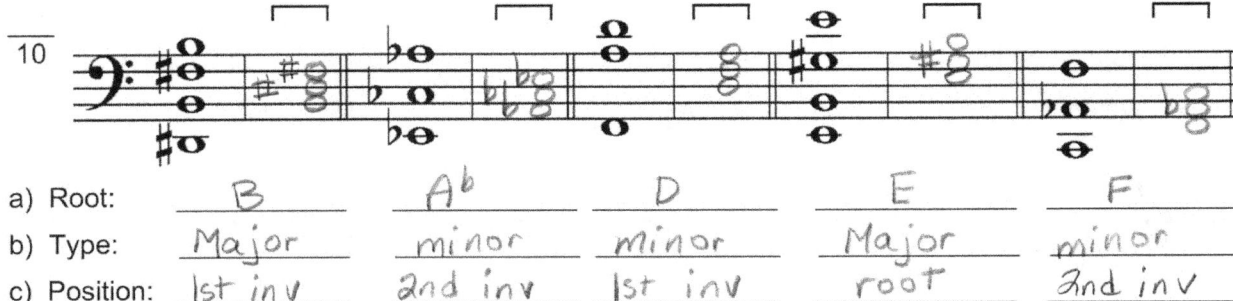

a) Root: B   A♭   D   E   F
b) Type: Major   minor   minor   Major   minor
c) Position: 1st inv   2nd inv   1st inv   root   2nd inv

4. Name the key of the following melody. Transpose it **UP** a minor third using the correct Key Signature. Name the new key.

Key: E Major

New Key: G Major

5. For each of the following cadences, name:
   a) the key; b) the type (Perfect, Plagal or Imperfect)

a) Key: F Major   f♯ minor   B Major
b) Cadence: imperfect   plagal   imperfect

a) Key: c minor   a♯ minor
b) Cadence: imperfect   imperfect

6. Name the following scales as Major, harmonic minor, melodic minor, natural minor, chromatic, whole tone, octatonic, blues, Major pentatonic or minor pentatonic.

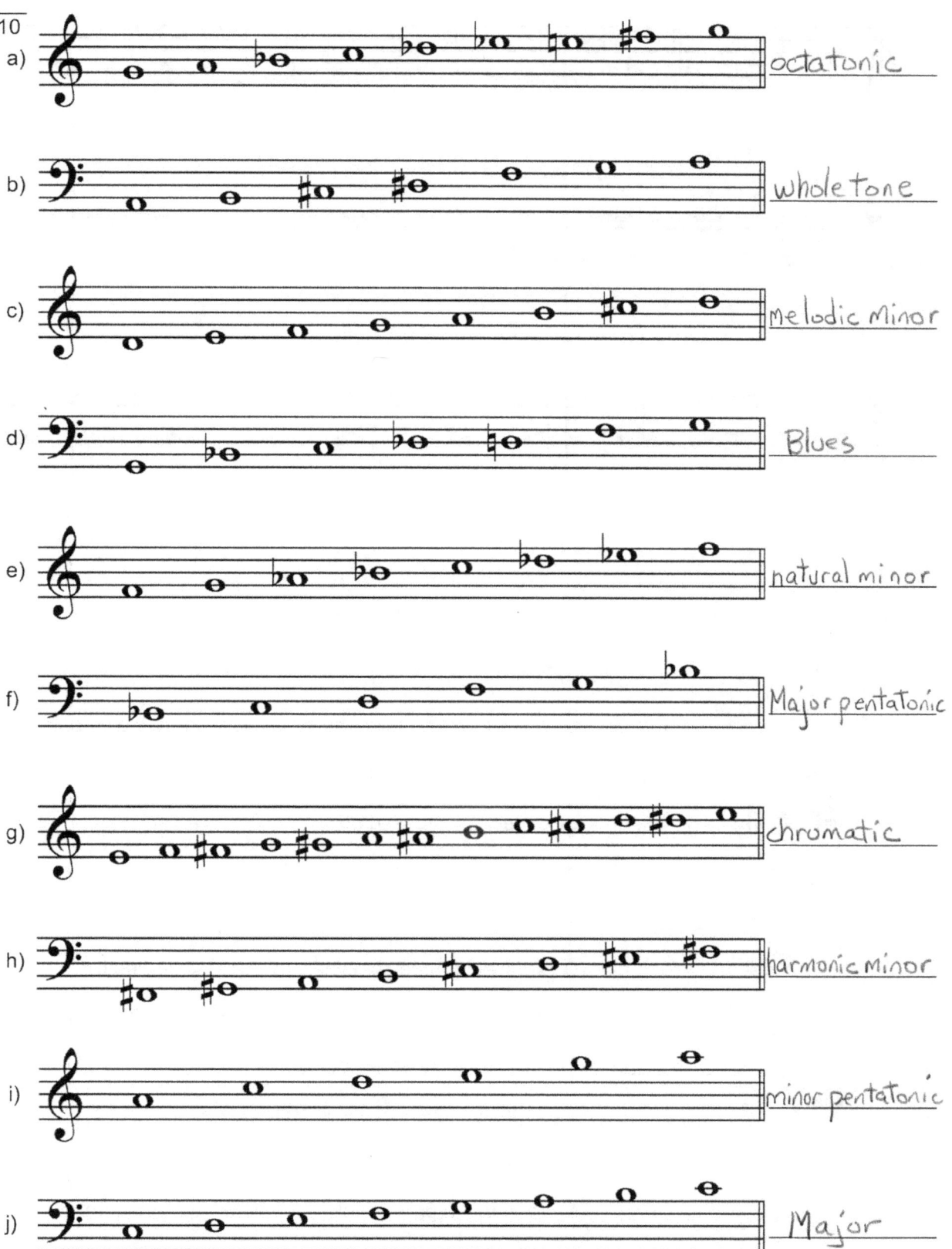

7. Add the correct Time Signature below each bracket.

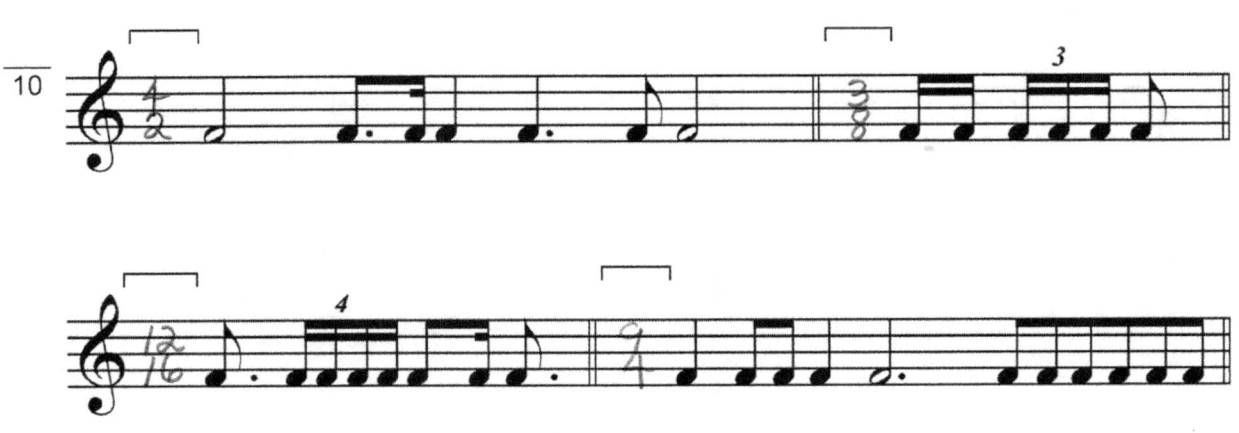

8. Match each musical sign with the English definition. (Not all definitions will be used.)

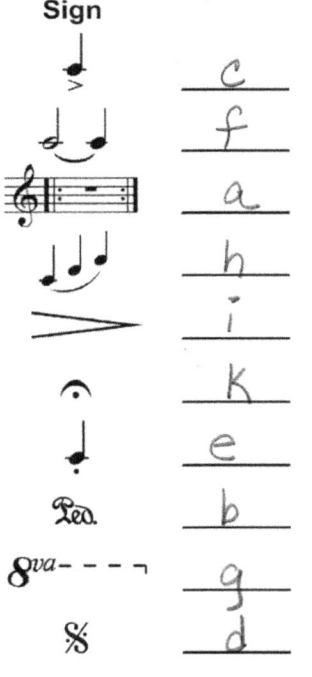

Sign	Answer
(accent)	c
(tied notes)	f
(whole rest)	a
(three notes)	h
(decrescendo)	i
(fermata)	k
(staccato)	e
Ped.	b
8va- - -	g
𝄋	d

a) *repeat signs*: repeat the music within the double bars
b) *pedale*: with pedal
c) *accent*: a stressed note
d) *dal segno, D.S.*: from the sign
e) *staccato*: play the note sharply detached
f) *tie*: hold for the combined value of the tied notes
g) *8va*: play one octave above the written pitch
h) *slur*: play the notes legato
i) *decrescendo*: becoming softer
j) *crescendo*: becoming louder
k) *fermata*: a pause; hold the note or rest longer than its written value

9. a) Name the **MINOR** key for each of the following Key Signatures.
   b) Give the **TECHNICAL DEGREE NAME** for each note. (Tonic, Supertonic, etc.)

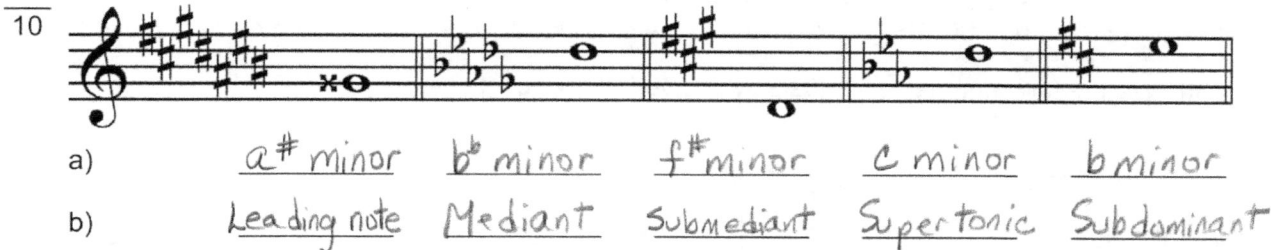

a) a# minor   b♭ minor   f# minor   c minor   b minor

b) Leading note   Mediant   Submediant   Supertonic   Subdominant

10. Analyze the following piece of music by answering the questions below.

    a) Add the correct Time Signature directly on the music.
    b) Name the composer of this piece. Johann Sebastian Bach
    c) Name the key of this piece. d minor
    d) How many measures are in this piece? 8
    e) Explain the C sharp at the letter **A**. raised 7th note of d minor harmonic
    f) Name the interval at the letter **B**. Major 6
    g) Name the interval at the letter **C**. dim 4
    h) Give the technical degree name of the note at the letter **D**. Leading note
    i) Locate and circle a diatonic semitone in this piece. Label it as d.s.
    j) Locate and circle a whole tone in this piece. Label it as w.t.

Lesson 12   Analysis, Italian Terms and Signs

ANALYSIS of a piece of music develops a deeper understanding of the composers ideas.
ITALIAN TERMS and **SIGNS** give direction to the musician for performance of a piece of music.

1. Analyze the following piece of music by answering the questions below.

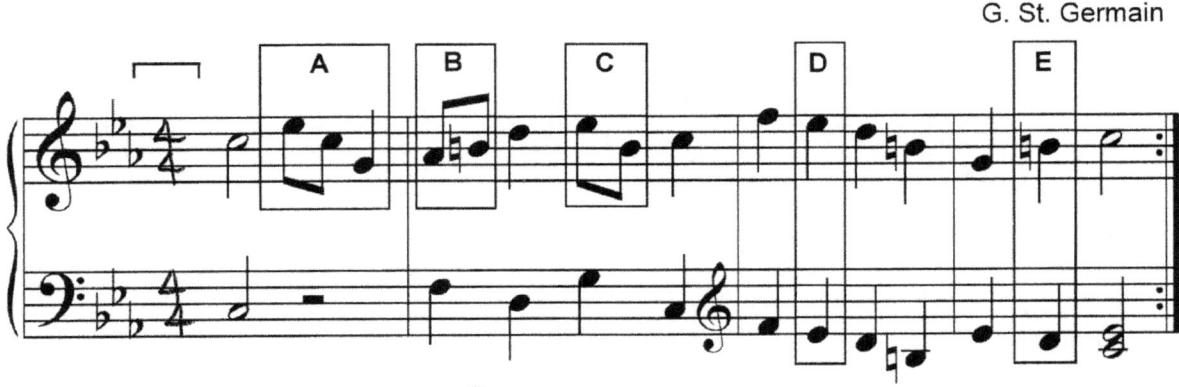

G. St. Germain

a) Name the composer. __G. St. Germain__

b) When counting the number of measures in a piece, a repeat sign WILL NOT affect the number of measures. How many measures are in this piece? __4__

c) When all repeat signs are observed, how many measures of music are played? __8__

d) When naming the key, look at the Key Signature. Check for the raised 7th note of the harmonic minor key to determine if the key is Major or minor. Check the last note of the piece; it will often end on the Tonic. Name the key. __C minor__

e) Write the Time Signature directly on the music below the bracket. Write it in BOTH clefs. Look for the easiest measures to determine the Time Signature.

f) When identifying triads, place the notes in root position (all lines or all spaces). The bottom note (when in root position) names the Root. Name the ROOT of the triad at the letter **A**. __C__

g) A triad may be written in SOLID (blocked) form or in BROKEN form. Name the form of the triad at the letter **A**. __broken__

h) When determining the type of triad (Major or minor), write the triad in root position. The bottom note names the key. If the Root to the 3rd is a Major third, the triad is Major. If the Root to the 3rd is a minor third, the triad is minor. Name the type of triad at the letter **A**. __minor__

i) When naming the position of a chord, first place it in root position. If the notes are all lines or all spaces, it is in root position. If the bottom note is the 3rd, it is in first inversion. If the bottom note is the 5th, it is in second inversion. Name the position of the chord at the letter **A**. __2nd inv__

j) When identifying intervals, count ALL the lines and ALL the spaces. Check for any clef changes. The clef may change from Treble to Bass in the upper staff, or from Bass to Treble in the lower staff. Check for any accidentals in the measure that would affect the note. Name the intervals at the following letters:

B __Aug 2__   C __dim 4__   D __Per 8__   E __Maj 6__

SIMPLE TIME and COMPOUND TIME REVIEW

SIMPLE TIME   COMPOUND TIME

Duple Time   2/4   6/8

1. Add rests below each bracket. Cross off the Basic Beat as each measure is completed.

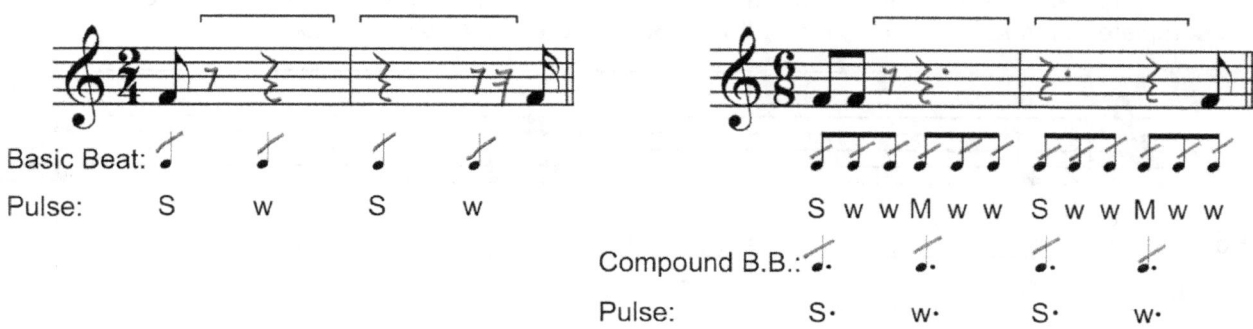

Triple Time   3/4   9/8

2. Add rests below each bracket. Cross off the Basic Beat as each measure is completed.

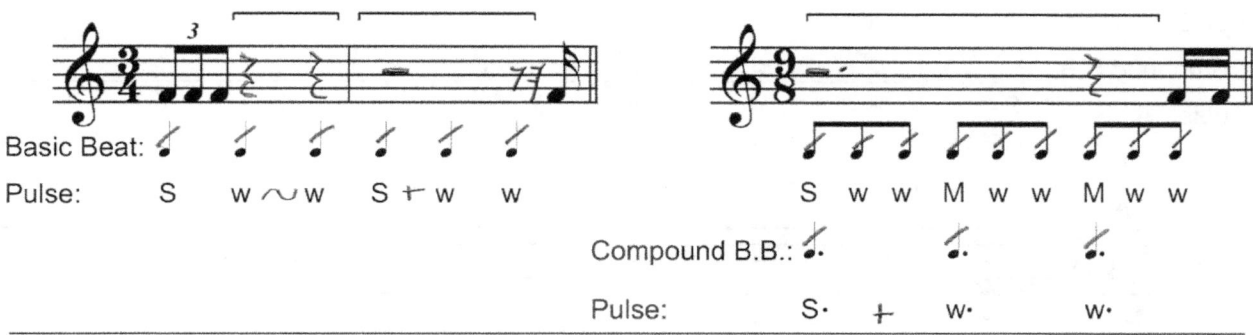

Quadruple Time   4/4   12/8

3. Add rests below each bracket. Cross off the Basic Beat as each measure is completed.

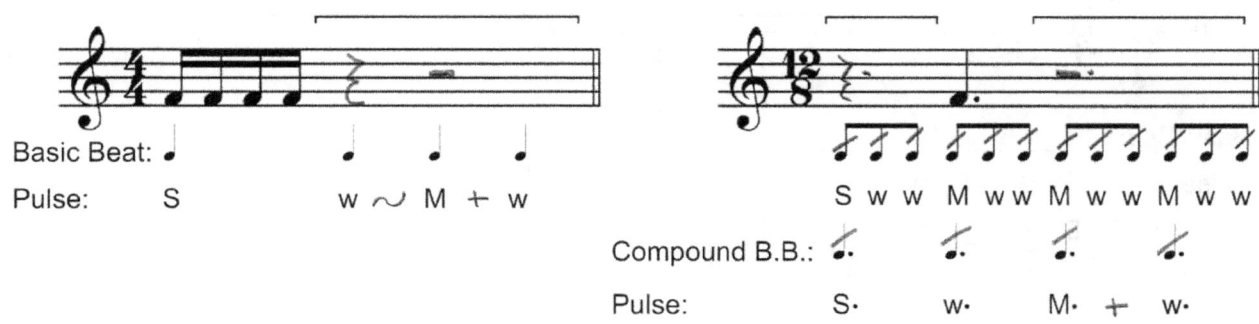

BASIC BEAT and PULSE REVIEW

BASIC BEAT is one note equal to one beat. **PULSE** is where the rhythmic emphasis falls.

♪ Note: A Strong pulse joins a weak pulse.   S + w   S· + w·

         A Medium pulse joins a weak pulse.   M + w   M· + w·

         A weak pulse can NOT join a weak or a Medium pulse.   w ~ w   w· ~ w·

                                                                                                                                     w ~ M   w· ~ M·

1. Write the Basic Beat and the pulse below each measure. Add rests below each bracket to complete the measure. Cross off the Basic Beat as each beat is completed.

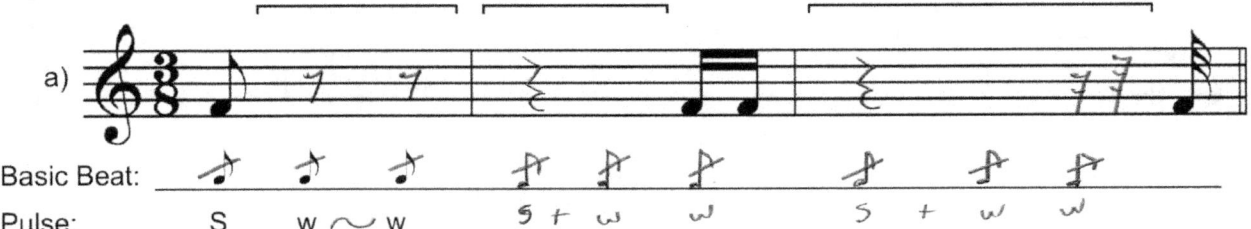

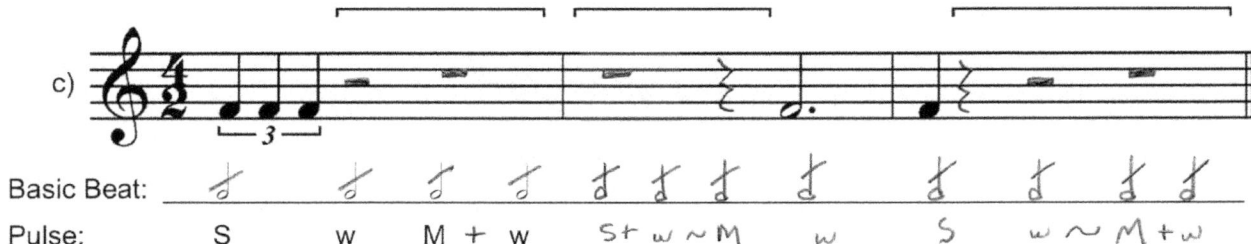

INTERVAL and TRIAD REVIEW

An **INTERVAL** is the distance in pitch between two notes. Inverting an interval is turning it upside down. The combined number of the interval and its inversion **ALWAYS** equals **NINE**.

♪ Note: When inverting intervals:
MAJOR	becomes	**MINOR**
MINOR	becomes	**MAJOR**
AUGMENTED	becomes	**DIMINISHED**
DIMINISHED	becomes	**AUGMENTED**
PERFECT	stays	**PERFECT**

Intervals may be **harmonic** (one note ABOVE the other) or **melodic** (one note BESIDE the other). The bottom note always names the Major key.

1. a) Name the following intervals. Invert each interval. Name the inversions.
   b) Identify each interval as **H** for harmonic or **M** for melodic.

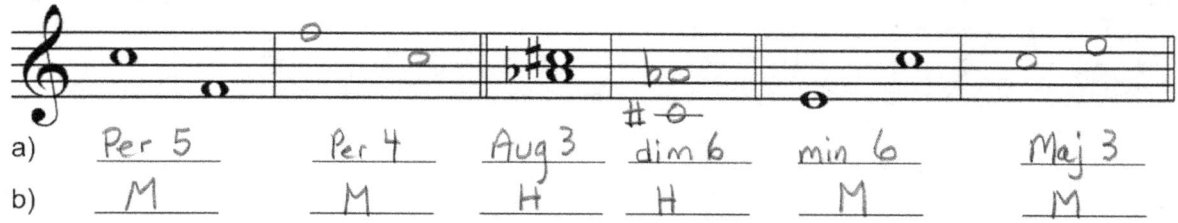

a) Per 5   Per 4   Aug 3   dim 6   min 6   Maj 3
b) M   M   H   H   M   M

A **TRIAD** is a three note chord. Four elements when identifying a triad are: the Root (name); the position (root, 1st inv or 2nd inv); the type (Major or minor); and the form (solid or broken).

The **ROOT** or name of a triad is determined by the bottom note when in root position (all lines or all spaces).

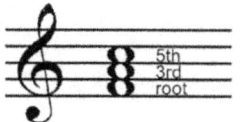

The **POSITION** of a triad is determined by the location of the Root note within the triad. Root position: the bottom note is the Root. (This note names the triad.) First inversion: the bottom note is the 3rd above the Root. Second inversion: the bottom note is the 5th above the Root.

The **TYPE** or quality of a triad is determined by the intervals in the root position triad. Major triad: Root, Major 3rd and Perfect 5th. Minor triad: Root, minor 3rd and Perfect 5th.

The **FORM** is determined as solid (notes played together) or broken (one note played after the other).

2. For each of the following triads, name:
   a) the Root; b) the position; c) the type; d) the form

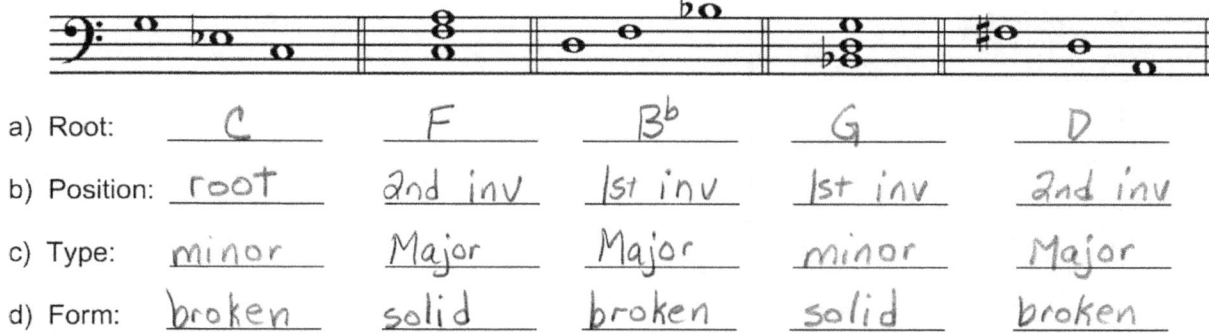

a) Root: C   F   B♭   G   D
b) Position: root   2nd inv   1st inv   1st inv   2nd inv
c) Type: minor   Major   Major   minor   Major
d) Form: broken   solid   broken   solid   broken

135

REVIEW: ULTIMATE MUSIC THEORY CHART - INTERMEDIATE

1. Complete the following to create the Ultimate Music Theory Chart - Intermediate.

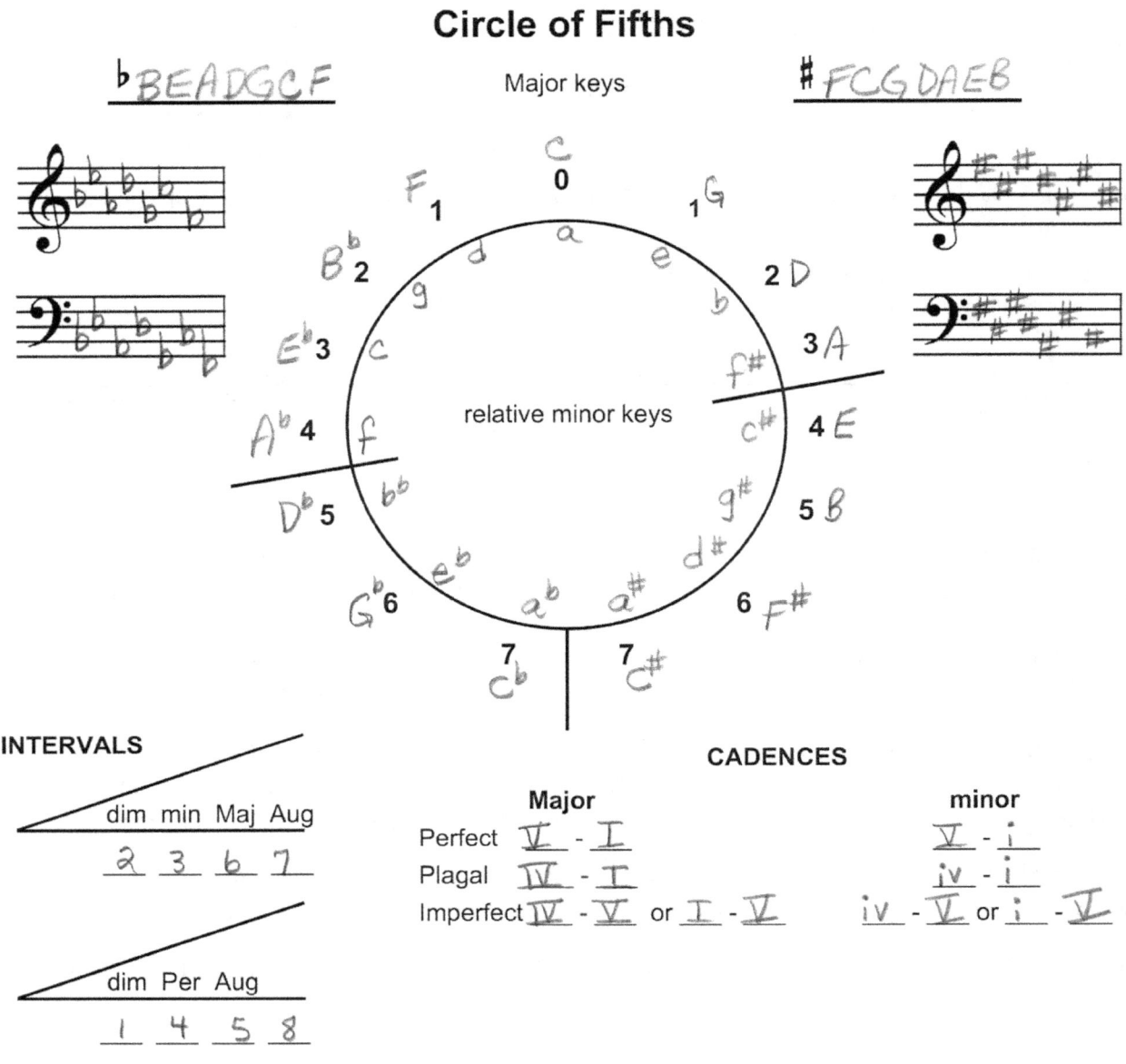

♭ BEADGCF   ♯ FCGDAEB

INTERVALS

dim min Maj Aug
2   3   6   7

dim Per Aug
1   4   5   8

CADENCES

	Major	minor
Perfect	V - I	V - i
Plagal	IV - I	iv - i
Imperfect	IV - V or I - V	iv - V or i - V

TECHNICAL DEGREE

- 8̂ (1̂) Tonic — octave Tonic note
- 7̂ Leading note — semitone (2nd) below Tonic
- 6̂ Submediant — 3rd below the Tonic
- 5̂ Dominant — 5th above the Tonic
- 4̂ Subdominant — 5th below the Tonic
- 3̂ Mediant — 3rd above the Tonic
- 2̂ Supertonic — 2nd above the Tonic
- 1̂ Tonic — 1st note of the key (Key note)

SCALES

Number of Notes:
- 13 Chromatic
- 9   Octatonic
- 8   Major/minor
- 7   Whole tone
- 7   Blues
- 6   Pentatonic

ITALIAN TERMS, SIGNS and DEFINITIONS - ARTICULATION, DYNAMICS and PREFIX

Articulation	Sign	Definition
marcato, marc.		marked or stressed
accent	♩̌	a stressed note
legato		smooth
slur	♩♩♩	play the notes *legato*
leggiero		light, nimble, quick
staccato	♩̇	play the note sharply detached
tenuto	♩̄	held, sustained

Dynamics

crescendo, cresc.	<	becoming louder
decrescendo, decresc.	>	becoming softer
diminuendo, dim.	>	becoming softer
forte, f		loud
fortepiano, fp		loud then suddenly soft
fortissimo, ff		very loud
mezzo forte, mf		moderately loud
mezzo piano, mp		moderately soft
piano, p		soft
pianissimo, pp		very soft

Prefix

alla, all'	in the manner of
assai	much, very much (ex. *allegro assai*, very fast)
ben, bene	well (ex. *ben marcato*, well marked)
col, coll', colla, colle	with (ex. *coll'ottava*, with an added octave)
con	with
e, ed	and
ma	but (ex. *ma non troppo*, but not too much)
molto	much, very
non	not
non troppo	not too much
più	more
poco	little
poco a poco	little by little
quasi	almost, as if
sempre	always, continuously
senza	without
troppo	too much

1. Write the definition for the following terms:

sempre ben marcato: __always well marked__

ma non troppo crescendo: __becoming louder but not too much__

non legato quasi leggiero: __not smooth, as if light, nimble, quick__

ITALIAN TERMS, SIGNS and DEFINITIONS - STYLE and PEDAL

Signs	Definition
D.C.	*da capo*, from the beginning
𝄋	*dal segno, D.S.*, from the sign
𝄐	*fermata*: a pause; hold the note or rest longer than its written value
M.D.	*mano destra*, right hand
M.S.	*mano sinistra*, left hand
M.M.	Maelzel's metronome
8va------┐	8va, play one octave above the written pitch
8va------┘	8va, play one octave below the written pitch
𝄞 Ped.	*pedale*: with pedal
‖: :‖	*repeat signs*: repeat the music within the double bar lines
♩‿♩	*tie*: hold for the combined value of the tied notes

Style

animato	lively, animated
brilliante	brilliant
cantabile	in a singing style
con brio	with vigor, spirit
con espressione	with expression
dolce	sweet, gentle
espressivo, espress.	expressive, with expression
grazioso	graceful
maestoso	majestic
tranquillo	quiet, tranquil
spiritoso	spirited

Pedal

con pedale, con ped.	with pedal
tre corde	three strings; release the left (piano) pedal
una corda	one string; depress the left (piano) pedal

1. Write the definition for the following signs:

    8va------┐ : <u>8va play one octave above the written pitch</u>

    8va------┘ : <u>8va play one octave below the written pitch</u>

    𝄐 : <u>fermata: pause, hold the note or rest longer than its written value</u>

ITALIAN TERMS, SIGNS and DEFINITIONS - TEMPO, CHANGES in TEMPO and TERMS

Tempo   **Definition**

Tempo	Definition
adagio	a slow tempo (slower than *andante* but not as slow as *largo*)
allegretto	fairly fast (a little slower than *allegro*)
allegro	fast
andante	moderately slow; at a walking pace
andantino	a little faster than *andante*
con moto	with movement
grave	slow and solemn
larghetto	not as slow as *largo*
largo	very slow
lento	slow
moderato	at a moderate tempo
presto	very fast
prestissimo	as fast as possible
vivace	lively, brisk

Changes in Tempo

Term	Definition
accelerando, accel.	becoming quicker
a tempo	return to the original tempo
meno mosso	less movement, slower
più mosso	more movement, quicker
rallentando, rall.	slowing down
ritardando, rit.	slowing down gradually
Tempo primo, Tempo I	return to the original tempo
rubato	with some freedom of tempo to enhance musical expression

Terms

Term	Definition
loco	return to normal register
ottava, 8va	the interval of an octave
tempo	speed at which music is performed
fine	the end

1. Write the definition for each of the following tempos:

larghetto: *not as slow as largo*   vivace: *lively, brisk*
grave: *slow and solemn*   presto: *very fast*
lento: *slow*   con moto: *with movement*

2. Write the definition for each of the following changes in tempo:

meno mosso: *less movement*   più mosso: *more movement*
accelerando: *becoming quicker*   rallentando: *slowing down*
rubato: *some freedom of tempo*   Tempo primo: *return to the original tempo*

3. Write the definition for each of the following signs:

𝄆 𝄇 : *repeat the music within the double bar lines*

𝄋 : *dal segno, D.S., from the sign*

𝄮 : *pedale: with pedal*

Lesson 12   Final Intermediate Exam

Total Score: ____ / 100

Write the Circle of Fifths on a blank piece of paper. Use it as a reference when doing the review test.

1. a) Name the following intervals.

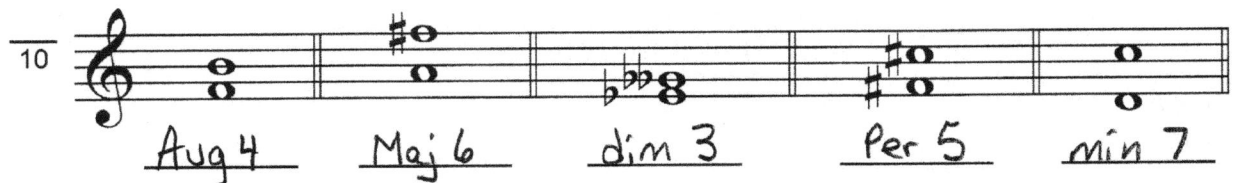

Aug 4   Maj 6   dim 3   Per 5   min 7

b) Invert the above intervals in the same clef. Name the inversions.

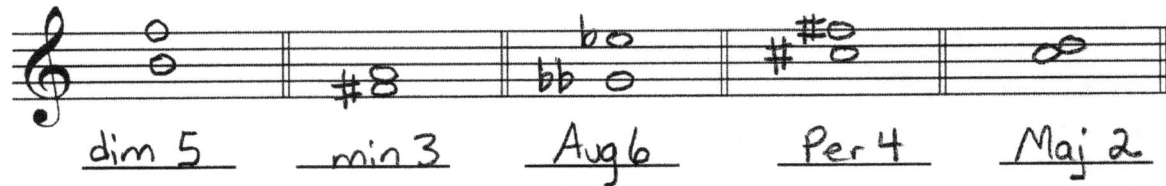

dim 5   min 3   Aug 6   Per 4   Maj 2

2. Write the **BASIC BEAT** and the **PULSE** below each measure. Add rests below each bracket to complete the measure. Cross off the Basic Beat as each beat is completed.

140

3. Name the **MINOR** key for each of the following Key Signatures. Write the following triads in the Treble Clef for each **HARMONIC MINOR** key.

__10__
   a) the **SUBDOMINANT** (iv) triad in first inversion
   b) the **DOMINANT** (V) triad in second inversion
   c) the **TONIC** (i) triad in first inversion
   d) the **DOMINANT** (V) triad in root position
   e) the **SUBMEDIANT** (VI) triad in second inversion

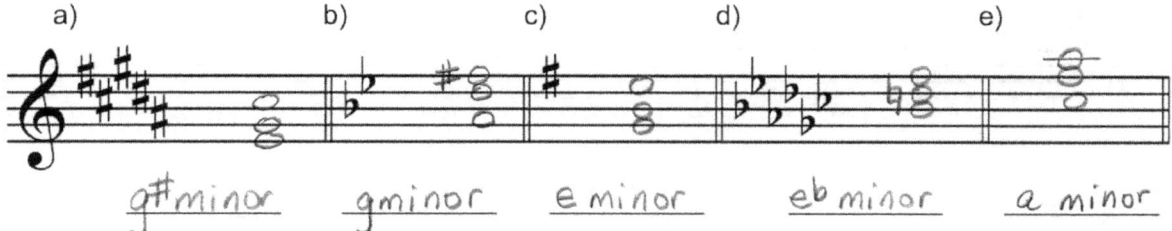

a) g# minor b) g minor c) e minor d) eb minor e) a minor

4. Name the key of the following melody. Transpose it **UP** an Augmented second using the correct Key Signature. Name the new key.

__10__

Key: Gb Major

New Key: A Major

5. Identify the following cadences using Roman Numerals.

Cadence	Major keys	minor keys
Perfect (authentic):	V - I	V - i
Plagal:	IV - I	iv - i
Imperfect (half cadence):	IV - V OR I - V	iv - V OR i - V

__10__

For each of the following cadences, name:
a) the key; b) the type (Perfect, Plagal or Imperfect)

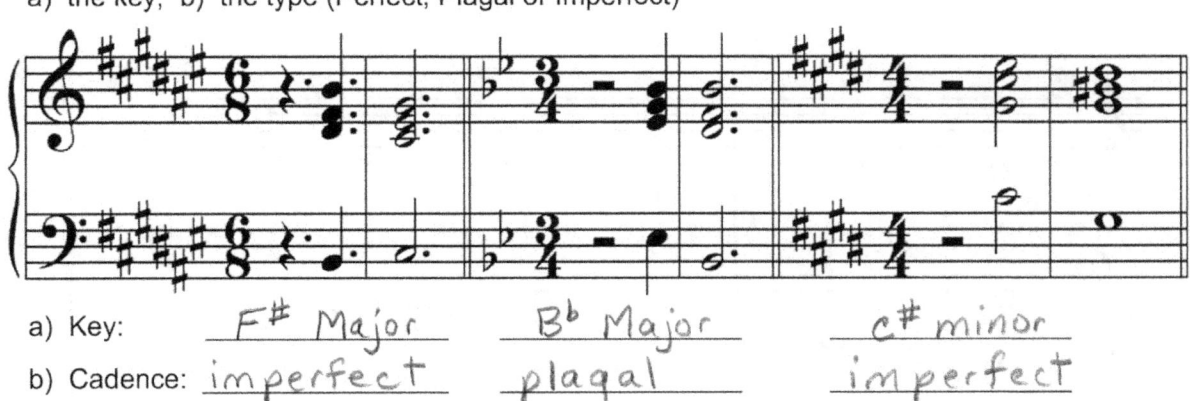

a) Key: F# Major, Bb Major, c# minor
b) Cadence: imperfect, plagal, imperfect

141

6. Write the following scales, ascending and descending, using the correct **KEY SIGNATURE** and any necessary accidentals. Use whole notes.

a) C sharp Major in the Treble Clef
10 b) relative minor, melodic form, of C sharp Major in the Bass Clef
c) Tonic minor, harmonic form, of C sharp Major in the Treble Clef
d) enharmonic Tonic Major of C sharp Major in the Bass Clef
e) enharmonic relative minor, natural form, of C sharp Major in the Treble Clef

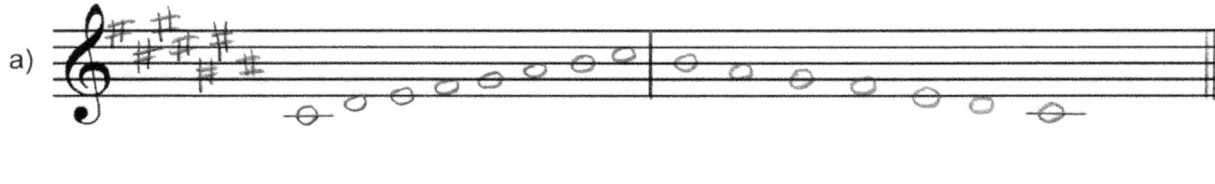

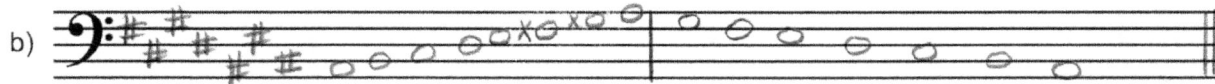

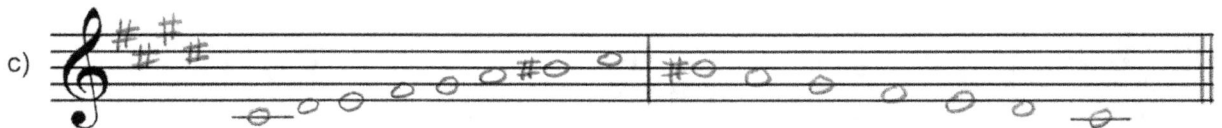

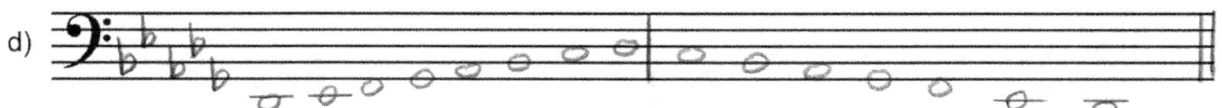

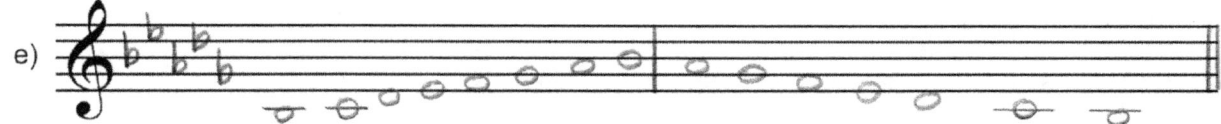

Name the following scales as chromatic, octatonic, Major pentatonic, minor pentatonic or blues.

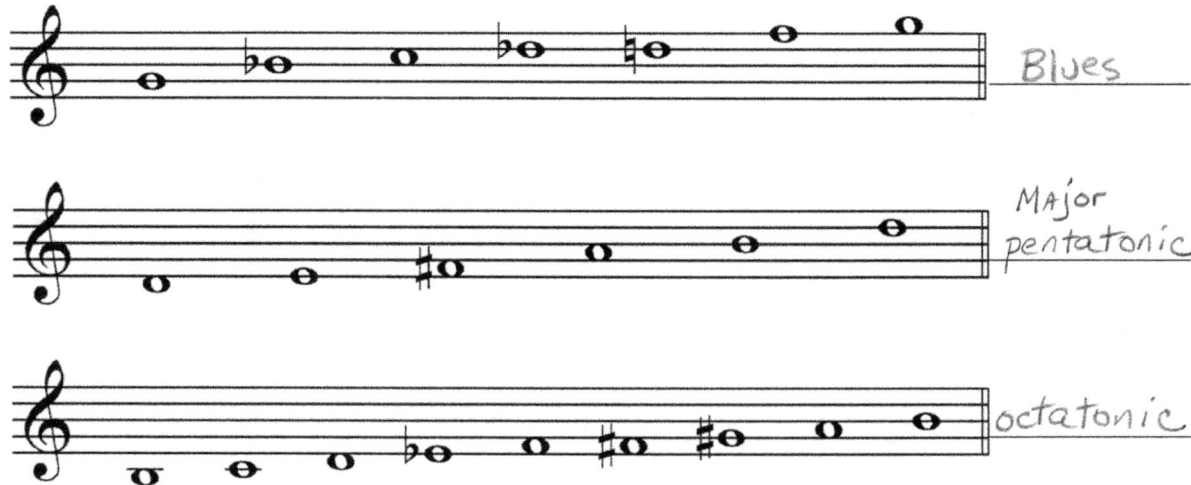

7. Add the correct Time Signature below each bracket.

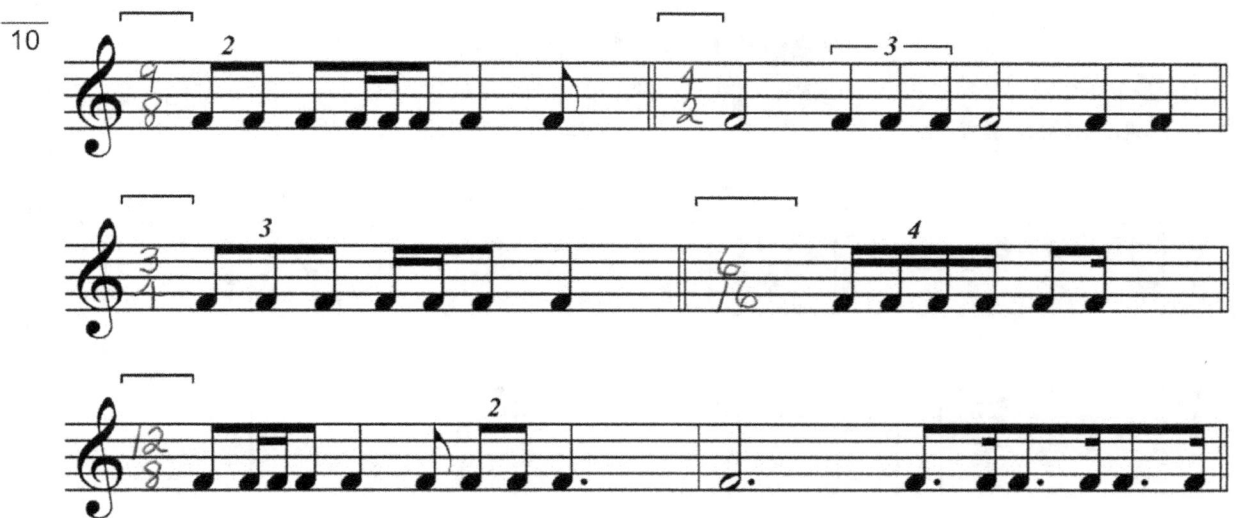

8. Write the following **NOTES** in the Bass Clef, using ACCIDENTALS instead of a Key Signature. Use whole notes.

   a) the **SUPERTONIC** of E Major
   b) the **MEDIANT** of b minor harmonic
   c) the **SUBMEDIANT** of G flat Major
   d) the **LEADING NOTE** of a sharp minor harmonic
   e) the **SUBDOMINANT** of F Major

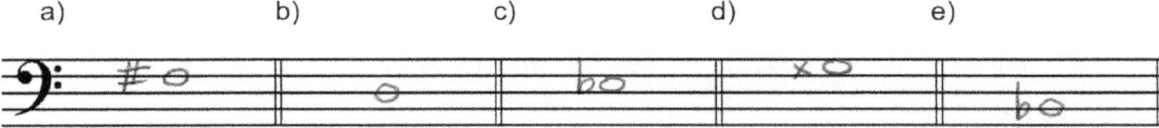

9. Match each musical term with the English definition. (Not all definitions will be used.)

Term		Definition
accelerando, accel.	g	a) majestic
leggiero	h	b) slowing down gradually
maestoso	a	c) graceful
fermata	k	d) sweet, gentle
cantabile	i	e) with vigor, spirit
con brio	e	f) less movement
senza	j	g) becoming quicker
meno mosso	f	h) light, nimble, quick
ritardando	b	i) in a singing style
grazioso	c	j) without
		k) a pause; hold the note or rest longer than its written value

10. Analyze the following piece of music by answering the questions below.

a) Write the correct Time Signature directly on the music.
b) Name the key of this piece. __D Major__
c) Explain the meaning of **Adagio cantabile**. __slow, in a singing style__
d) Name the intervals at the letters: **A** __Major 6__ **B** __Perfect 4__
e) Explain the sign at **C**. __dal segno, D.S., from the sign__
f) Identify the cadence at **D** as Perfect, Plagal or Imperfect. __Perfect__
g) Identify the cadence at **E** as Perfect, Plagal or Imperfect. __imperfect__
h) Identify the cadence at **F** as Perfect, Plagal or Imperfect. __plagal__
i) How many measures are in this piece? __12__
j) When all signs are followed, how many measures are played? __15__

UltimateMusicTheory.com

Ultimate Music Theory Certificate

_____

has successfully completed all the requirements of the

Intermediate Rudiments

_____   _____

Music Teacher   *Date*

Enriching Lives Through Music Education

ULTIMATE MUSIC THEORY GUIDE - INTERMEDIATE

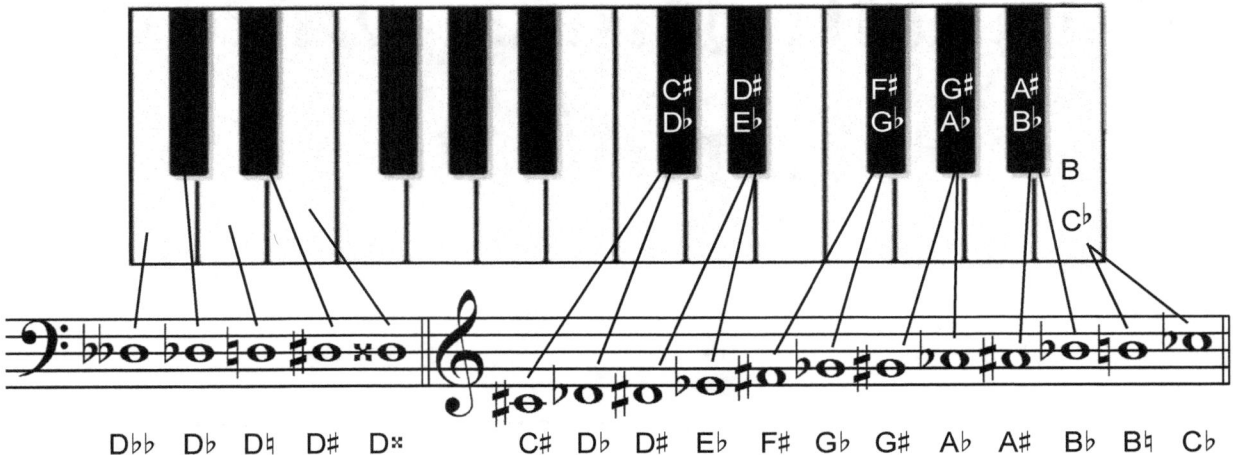

Double Flat, Flat, Natural, Sharp, Double Sharp   Enharmonic Equivalents

Scale Degree: $\hat{1}$ $\hat{2}$ $\hat{3}$ $\hat{4}$ $\hat{5}$ $\hat{6}$ $\hat{7}$ $\hat{8}$ $(\hat{1})$
Technical Degree: Tonic, Supertonic, Mediant, Subdominant, Dominant, Submediant, Leading Note, Tonic

MAJOR and MINOR SCALES
Relative Major and minor scales - same Key Signature. (D♭ Major - b♭ minor)
Tonic Major and minor scales - same Tonic note. (B♭ Major - b♭ minor)

ENHARMONIC SCALES
Enharmonic Tonic Major scale - same pitch, different letter name. (D♭ Major - C♯ Major)
Enharmonic Tonic minor scale - same pitch, different letter name. (b♭ minor - a♯ minor)
Enharmonic Tonic Major/minor scale - same Tonic pitch, different letter name. (D♭ Major - c♯ minor)
Enharmonic relative minor scale - same pitch as the relative minor, different letter name.
(Enharmonic relative minor of D♭ Major - a♯ minor)

20ᵗʰ CENTURY SCALES
Whole Tone scale - 6 consecutive whole tones beginning and ending on the same letter name.
Major pentatonic scale - Major scale omitting the 4ᵗʰ and 7ᵗʰ degrees.
Minor pentatonic scale - natural minor scale omitting the 2ⁿᵈ and 6ᵗʰ degrees.
Blues scale - minor pentatonic scale adding the "blue note" of the raised 4ᵗʰ or lowered 5ᵗʰ degree.
Octatonic scale - alternates between tones and semitones or semitones and tones.

CADENCES: Key of C Major   **CADENCES**: Key of a minor

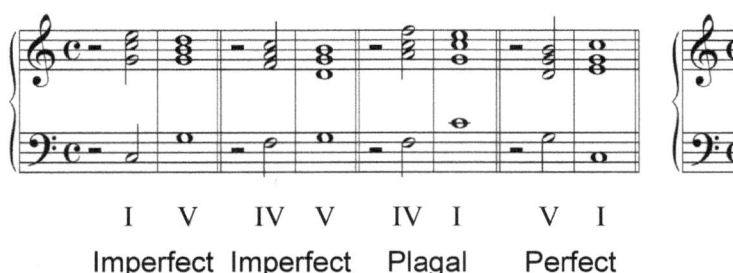 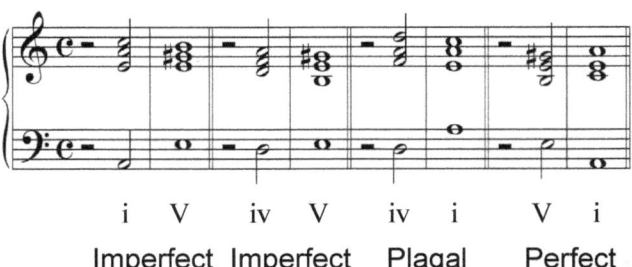

♪ **Note**: The **Dominant (V) Triad** is ALWAYS Major (raised 7ᵗʰ note of the harmonic minor key).

UltimateMusicTheory.com

ULTIMATE MUSIC THEORY CHART - INTERMEDIATE

Circle of Fifths

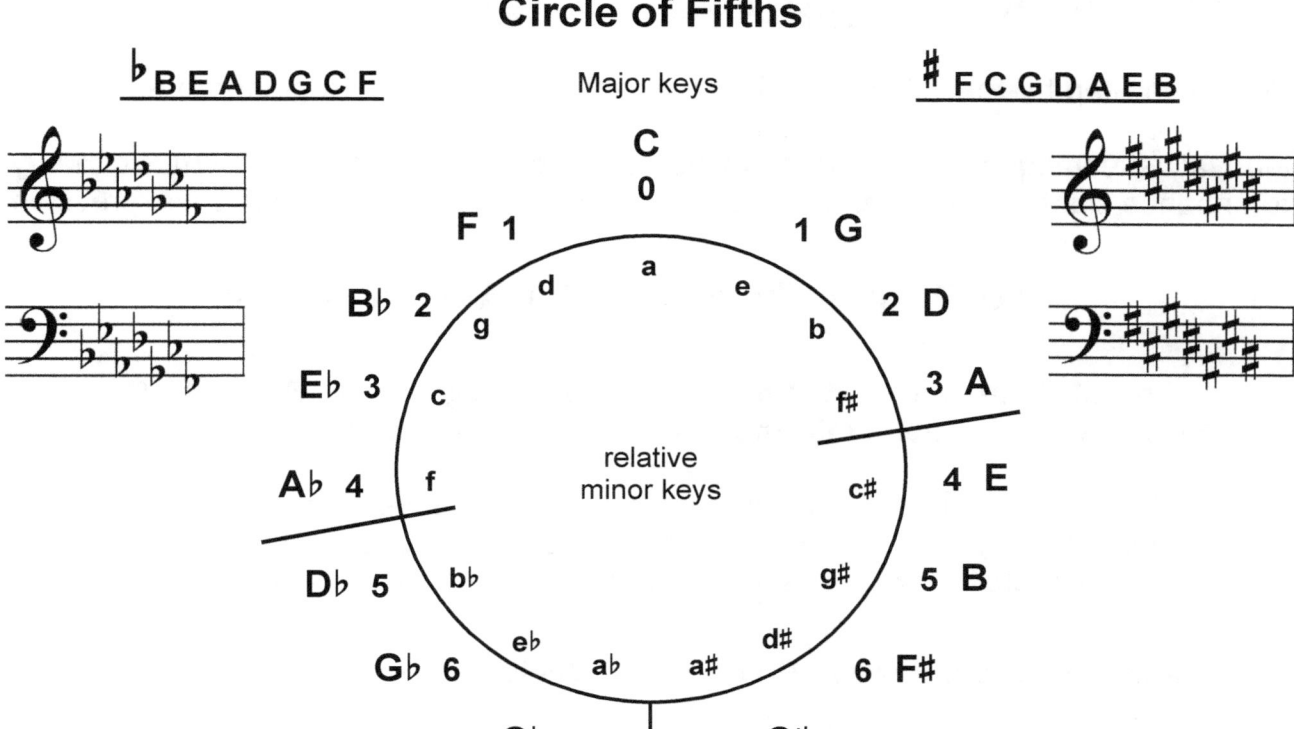

UltimateMusicTheory.com

Ultimate Music Theory
Workbooks, Exams, Answers, Online Courses, App & More!

A Proven Step-by-Step System to Learn Theory Faster - from Beginner to Advanced.

Innovative techniques designed to develop a complete understanding of music theory, to enhance sight reading, ear training, creativity, composition and musical expression.

All UMT Series have matching Answer Books!

The UMT Rudiments Series - Beginner A, Beginner B, Beginner C, Prep 1, Prep 2, Basic, Intermediate, Advanced & Complete (All-In-One)

♪ 12 Lessons, Review Tests, and a Final Exam to develop confidence
♪ Music Theory Guide & Chart for fast and easy reference of theory concepts
♪ 80 Flashcards for fun drills to dramatically increase retention & comprehension

Rudiments Exam Series - Preparatory, Basic, Intermediate & Advanced

♪ 8 Exams plus UMT Tips on How to Score 100% on Theory Exams

Each Rudiments Workbook correlates to a Supplemental Workbook.

The UMT Supplemental Series - Prep Level, Level 1, Level 2, Level 3, Level 4, Level 5, Level 6, Level 7, Level 8 & Complete (All-In-One) Level

♪ Form & Analysis and Music History - Composers, Eras & Musical Styles
♪ Melody Writing using ICE - Imagine, Compose & Explore
♪ 12 Lessons, Review Tests, Final Exam and 80 Flashcards for quick study

Supplemental Exam Series - Level 5, Level 6, Level 7 & Level 8

♪ 8 Exams to successfully prepare for nationally recognized Theory Exams

UMT Online Courses, Music Theory App & More

♪ UMT Certification Course, Teachers Membership & Elite Educator Program
♪ Ultimate Music Theory App correlates to the Rudiments Workbooks
♪ Free Resources - Teachers Guide, Music Theory Blogs, videos & downloads

Go To: UltimateMusicTheory.com

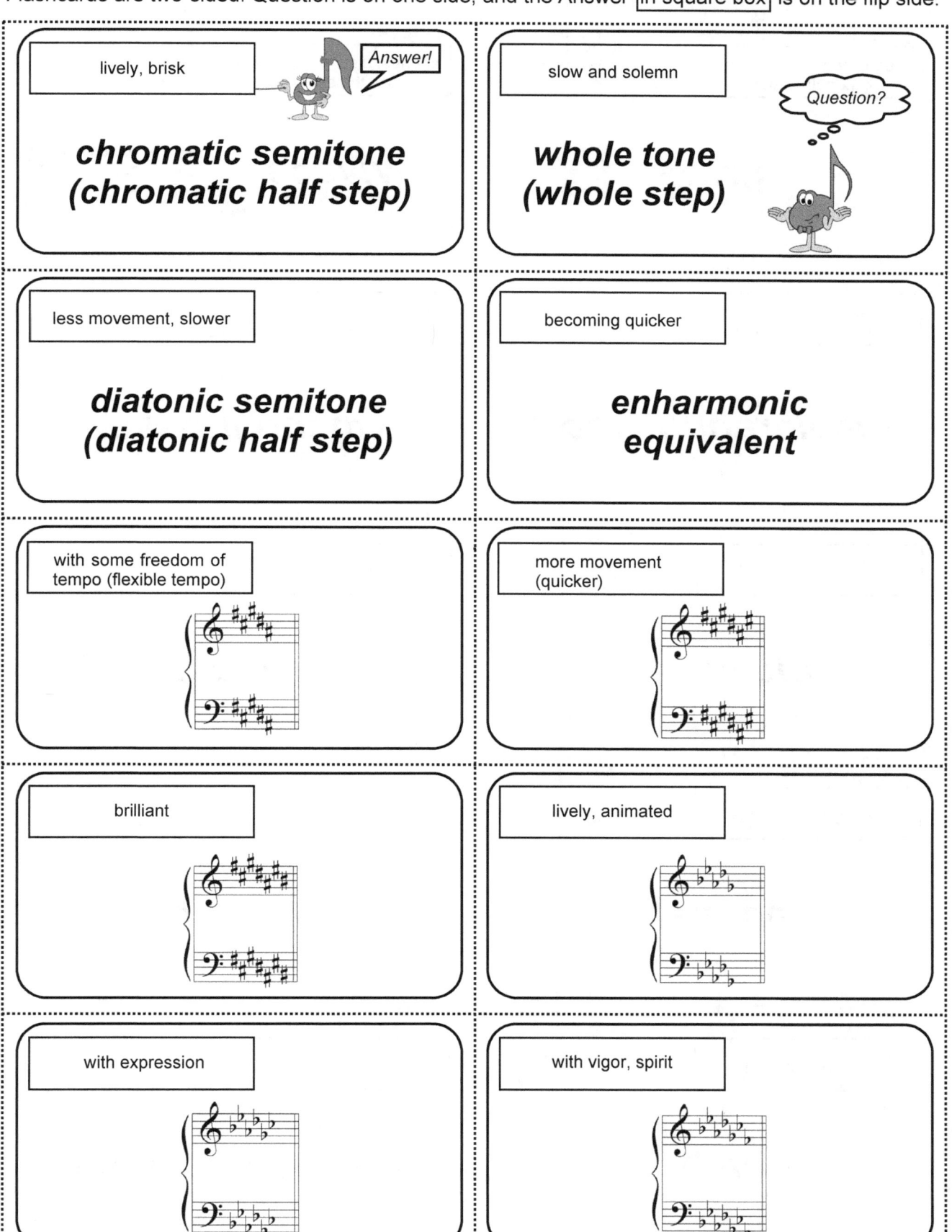

Study by cutting out the Flashcards, or by turning each page to check the answer on the other side.

Answer	Question
equal to two semitones (2 half steps) — **grave**	shortest distance between 2 notes, uses the same letter name — **vivace**
same pitch with different letter names — **accelerando, accel.**	shortest distance between 2 notes, uses different letter names — **meno mosso**
F# Major or d# minor — **più mosso**	B Major or g# minor — **rubato**
D♭ Major or b♭ minor — **animato**	C# Major or a# minor — **brillante**
C♭ Major or a♭ minor — **con brio**	G♭ Major or e♭ minor — **con espressione**

well	much, very much
con moto	**espressivo, espress.**

with	with
spiritoso	**tranquillo**

but	and
leggiero	**M.M.**

much, very	less
loco	**tre corde**

not too much	not
una corda	**alla, all'**

with expression, expressive	with movement
assai	**ben, bene**

quiet, tranquil	spirited
coll, coll', colla, colle	**con**

Maelzel's metronome	light, nimble, quick
e, ed	**ma**

three strings; release the left (piano) pedal	return to normal register
meno	**molto**

in the manner of	one string; depress the left (piano) pedal
non	**non troppo**

3/4	4/4
più	*poco*

6/8	3/8
poco a poco	*quasi*

12/16	3/2
sempre	*senza*

9/8	6/4
troppo	*fortepiano, fp*

9/16	12/8
Key: ____ Cadence: _____	Key: ____ Cadence: _____

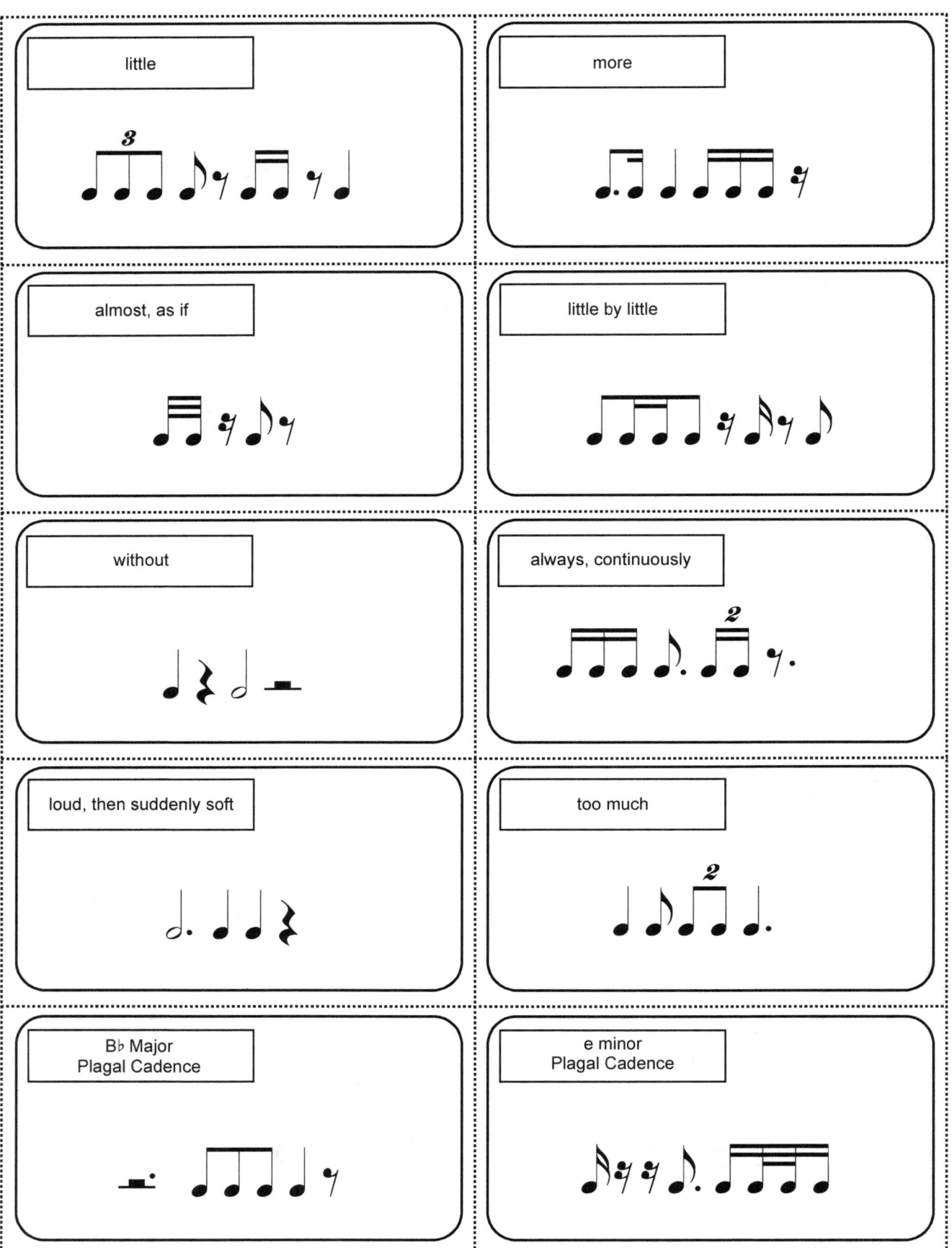

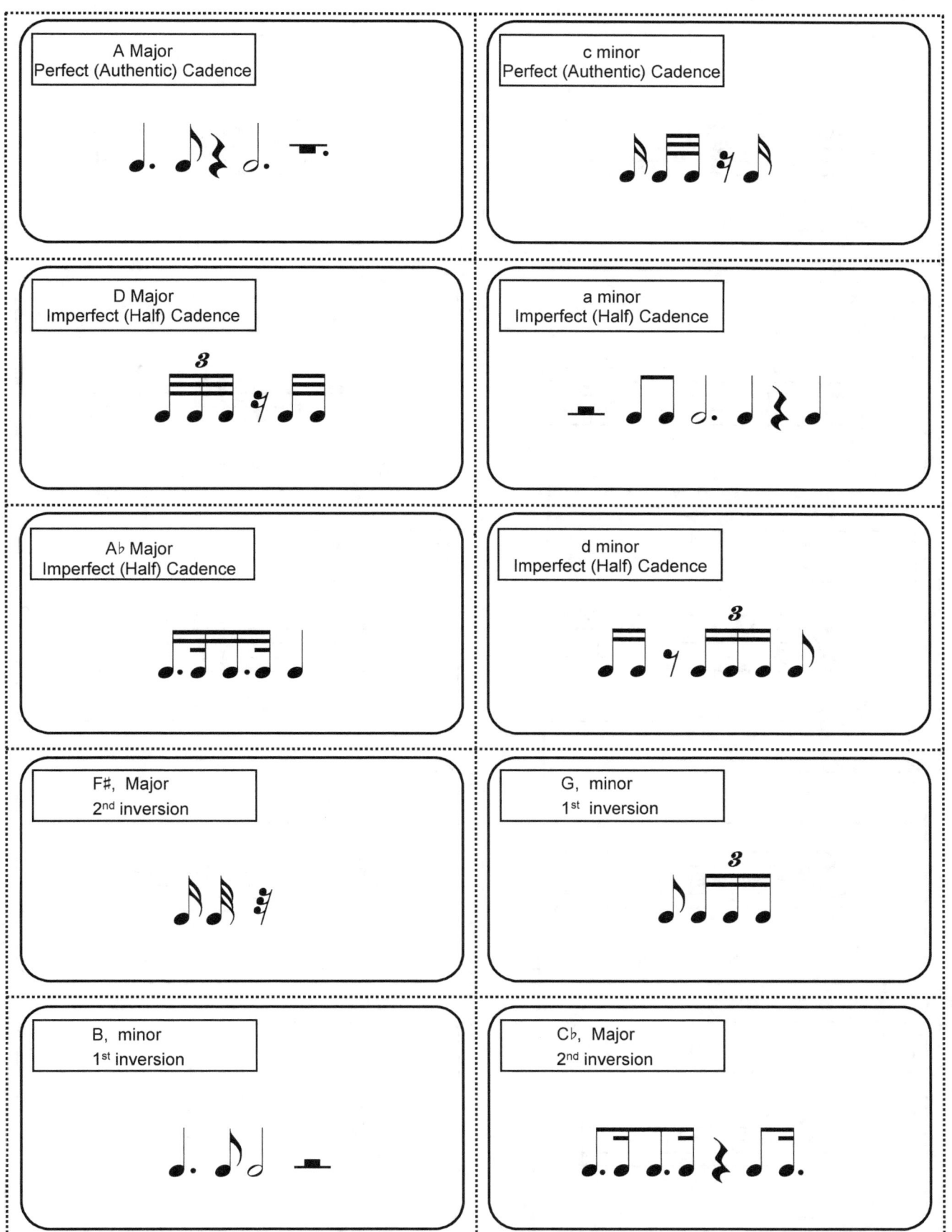

www.ingramcontent.com/pod-product-compliance
Lightning Source LLC
Chambersburg PA
CBHW060514300426
44112CB00017B/2667